A Yankee at Arms

A Yankee
at Arms

THE DIARY OF
LIEUTENANT AUGUSTUS D. AYLING,
29TH MASSACHUSETTS VOLUNTEERS

Edited by
Charles F. Herberger

Voices of the Civil War
Frank L. Byrne, Series Editor

THE UNIVERSITY OF TENNESSEE PRESS / KNOXVILLE

The Voices of the Civil War series makes available a variety of primary source materials that illuminate issues on the battlefield, the homefront, and the western front, as well as other aspects of this historic era. The series contextualizes the personal accounts within the framework of the latest scholarship and expands established knowledge by offering new perspectives, new materials, and new voices.

Four Mathew Brady photographs from *Mr. Lincoln's Camera Man*, 1946, are reprinted by permission of Russell & Volkening as agents for the author.

∞ The paper used in this book meets the minimum requirements of ANSI/NISO Z39.48-1992 (R 1997) (*Permanence of Paper*). The binding materials have been chosen for strength and durability. Printed on recycled paper. ✪

Library of Congress Cataloging-in-Publication Data

Ayling, Augustus D.
    A Yankee at arms : the diary of Lieutenant Augustus D. Ayling,
29th Massachusetts Volunteers / edited by Charles F. Herberger. — 1st ed.
    p. cm. — (Voices of the Civil War series)
    ISBN 1-57233-034-1 (cl.: alk. paper)
    1. Ayling, Augustus D.—Diaries. 2. United States. Army. Massachusetts Infantry
Regiment, 29th (1861–1865) 3. Massachusetts—History—Civil War, 1861–1865—
Regimental histories. 4. United States—History—Civil War, 1861–1865—Regimental
histories. 5. Massachusetts—History—Civil War, 1861–1865—Personal narratives.
6. United States—History—Civil War, 1861–1865—Personal narratives. 7. Soldiers—
Massachusetts—Diaries. I. Herberger, Charles F. II.
Title. III. Series.
E513.5 29th .A95 1999
973.7'444—ddc21   98-40114

Contents

ILLUSTRATIONS

Figures

Maps

Foreword

By the Civil War's end, Confederates would call most of their Northern enemies "Yankees" (often accompanied by a hostile adjective). Ironically in the world wars of the twentieth century, Southerners too would find themselves called Yanks. Yet in the Civil War many Union soldiers fit the original definition of the Yankee as New Englander. Such a Yankee was Augustus D. Ayling of Massachusetts. A resident of the most populous New England state, he was associated with the commerce and manufacturing that many saw as characteristically Yankee.

Above average in writing ability, he kept readable diaries of his war service. Because of the loss of his first diaries and because of later additions, Ayling's papers also have some of the characteristics of a memoir. Since he enlisted very early in a Massachusetts regiment, his writings cover much of the war. Ayling tells of participation in the Seven Days battles and on the fringes of Fredericksburg. The writer spent time in hospitals, including one on Bedloes Island, the future site of the Statue of Liberty. He also experienced the difficulties of wartime travel. His unit, the 29th Massachusetts, was one of the limited number of regiments that fought in both East and West. Ayling gives a good sense of the confusion of the Vicksburg campaign and of the problems of getting around in—let alone fighting in—Kentucky and Tennessee. Readers of this series may be especially interested in his account of hardships in Knoxville and elsewhere in East Tennessee.

While Ayling began as an enlisted man, he was soon commissioned and tells much of the positive and negative aspects of life as a company officer. He is unusually candid about the extent of his drinking ("moderate" as he liked to think), a prominent part of army life. He also wrote more frankly than most who preserved their diaries about a wartime romance with a Kentucky woman. Before the war's end, he took advantage of a seldom-cited War Department order for the mustering out of officers to get away from his colonel.

Since he missed military life, he then secured a staff position in the occupation force in Richmond. Some of the diary's especially revealing passages show the conquerors enjoying the fruits of their victory. Ayling also demonstrates much about the routine of a judge advocate in courts-martial. Perhaps less predictable is the indication that elite whites so recently engaged in combat were resuming social relations in the bonds of Freemasonry. Students of Reconstruction will be interested in Ayling's professed willingness to help put down a rumored uprising by the blacks of the former Confederate capital. The Yankee at Arms and former Rebels had already set foot on what one historian would call the Road to Reunion.

Frank L. Byrne
Kent State University

INTRODUCTION

In 1915 at the age of seventy-five, General Augustus Davis Ayling was in retirement at his home on Cape Cod. After a lifetime career in the army, he preserved his Civil War experiences by making a transcript of his diaries kept in the field. He introduces this document with the words:

> The following is a transcript from diaries kept by me while in the service of the United States during the Civil War 1861–5, supplemented by incidents and experiences, revived in my memory by memoranda in the diaries. It has been written at the urgent request of my family, and with the hope that in years to come, it may be of interest to those who shall come after me.
>
> Signed: Augustus D. Ayling

It is to be regretted that the original handwritten diaries were not preserved in addition to the typescript of 1915, which is now in the archives of the Centerville Historical Society in Massachusetts. It does not appear that General Ayling foresaw publication, yet it is clear that he is trying to preserve for posterity the immediacy and impact of his day-by-day experience. Each day's entry is dated, and it is obvious that he is transcribing his handwritten diaries from the field faithfully and accurately. Apparently he had also scribbled marginal notes, and he incorporates these to amplify the lived experience that he remembered. Since as he tells us that an early segment of the diary was lost, some early passages take on more of the nature of a memoir than a contemporary diary, although the work as a whole is presented in diary format. And while incorporating marginal notes, he may well have been influenced by postwar developments.

The circumstances under which the diary came to the archives of the Centerville Historical Society are worth noting. General Ayling's son, Charles Lincoln Ayling, was a very successful and prosperous businessman: he was the chairman of the board of John Hancock Life Insurance Company, among other business interests, and also a generous philanthropist. His mother, the general's wife, Elizabeth Cornish Ayling, was a Cape Codder, the daughter of a sea captain, and both he and his father spent their summers in Centerville on the Cape. That is why his philanthropy centered there. Cape Cod owes its major hospital and its major airport at Hyannis to Charles Ayling's initiative and endowment. Centerville is indebted to him for its library building, and the Centerville Historical Society owes him for a wing of its museum and a large part of its collection and endowment. It is evident that Charles Ayling appreciated the historical value of his father's diary and therefore presented it, together with his father's personal scrapbooks, letters, and collected Civil War records, artifacts, and mementos, to the Centerville Historical Society. It is not an accident that this significant document has been preserved.

The diary is remarkable for a number of reasons. It offers a personal view of the war through its entire duration, from Ayling's enlistment in response to Lincoln's call for volunteers in April of 1861 shortly after Fort Sumter to Lee's surrender at Appomattox in April of 1865. It also chronicles the aftermath of the war, as Ayling served in Richmond, the fallen Capital of the Confederacy, until January of 1866.

It also provides close-ups of almost all the important theaters of action: the naval encounter of the *Monitor* and the *Merrimack* at Newport News, Virginia; the Peninsula campaign of the Army of the Potomac under McClellan; Burnside's nearly disastrous advance and retreat at Fredericksburg; the Western Theater in Kentucky; Grant's army at the fall of Vicksburg; the campaign in the mountains of Tennessee and the encampment near Knoxville; Ayling's duty as an aide-de-camp on General Foster's staff in Richmond after the war; and also glimpses of conditions in military hospitals and railroad and steamship travel.

Augustus Ayling was born in Boston on July 28, 1840, the son of William L. and Margaret C. Ayling.[1] Both of his parents were theater people. Shortly after his death on March 11, 1918, a remembrance of his parents appeared in the *Boston Herald* as follows:

> The last time I saw Mrs. L. Ayling she was acting at the National Theatre. She was the mother of General Augustus D. Ayling, whose death has been recently recorded. He was a Civil War veteran of

distinction. For more than 27 years he was Adjutant General of New Hampshire. He was a native of Boston, and he died at Centreville, Cape Cod, universally respected. "Meg" Ayling was a bright and lively actress who began her stage career at the old Tremont Theatre. My mother knew her as a naturally talented young girl who was sure to make her mark. Her husband was a sensible, intelligent actor, always popular in Boston. My impression is that "Meg" Ayling performed here for the last time at the Continental Theatre, though I remember meeting her on the street afterward, when she was apparently unknown to the great majority of playgoers. My final glimpse of her at the National was as the leader of a female guard, for whom she asked three cheers when she was summoned enthusiastically before the curtain.[2]

It is significant that Ayling's parents were sensitive and artistically talented people. In dedicating the Centerville Public Library to his father, Charles Ayling remarked on General Ayling's lifelong interest in Shakespeare. Although he did not attend a university, he was a well-educated man, having attended Boston public schools and an elite private school, Lawrence Academy in Groton, Massachusetts.[3] That he was well read in good literature is evident from his style, and it is no surprise to find him quoting from memory a stanza from Byron's "Childe Harold's Pilgrimage," which, with its reference to "the unreturning brave," he says haunted him all day as he marched to the Battle of Fredericksburg.

As the French naturalist Buffon said, style is the man. The style of the diary is remarkably revealing of the kind of man Ayling was. It is lively, vivid, and dramatic when the events described demand verisimilitude, but it is also meticulously accurate in reporting factual details. That Ayling was by nature painstakingly conscientious and thorough is reflected in several ways. Before his enlistment he had been a clerk and bookkeeper for the J. C. Ayer & Company of Lowell, Massachusetts, a pharmaceutical firm, and he served as clerk to General Butler at Fort Monroe, Virginia, in the early days of the war. After the war as an adjutant general he voluntarily undertook the task of compiling a book, the *Register of the Soldiers and Sailors of New Hampshire in the War of the Rebellion.* This book, which he patiently researched over a period of ten years, gave complete factual details about every soldier, sailor, or marine of the state who served in the war. This work of 1,347 pages was published in 1895 under the auspices of the state legislature.[4] An article in the *Manchester*

Union states, "Accuracy has been General Ayling's governing idea, and no efforts have been spared to make each individual record accurate and complete."[5] There was nothing slipshod or careless about General Ayling, which made him a good soldier and also a reliable reporter and writer.

There is one more quality of his style that deserves to be mentioned. Augustus Ayling was a gentleman. Although he does not hesitate to call a spade a spade, his language is never crude, vulgar, or obscene. It is not a matter of language alone but also of conduct. His gallant and courteous behavior toward the "rebel" ladies of Baltimore, his restraint and self-control in the face of his incompetent superior, Colonel Pierce, and his respect and admiration for the Catholic nun who nurses him in the hospital all bespeak the sensitivity of a gentleman.

To sum up his style in general, one may say that it is clear and accurate in detail and also vivid, lively, and dramatic in evoking a sense of personal experience, whether what he experienced was the exploding of shells on the battlefield, the boredom of monotonous camp life, or the poignancy of parting with loved ones when responding to the call of duty in war. In its humanity and individuality, this diary is truly a significant voice of the Civil War.

The diary has been rendered verbatim from the existing document in the possession of the Centerville Historical Society. There have been no additions or deletions from the complete text, although a few obvious typographical errors have been corrected. Notes have been appended wherever necessary to identify persons, places, and things mentioned in the text that may be unfamiliar to nonspecialist readers. Although every effort has been made to identify persons and other specific matters mentioned by Ayling, a few remain unidentified. When junior officers or enlisted men are mentioned merely by last name and rank, without information being given on their regiment or state, and their last names are common to many, it is sometimes impossible to distinguish them with certainty from the general Army register. The division into chapters with commentary by the editor is done to place the narrative in the context of the major geographical and temporal aspects of the Civil War.

A Yankee at Arms

Chapter 1

ENLISTMENT AND FORT MONROE

At 4:30 A.M. on April 12, 1861, shore batteries commanded by General Pierre G. T. Beauregard opened fire on Fort Sumter in Charleston, South Carolina, and the Civil War began. On April 15 Lincoln called for volunteers, and on April 19 Augustus Ayling enlisted as a private in the 7th Battery, Massachusetts Volunteers. Ayling, who was born July 28, 1840, was twenty years old when he enlisted. After enlistment in Lowell, Ayling's company was stationed at Fort Monroe, Virginia, which was held by Federal forces despite the secession of the State of Virginia. Fort Monroe, overlooking Hampton Roads, was of strategic importance because it commanded access to the Norfolk Navy Yard and also to the James River, which was a waterway to Richmond, the capital of the Confederacy.[1]

April 16th, 1861

In April, 1861, I was a clerk in the office of J. C. Ayer & Company, Lowell, Massachusetts, where I had been employed for several years, working up from boy in the bindery to assistant bookkeeper. There had been a good deal of talk and discussion among my friends and in the office over the political situation, but few, if any, believed there would be war. Today, however, things looked more serious, and Lowell is full of excitement as the several city companies (4) left today for Boston to join the rest of the Sixth Regiment, when they are to go to Washington. I went to the railroad station to see them off and there was great excitement—men cheering and women crying. Wanted to go with them awfully and should have gone if mother had been home.

April 17th, 1861

Was blue and disappointed and felt like anything but work because I could not go with the "boys" yesterday. Am determined to go with the next company that is called for. Went to see Sheriff Hayes, who is talking of raising a company.

April 18th, 1861

Wrote mother today that I was going to enlist the first chance I had and that I knew if father was alive he would say, "Go, and do your duty."

April 19th, 1861

An important day in my life! I learned that a company was to be raised to join the Sixth Regiment at Washington, and in the evening went to the Armory and enlisted. Other companies are being raised in the city, but ours is considered the "crack" one of them all. Most of the men are educated, clean and from good families. Some are my intimate friends and we were schoolmates. All are supposed to be "picked men". A propos of the "picked" business, when I applied to enlist, Edward Hunt, who was in charge and was later on one of the lieutenants of the company, put me through a long questioning, endeavoring to impress me with the idea that the company was to be exclusive, and that he had some doubt as to my coming up to the standard; but "Billy" Farrar, afterwards First Lieutenant and who was a fine officer, promptly spoke up when he saw the drift of things, and said he would vouch for me. As to Hunt, who was the son of a wealthy family and quite well up socially, he went out with us, and then "went to the dogs", as a drunkard. I saw him in 1865 at Richmond. I was riding into the city with Col. Edmands as his Adjutant, and we met the Colonel of the 4th Massachusetts Cavalry with his orderly, who was none other than Ed Hunt. He had gone down and I had come up a little. Poor Ed, he was really a very good fellow, but a little bit snobbish.

I felt much pleased to get into this Company, as it was really a nice lot of fellows and many wanted to join but were told there was no room. We chose the name of the Company and voted to name it "The

Richardson Light Infantry" in honor of Hon. George F. Richardson, to whom we were indebted for the money for our uniforms etc. Mr. Richardson was at the beginning, all through the war, and to the present day, has been, a warm friend to every member of the Company. We all respect and love him.[2]

April 20th, 1861

The excitement and war talk is increasing all the time, and we expect to be ordered to the front next week. In order to have our uniforms the first of the week, the Company has divided into squads and with the cloth distributed among the tailors of the city, who are to work all night and tomorrow (Sunday), so we can be ready to go to the front when ordered.

April 21st, 1861

Lowell never had so exciting and unusual Sabbath in its history. Rumors and reports regarding the attack upon the Sixth Regiment on its passage through Baltimore were the topics of conversation among excited groups at the street corners.[3] Flags were flying from every available place, including many church spires. Everybody was ugly and ready to fight the rebels if only given a chance. From the above date until May 21st my time was spent, part of the time in the office, where I would work a few hours some days, and the rest of the time drilling either in Armory or out of doors. The Company had elected officers as follows: Phineas A. Davis, Captain; Israel H. Wilson, 1st Lieutenant; William E. Farrar, 2nd Lieutenant; Edward S. Hunt, 3rd Lieutenant. The Captain was a splendid officer, as was also Farrar. The 2nd Lieutenant, Wilson, who was later a Captain in the 29th Regiment when I joined it, was a good natured, easygoing man, but not brilliant as an officer. Hunt went out with the Company, but United States Army regulation did not allow a 3rd Lieutenant to infantry companies, and he was commissioned into the Union Coast Guard, so called, but did not stay long, finally drifting into the 4th Massachusetts Cavalry as a private, as I have previously stated.

April 23rd, 1861

I wrote a letter for Captain Davis to General Butler, asking that

Private Augustus D. Ayling, 1861.
Centerville Historical Society Archives

he have us ordered to Washington. We have learned that we are to be Company G of the 6th Regiment and are glad we are to be a part of that gallant regiment that fought its way through Baltimore.

April 25th, 1861

We underwent our physical examination, which I did not dread as I was in splendid condition, thanks to my gymnasium practice and training.

April 28th, 1861

I received my uniform this morning and like it very much. Cadet gray—cap, coat and trousers trimmed with black. I was quite proud and felt, as I fancy others of the Company did, that I could whip an unlimited number of able bodied "Rebs". At half after ten o'clock we formed at the Armory and marched to Rev. Dr. Cleaveland's church, where we had a fine service and a rousing patriotic sermon, the church of course being crowded.

May 1st, 1861

At nine o'clock the Company formed and marched to the station and took the cars for Billerica. On arrival, we marched to a large field where we drilled all the forenoon. It was a bright, sunny day and everybody was in fine spirits. The citizens received us with much enthusiasm and at noon gave us a collation in the hall. We drilled about until five o'clock, then started for a march home to Lowell, some four or five miles. Had a good time on the route and was not very tired. This was somewhat different from the marches I had to take later on. At a meeting of the Company in the evening, we voted to go into camp at Billerica, tents having been arranged for.

May 2nd, 1861

The next morning we got all ready and after dinner started on a march for the camp ground of yesterday. We had to pitch our tents after we arrived, and as everybody was "green" it took lots of time and labor before we got them up. The night was very cold and we were half frozen. At two o'clock I was so cold I couldn't stand it any longer, so I stirred up Charley Brigham, and together we woke up the whole camp. No one had any more sleep that night.

May 3rd, 1861

The next morning we were "drummed up" at 5 o'clock and on going to a pond to wash, found the water frozen quite hard. At night we went with Sergeant Wooster and others to serenade Mr. Talbot (afterwards Governor). He invited us in and we had hot coffee, cake, etc. A real nice time!

May 4th, 1861

The next day drilled in the morning and at eleven o'clock marched to Billerica Center, some three or four miles, where we had dinner and dress parade, then marched back to our camp, where, on arriving, we found a lot of ladies and gentlemen from Lowell waiting to greet us. We gave them a dress parade.

May 5th, 1861

The next morning we were awakened at 5 o'clock by the "Tattoo" (as my diary calls it, showing I was "green" enough not to know the difference between Tattoo and Reveille). The pond was frozen again and we had to break the ice in order to get our morning wash. About half after six we started on our march for Lowell without any breakfast. Arrived about eight and went home for a big breakfast, after which went to the Armory and with the Company marched to the First Unitarian Church of Rev. F. Hinckley. A good sermon and the church was crowded, but the Company was pretty sleepy and tired when dismissed. Went home and slept until supper time. We heard today we were ordered to go to Alexandria, Virginia, by first boat, but as the air has been full of rumors for some days, don't place much confidence in them.

May 6th, 1861

A most impressive and exciting day. In the morning the first platoon went to Boston to receive the bodies of the two Lowell men killed by the mob in Baltimore on April 19th—Luther C. Ladd and Addison O. Whitney. The second platoon to which I belonged was detailed to

Attack on the 6th Mass. Vol., Baltimore, April 10, 1861.
From J. T. Headley, *The Great Rebellion,* vol. 1, 1862.

fire the volleys, which by the way, were five. Everybody said they sounded like one gun. On arrival of the bodies and escort in the P.M., we received them at the station and marched to Huntington Hall where the funeral ceremonies were held. The city was literally in mourning, the streets and stores hung with black, and over all a solemn hush. The Hall was draped heavily with black and near the platform a catafalque was erected under which the bodies rested. At each corner of the catafalque a member of our Company was stationed as guard of honor, and I was much pleased and very proud to be detailed as one of the four. The ceremonies were most impressive, and the sobs of the families of the dead soldiers, and the betrothed of one of them, could be frequently heard. At the close, we marched to the cemetery in a driving rain, where our platoon fired the volleys. When I got home was wet to the skin. Surely a memorable day.

May 7th, 1861

Felt a little stiff and sore from yesterday's soaking and marching. Another rumor today that we are to go to Annapolis Thursday. We are under orders to be ready to on three hours notice.

May 8th, 1861

Got a pass and went to Boston this morning. Called on Uncle Henry and Uncle Isaac. They are both very patriotic and were glad I had enlisted. Each gave a present of money. Went back to Lowell in the P.M. and went around bidding my friends good bye. There really seems to be a probability of our getting away.

May 9th, 1861

I had a sad, hard time this morning bidding good bye to mother and Mary [his sister]. They felt bad to have me go, and I felt bad to leave them. When I got to the Armory found we were not to leave today after all. There was a pretty mad crowd for a while, and we were disgusted as we had said our good bye, and there was a crowd of our friends to see us off, but after Mr. George F. Richardson, for whom we are named, had talked to us, we calmed down. We had out-door drill in both A.M. and P.M. At the end of the afternoon drill, we left our guns in the Armory and marched to French's Restaurant, where we were given a nice supper. We had a message from Captain Davis from Boston that we were to go on Monday next. We are to be quartered in Chesley's Hall hereafter, as long as we remain here, and are to be fed by the city.

May 10th, 1861

The usual routine of drills, etc. for the next two or three days with the usual talk of being ordered off in a "few days." We have got so that we don't and shall not believe anything until we are fairly off. We like our quarters very well. The living is good and we sleep on mattresses on the floor quite comfortably.

May 13th, 1861

Orders were received tonight from the Governor announcing that no more three-months men would be received, only men who would enlist for three years.[4] This would let us out as we enlisted to go for three months only. After some talk the Company voted almost unanimously, only one man dropping out, to go for three years. The Company is to be recruited up to the U.S. standard of 101 men, so there will be more delay.

From this date to May 21st, when we finally got away, we lived and were quartered in Chesley's Hall, getting our meals at the restaurant at the city's expense. Had roll calls and drills regularly, street parades, etc., and the most exciting incidents were the presentation of a silk flag, marches to the houses of prominent citizens for speeches and collations, and a visit of the Company *en masse* to a circus where seats were reserved for us.

May 21st, 1861

Orders were received last night for us to go to Boston today to take boat for the "seat of war", and it now looks as if we were really to get away. Was busy all the morning saying good byes, and making final preparations. At ten o'clock the Company was formed and escorted by the Hill Guards and Butler Rifles, marched to Huntington Hall, which was crowded with men, women and children. The Mayor, clergymen and prominent citizens made speeches and bid us God speed! Before marching to Huntington Hall the Company was photographed at Park Square, Belvidere, with Mr. George F. Richardson and his little daughter, "Meta", as daughter of the Company. At 12:20 we took the cars for Boston. On arriving were met by a battalion of the First Regiment under Captain Snow and escorted to the State House where drawn up in line and with heads uncovered we took a solemn oath of allegiance to our country.[5] At request of the Company the oath was administered by our friend and sponsor, Mr. George F. Richardson. We were then regularly mustered in and became Uncle Sam's boys. We were quartered for the night at the Hancock House, Court Square, where we received our equipment of knapsacks, haversacks, canteens, dippers, knives, forks, spoons, etc.

May 22nd, 1861

At half after eleven, we embarked on the propeller "Pembroke" for Fort Monroe, Virginia, with one other Company, Whightman Rifles, Captain Clarke.[6] This latter Company became a part of the 29th Regiment to which I was commissioned later on, and Captain Clarke was a very good friend to me. The steamer on which we sailed was formerly a coal boat and was much too small for two companies, many of the men being obliged to sleep on the deck. She carried two thirty-two pounders, one at the bow and one at the stern, and was supposed to be able to make a fight if necessary, but fortunately we did not meet any rebel craft. We had a very pleasant trip for those who were not seasick, and most of the men were so sick that to this day the name "Pembroke" carries a feeling of nausea. Old ocean and I being good friends, I was not troubled any and consequently was detailed as one of the eight boat guards whose duty it was to wear our belts and bayonets night and day and in case of an alarm to guard the boats and keep off any rush of frightened or panic-stricken men. The signal for us was three bugle calls, and it was sprung on us once or twice, but found us ready for business at our posts. We came in sight of Fort Monroe early today and as we steamed towards the wharf were saluted by the blockading fleet. On landing, we were quartered at or in the Hygeia Hotel, formerly a swell watering place hotel outside the fort. I was detailed for guard duty the first night and was posted at the main entrance with strict orders to allow no one to enter the hotel "without the countersign". Late in the night a certain officer who evidently was somewhat intoxicated attempted to pass me without countersign or any other evidence of right to enter, in spite of my warning, and allowed himself to run against the point of my bayonet, getting a slight prick, which frightened him and he left vowing vengeance. I was somewhat scared myself as I did not quite know just how literally I was to obey orders and did not know enough to call the "Corporal of the Guard". We remained at the Hygeia about a week and were then moved to the Fort and quartered in barracks alongside the "regulars", as part of the garrison and conforming to the routine in everything. One of the things that galls us is morning police duty. Immediately after reveille roll call the Company was deployed in front of our barracks, each man having a basket or box and then we moved slowly across the parade ground picking up pieces of paper, cigar stumps, and all kinds of litter, a very proper and necessary thing to do, but we did not like it. We were kept quite busy with not only infantry but heavy artillery mortar and casemate howitzer drills, also helped mount the big "Union Gun" which arrived from Baltimore and is mounted outside the Fort commanding the channel. It is a big one sixteen feet long weighing 52000 lbs. Early in June I was detailed as clerk in the office of General Butler commanding the Department.[7] My hours in the office were such that I kept up with many of the drills of the Company. General Butler, who used to know father, was very kind to me and life was very pleasant, though I did not feel that I was doing much to put down the rebellion. One thing I remember which is interesting. General Butler stood at my side and dictated the plan of the Big Bethel attack, from which plan orders to the different commanders were made, and I have always held that if the orders and plan had been carried out as the General intended, the attack would have been successful. I retained the original draft as the General dictated it, but it was captured the next year with my baggage, which included a new uniform with overcoat and my '61 diary[8] at White House Landing on the Pamunkey River, when Stuart made his raid around McClellan's army on the peninsula.[9]

June 10th, 1861

The battle of Big Bethel, which is about nine miles from Fort Monroe, was fought on this date and the same afternoon and evening the wounded and some of the dead were brought to the Fort.[10] I helped in the evening to make boxes to be used as coffins and saw some of the bodies. The first men I had seen killed in battle. Lieut. Greble of the regular artillery was killed and his funeral was on June 12th; all the troops including our Company escorting his body to the wharf from whence it is to be sent to Philadelphia—a pretty solemn time for us and we begin to realize the seriousness of war. Major Winthrop of General Butler's staff was also killed at Bethel and buried on the field, but the body was brought in and sent to New York June 18th, all the troops acting as escort. While clerk for General Butler, he called me in one day to go with him as orderly to the Rip Raps, an artificial island in the channel, just off the Fort, where there was a fortification being erected, and as I had no side arms with me, he told me to borrow the sabre from his cavalry orderly. This was the first time I had ever worn a sword, and above all a long cavalry sabre, and was constantly falling over it, and had no end of trouble in trying to appear in an easy, soldierly manner as if I had been born with a sword on.

I was relieved from duty in the General's office after a time, at my own request, that I might have the advantage the Company was having drilling on heavy guns under regular army sergeants. One afternoon after drill, I came in hot and dirty, and after washing, threw the dirty water very carelessly out a window towards the parade ground. In a short time Captain Davis appeared in a towering passion and said someone had thrown dirty water on Lieut. Sanger of the regular artillery, and he wanted to know who did it. At least half of the men in the room must have known it was I, but not a soul spoke, and I could not for fright. Finally the Captain said he would give fifty dollars to find out, and was going to. He then went back to his quarters, and there was a solemn pause in the room, everybody looked at me and shook their heads in sympathy with me. We all thought that nothing less than shooting would be my fate, and as for me, I fully expected it, unless they substituted hanging. I was scared "blue" and utterly miserable. At last I could stand the suspense no longer, so plucking up courage to meet my fate, I went to Captain Davis' quarters and told him it was probably I who threw the water on the officer, but that it was entirely carelessness, not design, as he thought. In my innocence I even offered to go and make an apology to Lieut. Sanger, not realizing the absurdity of the proposition. Captain Davis, having gotten over the worst of his anger, was real nice to me, saying he would explain matters to the Lieutenant, and cautioned me about throwing out water. I returned to the barracks with a great load lifted from my mind, but I was badly scared.

Life in the Fort was pleasant, with drills, guard mount and inspection coming at regular intervals—the living was fair. About the first of July a volunteer clerk was called for from the Company to go with a Dr. Morton, detailed by the War Department to collect statistics and data from smallpox camp at Newport News. I volunteered and was accepted after a warning from the doctor regarding the risk of taking the disease. He was immune. There were hundreds of cases in tents and the doctor would ask such patients as could talk their age, name, birthplace, residence, etc., and see if they had ever been vaccinated, appearance of scars, if any, and various other matters for his report to the government, while I took everything down in a book. I had no fear of the disease and really enjoyed the work for a change. Dr. Morton was a gentleman and very nice to me.

The Secretary of War (Cameron) visited the Fort in July and reviewed all the troops, including our Company, and complimented us very highly, as have also the regular officers, the latter saying that we were the finest volunteer company they had ever seen.[11]

I am unable to say just how long I was with Dr. Morton, as my '61 diary was lost as I have said, but probably not more than a week or so, when I returned to duty with the Company and drilled on the big guns and mortars.

We had numerous alarms. The "long roll" would sound and everybody jump to his post expecting an attack, but nothing happened until a night in August.

August 7th, 1861

At about 12 o'clock we were called up and found the Rebs had set the village of Hampton, two or three miles from the Fort, on fire. We stood on the parapet and watched the fire the rest of the night. It was an exciting time for us. My post was at one of the parapet guns, 8 inch columbiads, and we were very anxious to be attacked, that we might show our efficiency. We could handle the heavy guns quite well and got lots of praise from the old regulars who instructed us. Sometime in the early part of August, General Butler appointed me Provost Marshal on the "Adelaide", a steamer running between Fort Monroe and Baltimore in the government service, but allowed to carry passengers. This was a very singular appointment and shows the irregular way things were done in the early days of the war. I was only a private and had a guard of a Lieutenant and twelve men practically under my orders, as was also the Captain of the boat. My duties were to stand at the gang-way with a guard of two men with their rifles, and take the name, residence, business and object in going to the Fort, of every person desiring to make the trip from Baltimore, and on arriving at the Fort no passenger was allowed to leave the boat until I had taken the list to General Butler, who would designate those who might land. The others were kept on the boat all day and sent back to Baltimore at night. I had authority to prevent anyone coming on the boat at all, if I did not like their looks, or believe their story, and could make the Captain anchor under the guns of Fort McHenry, just out of Baltimore, if I judged it necessary, there being fears that the secessionists in Baltimore might try to capture the boat, as had been done on the Potomac, by getting on board disguised but heavily armed. Another of my duties was to examine the baggage of persons who armed with a permit from the Secretary of War or the Secretary of State were going south via Fort Monroe and flag of truce to Norfolk. This was not particularly agreeable duty and sometimes very disagreeable, as when some bitter female "Reb" would refuse to give me the keys to her trunks until I threatened to break them open, and stand and abuse me to her best ability, while I was making the examination. Some would give up their keys willingly, or at least without making any face, when I explained that I must obey orders and search their baggage for contraband articles, some of which were, as I remember, quinine, sewing silk, needles, surgical instruments. One particularly sad case was that of a lady (one of the few ladies I had to deal with, the others were—

well not ladies) who came aboard with a pass to go south from the
Secretary of State, and when I told her I must examine her trunks, gave
me the keys willingly, but begged that I would not open one small
trunk, assuring me there was nothing in it I could object to. Of course,
I had to open all trunks, and when I came to the little one she referred
to, it contained toys and baby clothing of an infant she had very recently lost. The poor mother stood sobbing and crying all the time I
was looking through the things and I sympathized with her. I handled
everything carefully as possible and put the things all back as gently
as I could. The ugly, saucy people did not get their property handled
so gently. I liked my position very much, and it certainly was a soft
job for a private. I had a nice stateroom and had my meals on the boat,
living much better than if with the Company. We made the trips at
night, leaving at 6 o'clock in the afternoon and arriving at about the
same hour the following morning. This gave me, alternately, a whole
day at each place, the Fort and Baltimore, and enabled me to become
well acquainted with the latter city. With a few exceptions the people
were awfully bitter, and if I wore my uniform, young women and girls,
many wearing secession colors, and some with dainty pearl-handled
pistols in their belts, would sweep their skirts aside as they passed and
occasionally would spit towards me. I took no notice of them however, which probably worried them more. I made the acquaintance of
an old gentleman named John Hanna, a red-hot Union man, who with
his son, kept a fine cigar store on North Calvert Street, and made my
headquarters there, learning much about the city and having pointed
out to me some of the prominent "Rebs" and "The Uglys", as the
toughs who had terrorized the city were called. It happened to be my
day in Baltimore on Christmas and with Charlie Brigham of my Company, who was Provost Marshal on the companion boat to mine, we
called on a number of Union people whose acquaintance we had made
and were nearly swamped with egg-nog, which was pressed upon us
everywhere we went. Everybody kept open house and the Union people
could not do enough for us.

Chapter 2

THE *MONITOR* AND THE *MERRIMACK* AND NEWPORT NEWS

By April 1861, the Norfolk Navy Yard was in Confederate hands, and the scuttled steamer *Merrimack* was raised, repaired, and fitted as an ironclad ram renamed the *Virginia.* Hampton Roads was an assembly point for Federal naval power. As Ayling relates, General Burnside's expedition to North Carolina assembled vessels there on January 10, 1862. On January 17, 1862, Ayling visited the steamer *Constitution* there. The *Constitution* was part of the naval force under General Butler that joined Farragut's fleet at New Orleans on May 1, 1862. Ayling was commissioned second lieutenant in the 29th Massachusetts Volunteers on January 4, 1862, under Col. E. W. Pierce, and he was stationed at Newport News. On March 8, 1862, the *Merrimack* sailed into Hampton Roads under Commodore Franklin Buchanan and attacked the Federal ships there. She rammed and sank the *Cumberland* and destroyed the *Congress.* On the following day the Federal ironclad *Monitor* engaged the *Merrimack* in the first naval battle of two ironclad ships and revolutionized naval warfare. The battle was a draw, but the *Merrimack* was forced to return to Norfolk and failed to get to the *Minnesota,* which otherwise would have been a victim. The rebuff also saved the Federal forces at Newport News, which otherwise would have been easy prey to General Magruder's land troops.

January 8th, 1862

I received today a nice letter from Uncle Henry saying I was to be commissioned as 2nd Lieutenant in the 29th Massachusetts Volunteers. I was, of course, delighted, and felt very grateful to him for it was to his efforts I was indebted for my promotion. I supposed I should have to be examined before muster-in as an officer, and immediately commenced to "cram" on tactics. Fortunately, however, no examination was required, but the hard study I put in for several days and nights was of considerable benefit to me, as I found out later, when I joined the regiment. I knew fully as much, and perhaps a little more than the other officers of my company. I found on the night of January 16th I had as a passenger Col. E. W. Pierce, Commander of the 29th regiment, so after supper, I introduced myself to him. He told me he had my commission and would like for me to report as soon as possible, or as soon as I could get my uniform, etc., which I had ordered in Baltimore. I did not fancy the Colonel's looks much. He was anything but my idea of the ideal officer.

January 10th, 1862

General Burnside's expedition for Hatteras and points on the North Carolina coast rendezvoused at the Fort, or rather in Hampton Roads, where the anchorage is. As there were over 80 vessels, it was an impressive sight. At night all the vessels were illuminated, bands playing and men singing. It was a scene never to be forgotten.

January 17th, 1862

The big steamer "Constitution" with a part of General Butler's New Orleans expedition came into Hampton Roads, and as I knew there were a lot of Lowell boys on board, I got a boat and went out to see them, found a number of old friends and stayed to supper and all night. Wished I was going with them.

January 18th, 1862

Went up to Newport News, where the 29th Regiment is stationed, and reported to Colonel Pierce. Got leave to go to Baltimore and hurry up my uniform. Went up on the boat the next evening and had turned in when aroused by a wild yell, shrieks from women and the smashing of glass. I dressed quickly, took my revolver, and went into the saloon, and found that a big six-foot Vermont soldier who had been discharged and was on his way home, had gone crazy and with a cavalry sabre was chasing the passengers through the saloons, striking at any one who came within reach, and incidentally smashing the lamps. One man had his coat and waistcoat cut through and his skin grazed. Finally, one of the guards knocked the man over with the butt of his rifle and it took six or eight of us to tie him and get him into a bunk, where we tied him down. It was a pretty exciting time for a while. I pitied the poor fellow. Possibly he went crazy from nostalgia, or homesickness, as many of the Vermont regiment were really very ill and off duty from the disease. The surgeons recognized it as a disease.

January 25th, 1862

Took the boat this A.M. and went to Newport News and reported to Col. Pierce, who mustered me and assigned me to Company D as 2nd Lieutenant. The Captain was Charles Brady and 1st Lieutenant, Henry A. Kern. The Company was from Sandwich on Cape Cod and had among its members many glasshouse men from the Sandwich Glass Works, as were the Captain and 1st Lieutenant. The latter were very good fellows and treated me well, but there were some pretty tough specimens in the Company. However, I got along with them all right and never had any trouble, or had to punish a man, and there is not a man in the Company or the Regiment I would not be glad to meet.

The first time I had to go out with the Company on Inspection Parade, or drill, I was pretty nervous. The situation was considerably different from that to which I had been accustomed and I knew I was being watched closely, but I got through all right fortunately. I don't think my appointment to the regiment was entirely agreeable to all. I was an outsider and there was a feeling that my commission should have been given to some sergeant of the regiment. However, this feeling was not shown very much and soon passed away. Soon after reporting to the regiment, I received a letter from Uncle Henry with a check for $150 to help me in getting fitted out as an officer. What a dear, good man he was, one of the very best the Lord ever made. I figured up, one day, the cost of my outfit and found it to be just $205.

February 8th, 1862

Today I was detailed as officer of Picket Guard, and as the ceremony of Guard Mount is made a good deal of here, and as all the officers and most of the men were out watching, I was somewhat anxious. It was the first time I had ever commanded men, and it was a very peculiar sensation to stand before a line of men knowing they were waiting for me to give them certain orders. The regiment had what was called "No. 5 picket" to guard and there being no enemy near, there was no firing. Everything was peaceful, and the duty was not all disagreeable. There was a very singular thing connected with No. 5 picket which seems worthy of note. Every night a small dog would make his appearance from no one knew where, and visit all our posts and the reserve. The men would share their food with him and he would stay with us until morning, when he would disappear. Nothing would induce him to stay after daylight or to go to camp. There was no inhabited house within six or eight miles, and where he came from, or went, and why he visited our picket only, which was the fact, was a mystery. The men named him "Picket" and he would answer to it readily. We all became very fond of the little fellow.

Just back of our line of officer's quarters, on the bluff overlooking the river, was a Water Battery of four guns, 5 inch rifles and 8 inch Columbiads (smooth bore). The battery was divided, a detail from a New York regiment manning the right half and a Lieutenant with men from the 29th Regiment manning the other half, which consisted of a Sawyer Rifle and a Columbiad.

February 11th, 1862

A sad accident occurred today which cast a gloom over the whole regiment. The Secretaries of State and War (Seward and Cameron) and Senator Wilson visited our camp, and to entertain them the Sawyer gun of our battery was fired to show its extreme range, being given an elevation of 30 inches.[1] This almost nullified the recoil and the gun burst, killing two men, one of whom belonged to my Company, and wounding Lieut. Smith, commanding the battery and several others of the gun squad.[2] A large crowd of officers and men were near the gun, watching to see the shell strike, and it was almost a miracle that more were not killed or injured. Several had very narrow escapes.

March 8th, 1862

This was an eventful day for me, being my "baptism of fire", but a much more eventful day for the nation and the world. Naval warfare was revolutionized, and it was surely demonstrated that the day of wooden vessels of war had passed. In the morning, I had obtained leave of absence for the day and took the boat for Fort Monroe, expecting to spend the day with my old Company. I spent the forenoon with the boys, and was invited by Captain Davis and Lieutenant Farrar to dine with them, but just as we were about to go to the officer's quarters, the alarm gun at the Guard House was fired and the "long roll" sounded to call the garrison to arms. The Fort was at once buzzing with excitement, officers and men of the artillery hurrying to their stations at the guns, the infantry forming, and the guard turning out. Everybody was excited. Everybody asking, "What is it?" "What is the cause of the alarm?" Being on leave, away from my regiment, being under nobody's orders and having no station to report at, in my "greeness" I was somewhat at a loss to know just what to do with myself. I followed a squad of artillery men to the ramparts and then saw the cause of the alarm was the appearance of the rebel steamer "Merrimack" as we called her, or "Virginia" as the rebs called her. She had been the United States Sloop of War "Merrimack", captured with the Navy Yard at Norfolk by the rebels, cut down, and her deck covered with railroad iron in the shape of the roof of a house. We had heard rumors that the enemy was building a formidable ironclad vessel with which our navy was to be destroyed, but did not take much stock in the report. She was a black, wicked looking craft and appeared to be headed for Newport News, so I felt that my place was there with my Company and regiment, and started for camp by land, as of course, the boat had stopped running. The scene at the Fort was very exciting. The U.S. ships "Minnesota", "Roanoke" and "St. Lawrence" were firing, as was our fort on the "rip raps", so called, and the rebel battery on Sewall's Point was adding to the turmoil of heavy gun firing. I found two officers who were also bound for Newport News. We started for the camp through Camp Hamilton and engaged a "contraband" with a horse and cart to take us the few miles we had to go.[3] The roads were fearfully muddy, almost up to the hubs. As we drew nearer to the firing, our driver became badly frightened, and it took some money, considerable urging, and a few threats to keep him going.

We soon began to meet refugees from the front. Women, non-combatants and negroes, all telling dreadful stories of what was happening, and what was going to happen to the troops at the camp, which with an occasional shell crashing through the woods, utterly demoralized our driver, so we put some women into the cart and sent him back to the Fort, finishing our trip on foot. We reached camp just after the "Cumberland", rammed by the "Merrimack" went down, firing until her guns were down to the water, and with flag flying. I at once reported to my Captain, Brady, and he and Lieutenant Kern were glad to see me. Lieutenant Colonel Barnes, commanding the regiment, was kind enough to compliment me for reporting when my leave of absence had not expired, and under the rather ominous circumstances.[4] The whole camp was in a somewhat demoralized condition. Everybody realized that the rebel ironclad was more than a match for anything we had on sea or land. She had sustained, without apparent injury, and at close range, the heavy broadsides of our war ships, and the fire of our shore batteries of Columbiads and rifled guns, had sunk the "Cumberland", driven the "Congress" ashore and on fire, and now lying off where she could get a range was sending a few of her eleven inch shells over and through the camps. One shell struck the little house on the bluff, used by the commanding officer, General Mansfield, as headquarters, and within a short distance of where I was standing, knocking down the chimney and making a big hole, sending the old general out bareheaded and covered with dust and mortar, but fortunately injuring nobody.[5] Another shot struck a log Guard House knocking the logs in all directions. The "Merrimack" after a while, withdrew toward Norfolk, and darkness settled down upon as discouraged and disheartened a set of men as ever wore the blue. We stood on the bluff all the evening, the "Congress" burning, and it was a grand sight to see her masts and yards all aflame, and the fire bursting from her ports. Many of her guns had been left loaded when she was abandoned, and as the fire reached them they were discharged, some of the shots passing over our camp and one striking and sinking a supply schooner lying at our wharf. About midnight the magazine blew up—a magnificent and awful sight, and all that was left of the "Congress" was that which we saw the next morning blackened and shattered timbers sticking just out of water. We went to our quarters with heavy hearts, wondering what would happen next.

The Signal Corps, at the Fort, had signaled during the evening that the "Monitor" had arrived, but that did not mean much to us. We did

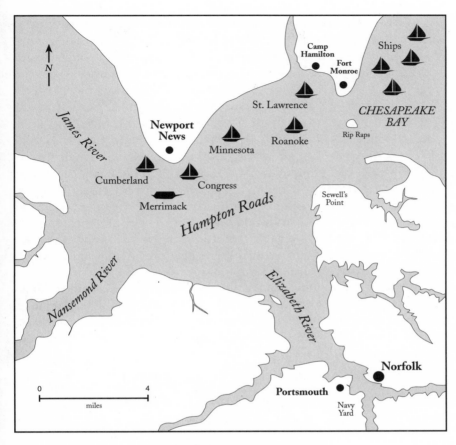

Hampton Roads, Virginia, 1862.

not know what a "Monitor" was, and the news gave little satisfaction. We also learned that the enemy was coming down from Yorktown to attack us. It was a "blue" time and there was little sleep in camp that night.

March 9th, 1862

The next morning I turned out early, wondering what the day would bring forth. We could see the "Merrimack" lying at anchor off Sewall's Point, and at about seven o'clock she started out with the intention, evidently, of destroying all our ships in Hampton Roads. As she headed for the "Minnesota", we saw coming out from behind the big war vessel a little craft, which we later learned was the "Monitor", aptly called by the rebels "a cheese box on a raft", and that is what she looked like. She boldly headed for the enemy's big ironclad, and we wondered what kind of a vessel it would be to dare to meet the huge and apparently invulnerable monster. We soon saw that the little "Monitor" was not afraid, for she steered straight for her big adversary, and for nearly four hours it was "give and take". Several of us officers went to the Point and watched the fight. I had a glass and could see every movement quite plainly, as the two vessels were not more than three or four miles away. We could not tell the result of course, but distinctly saw the "Merrimack" turn and start for Norfolk, twice, and the "Monitor" which was quicker in her movements, darted around her and turned her back. After a time, both seemed to have had enough, the "Merrimack" returning to Norfolk, and our little defender going to her former anchorage near the "Minnesota", which she had saved, as she had the other ships.

We had just finished dinner when some horsemen from the outposts dashed into camp with the report that the enemy was coming to attack us. The long roll sounded, and we hurried into line with the other troops, and were posted at the breastworks on the land side.

Naval encounter of the *Monitor* and the *Merrimack (Virginia)* at Hampton Roads, 1862. from *Battles and Leaders of the Civil War,* vol. 1, 1884.

While we stood anxiously watching the woods in our front, from which the enemy would probably come, Lieut. Col. Barnes, commanding the regiment in the absence of Col. Pierce, rode out to the front and said, "We may be called upon to meet the enemy this afternoon. You are the only Massachusetts men here." I shall never forget that moment nor the thrill that went through me at Col. Barnes' words. The enemy did not come within sight of the edge of the woods, but finding the position well entrenched and defended by a pretty strong force, withdrew without attacking. The garrison at Newport News at the time consisted of my regiment, 29th Massachusetts, the 1st, 2nd, 7th and 20th New York; the 7th New York being volunteers and not the famous militia regiment of the same number; the 7th and 20th were both composed entirely of Germans, the 7th (Steuben Rifles) being commanded by Count von Schack, an officer in the Prussian Guards.[6] There were also the remains of Ellsworth's famous regiment, 11th New York, and a regular Light Battery (Lodor's).[7] I guess we could have made a pretty good fight if attacked by land. We remained under arms all afternoon, and at night were dismissed with orders to be ready to move at a moments notice with one day's ration. We had two pretty exciting days and we all feel the effects of the excitement and anxi-

Officers of the *Monitor*, 1862. Mathew Brady photo, from *Mr. Lincoln's Camera Man*, 1946. Reprinted by permission of Russell & Volkening.

ety. We learned later if the rebel ironclad had been successful in destroying our navy, she was then to shell us out of our entrenchments, which she could easily have done, and General Magruder, who was waiting, would have killed or captured the whole force, we being entirely cut off from Fort Monroe.[8] The plan failed because of the timely arrival of the "Monitor", and her plucky fight which saved both navy and us. We were not disturbed by the enemy, after the first alarm, although the pickets on a part of our front were attacked once or twice. The days were devoted to drills, Company, regimental and brigade. I was in command of my Company quite a little, the Captain being on Court Martial, and the First Lieutenant on guard or picket. I really enjoyed the experience.

March 12th, 1862

I was officer of No. 5 Picket today, and at night the officer of the day came around and directed me to be very vigilant, as there was a large body of the enemy in the vicinity. I cautioned my men and waited anxiously all night, but no enemy came near my post.

March 18th, 1862

The past week has been full of rumors of impending attack, but nothing has happened. Today the regiment went out into the country seven or eight miles with seventeen wagons after wood. I went in command of "D" Company. We met several scouting parties, both cavalry and infantry and heard heavy firing in the direction of Yorktown, but we were not disturbed by anything or anybody and got our wood. It was a nice day and I enjoyed the trip very much.

March 19th, 1862

We had orders today to pack and be ready to move at short notice, so got my things together and am ready. In evening was in Captain Osgood's quarters.[9] I have become quite intimate with him and like him very much. He is a gentleman. I would much prefer being with him in "K" Company than in "D", for though the Captain and 1st Lieutenant are good fellows and nice to me, they are not quite so congenial as some others.

March 23rd, 1862

Sunday "inspection" today and our Company made so good an appearance, we were given the honor of "taking in the colors".

March 24th, 1862

There was quite a good deal of excitement in the regiment today on account of the alleged loose and disgraceful actions of our Colonel Pierce, and those of us among the officers, who are not his creatures or toadies, have strong hopes that he will resign. If he does not, I fear some of the best of the officers will, as Pierce is a poor specimen of a man and utterly unfit for the command of a regiment. How Governor Andrew could have been induced to commission him, I can not understand.[10] Later on, serious charges were preferred. He was court-martialed and dismissed from the service. The proceedings were approved by General Mansfield, but disapproved by General Wool.[11] What reasons he had for disapproval we did not know, but the result was disastrous to the regiment as it saddled Pierce upon us.[12]

March 26th, 1862

Was on picket yesterday and on coming off this morning found I had been detailed to command a section of the Water Battery on the bluff, relieving Lieut. Smith of my regiment who had resigned. This is very pleasing to me, and I suppose comes from my having had experience in heavy artillery drill while with my old company at Fort Monroe.

March 27th, 1862

Reported this morning to Col. Nauman, USA, commanding the artillery here, having received the order detailing me for duty with him.[13] He is a fine officer of the old school. My battery consists of one 8 inch Columbiad, smooth bore, and one 5 inch rifled gun. I have a fine lot of men in my detachment, from the 29th, and am quite at home in the drill for these guns. In the P.M. went out on battalion drill with my Company, as I want to keep up my infantry drills. In the evening was in Captain Osgood's quarters when a corporal of my detachment came and said the General wanted me at the battery. Hurried out, got my men, served out ammunition, and in a very short time was ready for business. It was reported that a rebel steamer was going to run by, but the night was intensely dark and we could see nothing, so after a time, by direction of the General, I dismissed my men and turned in.

March 28th, 1862

In the A.M. had gun drill and in the P.M. took my Company out on battalion drill. In the evening went to a meeting of the officers in Captain Clarke's quarters to consider a proposal of Col. Pierce to resign, but nothing was accomplished.

March 29th, 1862

No drills. Wrote a number of letters. In the evening, at the officer's mess, we gave a farewell spread to Lieut. Smith, who leaves for home next week—oysters, punch, etc. Had a fine time.

March 30th, 1862

It was so stormy today we had only inspection of quarters. At noon the regiment was paid, but I declined to sign the payroll, as there was a mistake of $50 against. In the evening had a session with the paymaster and got the correction made and received the full amount due, $200, my first pay as an officer, and somewhat different from the private's pay I previously had been receiving.

March 31st, 1862

This morning Vice President Hamlin and a party of ladies and gentlemen from Washington came up from the Fort rather unexpectedly, I guess, and I was ordered to fire a salute of seventeen guns.[14] I had only about five minutes notice, so had to hustle, but got through all right. In the P.M. a lot of us went down to the Fort to see Lieut. Smith off for home. The place was crowded with troops, wagons, etc. Looks as if something was going to be done.

April 1st, 1862

Was busy straightening out things at the battery. I want things in better shape than they have been.

April 5th, 1862

Yesterday a lot of troops passed our camp going in the direction of Yorktown, and today we have heard heavy firing in that direction, which has caused much excitement.[15]

April 11th, 1862

The past week has been quiet with the usual drills and occasional "alarms", but today there has been real excitement. In the early morning we received notice that the dreaded "Merrimack" was coming out again. Went to the battery and remained all day, but we saw no rebel vessel. At noon the regiment received orders to move out of the works if the "Merrimack" should shell us.

April 12th, 1862

This morning the rebel ironclad came out in plain sight, lying at the mouth of the Elizabeth River all day, but did not come within range. At dark a strange steamer appeared heading for us. Got all ready to fire on her, but just in time discovered she was one of our boats. In the evening a lot of officers came in the quarters which I have to share with the 1st Lieutenant, and there was a lot of drinking and carousing, which I do not enjoy, but under the circumstances, can not help.

April 14th, 1862

Lieut. Gould, who commands the right section of the water battery, and I were busy with our details building a target to be moored out in the stream for target practice, which we need badly. Gould belongs to a New York regiment and is a very nice fellow.

April 15th, 1862

Gould and I got our target of pork barrels on a raft afloat and were just going out with a boat to moor it when General Mansfield told us we had better wait a few days as we were probably to be attacked by the rebel steamers "Yorktown" and "Jamestown". Was much disappointed as we really should have practice if they ever expect us to hit anything. Captain Drake DeKay of General Mansfield's staff invited Gould and me to take a ride with him in his boat, and we were rowed out to the wreck of the "Cumberland", whose top masts are out of water, and then over to the remains of the "Congress". Mighty sad sights. Just after dinner a large body of troops came out of the woods and halted on our parade ground. Found it to be General Casey's division of ten or twelve regiments and three light batteries.[16] They made a fine appearance. After a short rest they moved off in the direction of Yorktown. In the evening had the men of the Company at my quarters to sign the clothing rolls, and afterwards walked out on the bluff with Captain Osgood, and watched signal lights that the enemy were showing. Also had a fine view with the Captain's glass, which is very powerful, of the moon, which is very unusually bright tonight.

April 17th, 1862

In the morning Lieut. Gould and I with our men took our target out and moored it about two thousand yards from shore, and got ready for practice, but we were allowed only one shot for each gun, so the firing was not very good, although Col. Nauman and General Mansfield were quite pleased with our shooting.

April 18th, 1862

The regiment went out today some three or four miles in heavy marching order. Being on detached service, I did not have to go and was glad to escape the heat and dust.

April 20th, 1862

Another alarm. We are getting lots of them nowadays. At night all lights were to be extinguished as a rebel steamer was reported to be coming up the river. Manned my guns and stayed at the battery for a while, but as usual, nothing happened. It was so dark I couldn't have seen anything anyway.

May 3rd, 1862

The days have passed in the usual way, with the usual drills and the usual alarms, which latter always come at night with the hurry to the guns and so far, for nothing. However, I suppose it is well to be on the safe side. Most of the evenings, when not on duty, I spend in Captain Osgood's quarters playing "500". This evening was out on the bluff with Lieut. Brooks enjoying the beautiful moonlight and its effects on the water. First Lieutenant Kern of my Company was placed under arrest today but we don't know the reason.[17] It is evident that fighting has commenced somewhere in the direction of Yorktown, for all the evening we have heard "the grand diapason of the commands" through the calm air of the beautiful night.

May 6th, 1862

Another alarm. Was called at 3 o'clock this morning by the sergeant of the guard who said there was a steamer going to run by. Manned the guns and was about to open on her as I could see her quite plainly, and she was a rebel without doubt, but was stopped by Col. Nauman, my chief. He would not let me fire. Can't understand why, unless we are short of ammunition, or perhaps it is feared that if we open fire it may be returned and the camp shelled. I don't like this being called constantly, at all hours of the night, to man the guns, and not being allowed to "blaze away" at something. Orders were received today for each company to devote a certain amount of time to skirmish drill instructions. Something we have never had. Captain Brady told the 1st Lieutenant, Kern, to instruct Company D, and Kern told me, so as I did not have anybody I could put it on, I had to take it, and commence to study up.[18] I really enjoyed the work and I think made a success of it, for Company D could deploy, rally or assemble with the best of them. While out with the Company drilling this A.M., the long roll sounded in camp and came in on the "double quick", and as usual, another false alarm. Received orders for the regiment to prepare to leave at once, a very familiar order, but we didn't go. In the P.M. battalion drill under Colonel Pierce, and a mighty poor drill it was. He is the poorest specimen of regimental commander I've ever seen or heard of. Wish Barnes was Colonel. It certainly does look as if we were going somewhere soon. I have my things packed all ready. Am a little afraid I may have to stay with the battery if the regiment moves, but am bound to go with it if possible.

May 7th, 1862

Had a fine battalion drill today under Lieut. Col. Barnes. He knows his business and is an officer and a gentleman. Pierce is neither. Was in command of Company as usual. Neither the Captain nor the 1st Lieutenant like to drill, if they can get out of it. In the evening, Colonel Nauman asked me to stay all night at the battery with my squad, as it was reported that a rebel steamer loaded with ordnance stores, was going to try to run our batteries and go up to Richmond. We took our blankets and spread them on the gun platforms and laid down, but of course no one slept. At midnight, I told the men to get some sleep, and they curled up in their blankets. I sat watching and waiting, but nothing happened. At daybreak I dismissed the men and went to my quarters.

May 8th, 1862

What season of alarms this is! Just after breakfast the long roll sounded, and I hurried to my station at the battery, and saw a lot of warlike looking ships coming up the river. They proved to be friends: the "U.S.S. Octavia", the ironclad "Galena", and several others. I remained at the battery all the A.M. watching our ships fighting some batteries up the river. Later they attacked the Sewall's Point battery and there was much noise and excitement. The New York detail at the right section of our water battery was relieved today by a detail from the 29th Regiment under Lieutenant Adams.[19] About all the regiments here are going up the river with General Mansfield, except the 29th, but we shall have to stay around here on account of our miserable Colonel, as it is reported the General will not take the regiment while he, Pierce, is in command. Too bad we are saddled with him.

May 9th, 1862

Heard we are to leave tomorrow, sure, but have heard that too often to place much confidence in it. Target practice, and brigade drill. Was in command of "D" as usual. I am getting good experience anyway.

Chapter 3

An Infantry Officer in the Army of the Potomac

On May 10, 1862, Ayling was relieved from artillery duty and was assigned as a second lieutenant of infantry in the 29th Massachusetts Regiment. The objective of General McClellan's Peninsula Campaign, between the York and the James Rivers, was to capture Richmond. The advance began on April 4, 1862, but was halted by the Confederates before Yorktown. After General Huger withdrew from Norfolk, destroying the *Merrimack* so that it would not fall into Federal hands, it was possible to support Union troops by a river fleet on the James.[1] But this fleet was repulsed at Drewry's Bluff on May 15. The slowness of McClellan's advance allowed the Confederate forces to consolidate. The climax came in the Seven Days battles beginning June 25. Ayling took part in the encounter at Gaines's Mill on June 27, the third of the Seven Days battles.[2]

May 10th, 1862

We are really off at last, and I have been relieved from the artillery. Started about six A.M. and marched to Camp Hamilton, near the Fort, about twelve miles, leaving baggage to follow later on by wagon. It was quite hot and we suffered some from heat and dust. Arrived at the camp about two P.M. and after a long and seemingly needless tramp around the grounds, went to the stables just vacated by a Pennsylvania cavalry regiment. Supposing we were to remain here all night, we got ourselves as comfortably fixed as possible, when we had to move.

Marched to Fort Monroe and halted in front of the Hygeia Hotel for a time, just before dark. Saw a number of the boys of my old company. Andrew Devol gave me a bottle of whiskey. We hung around until about ten o'clock and then went on board the old "Adelaide", the steamer I was Provost Marshal on a few months since, and we headed for the opposite shore at Willoughby's Point. Had a nice chat with my old friends, the officers of the boat. We landed between eleven and twelve and marched some three miles to a deserted rebel cavalry camp. We found the fires burning and evidences that the rebels had left hurriedly. Slept on top of a horse shed since the barracks were too filthy, and woke up in the night very cold. We had no blankets as it was expected that we would have a fight here, and all baggage was left behind. I found a vacant cook house off one side and slept there on the floor until morning. We have had a pretty hard day for beginners. Marched about fifteen miles in heat and dust with very little to eat.

May 11th, 1862

Woke up this morning feeling pretty "seedy". For breakfast had one piece of hard bread and a drink of coffee. Started early and marched into Norfolk, the enemy having gone out one side as we went in the other. Marched all over the city and then out to the entrenchments, where we camped for the night. Was detailed for guard; didn't enjoy this much as I have had no sleep for three or four nights to amount to anything. We passed Captain Davis and my old company on the road today. Was glad to see the old crowd. We heard early this morning while on the march a loud report or explosion off toward the river and somebody started the report that the rebels had blown up the "Merrimack", which proved to be true.

May 12th, 1862

On being relieved from guard, fixed a little shelter from the sun, and laid down and slept until afternoon. When I woke up, I found some of my men were building a shelter of boughs over me to protect me from the hot sun. Was very much pleased to think they had so much interest in making me comfortable. At night managed to get into a deserted house with some of the officers.

May 13th, 1862

Got a pass this morning to go to Norfolk, and took with me two of my former gunners, Corporals Fisk and Tighe, fine fellows both.[3] We went all around the city and over to the Navy Yard where the 16th Massachusetts is encamped. There are three Lowell companies in this regiment and I met a lot of acquaintances. Went back to Norfolk at noon and to a confectionery store to get some dinner. Had a nice chat with a very handsome woman and her husband, proprietors of the store. On returning to camp, found we are to move in the morning, and that orders were that one officer of each company must sleep with the men. In my Company, that of course meant me, so I crawled into the shelter the men had fixed for me and had a good night's sleep and rest.

May 14th, 1862

Started at sunrise and marched through Norfolk and over the river to Portsmouth to the Naval Hospital, where we are quartered for the present. A beautiful place and beautiful grounds, tastefully laid out. We officers have rooms in the building and are nicely fixed.

May 17th, 1862

On guard today with Company D at the hospital bridge. Some of the posts are in the city and I enjoyed the duty very much. In a house near guard headquarters were two little girls who amused us very much by singing rebel songs to us. "Bonnie Blue Flag", "Maryland, My Maryland", etc. About everybody around here is "secesh", and haven't much use for us.

May 18th, 1862

Captain Osgood and Lieut. Burbeck of Company K have resigned.[4] I am very sorry as the Captain has been my most intimate friend.

May 19th, 1862

Kern, 1st Lieut. of Company D resigned today. Hope I may be

promoted to fill the vacancy. Wrote Uncle Henry asking him to see if anything can be done towards my promotion. A pretty little dog attached himself to me today and sticks to me as if I were his master. No "secesh" about him.

May 20th, 1862

Company D on guard today. The regiment left us on guard and moved back to the Navy Yard. By Captain Brady's direction, went with the regiment to arrange for our quarters and to look after things. Tried to get tents for the Company but got only two. Got our baggage and things into one of them and straightened things out for the night as far as possible. Our camp is outside the Navy Yard in a swampy place. Rations are short all around. Had a piece of hard bread for supper. The men call this "Camp Starvation". There does not seem to be any need of a shortage of food here.

May 21st, 1862

When Captain Brady came in from guard this morning, he was cross and disagreeable. Nothing suited him although I had done the best I could to get things in shape for him. Don't like him a bit, or his way of doing things. Shall try to get out of Company D if possible. Today we are getting rations in plenty and the men feel better. In our mess today we have strawberries brought in by some darkies. Have been in service just a year today.

May 22nd, 1862

Was in charge of a fatigue party and went out in the woods for fuel. A very hard shower came up with a high wind. Got wet through. When I got back to camp, found my tent had blown down and blankets and everything soaking wet. Had a letter from Mary Crowell saying she was going to be married. Was much surprised. Another "wet blanket".

May 24th, 1862

Moved camp again today. We certainly do move some! Short of rations again. My dinner was hard bread and "salt horse".

May 25th, 1862

Got a pass to go to Fort Monroe. Had a nice sail and a chance to see the strong works the rebels had thrown up to defend Norfolk and the Navy Yard. I don't see why they gave the place up without fight. Had a delightful day with my old company, which has been turned into a light battery. Captain Davis and Lieut. Farrar insisted upon my being their guest and took good care of me. This morning had a letter from Uncle Henry saying there was no chance for me to get the First Lieutenantcy in Company D. I can fully understand the situation. One must be a toady to Col. Pierce to get anything in this regiment and that I will not be.

May 27th, 1862

Was with friends at the Fort all day. Lieut. Farrar and I took two of the battery horses and rode over to Camp Hamilton. Took the night boat to Norfolk, and found the regiment had moved again about a mile and are now an advanced post outside the entrenchments. Found Captain Brady surly and disagreeable as he is a good part of the time. He is probably disgruntled because I left him to go to the Fort. He does not like work.

May 31st, 1862

Very hot. Fortunately was not on duty as it was the hottest yet. Engaged a servant, which I was entitled to by regulations. He is a contraband named Bob and seems quite bright and intelligent. Can make him very useful.

June 3rd, 1862

At half past twelve this morning Lieut. Col. Barnes came to the tent, woke us up and directed that the men be aroused and made ready to march at once. I naturally had this duty and after getting the men up and all ready, found we were not to move until morning, so went back to bed and slept until reveille. We started about seven for Suffolk. Very hot day and Col. Pierce kept us going with few halts. After one halt in the blazing sun I attempted to rise, but everything grew black and I should have fallen if the Captain had not caught me. After being attended to by the surgeon, I felt better and kept on the road. Came near a sunstroke, I guess. The regiment suffered much on this march. Captain Leach fell senseless by the side of the road, and several men had convulsions.[5] We reached Suffolk about eleven at night, having made a forced march of twenty-five miles on a terribly hot day without the slightest necessity, and the men having had very little experience in marching. Col. Pierce is responsible and is totally unfit to command a regiment.

June 4th, 1862

Rained hard all day. Felt wretched but had to be out and about getting the Company street laid out and tents pitched. Company D was ordered for guard tonight and I had to go, although I feel quite miserable, as Captain Brady is off duty, as usual, when there is anything to be done.

June 5th, 1862

On coming off guard duty this morning felt quite sick. My blanket was soaking wet so could not lie in my tent. Captain Doten of Company E, a dear old man, took me into his tent and I tried to get some sleep, but my head ached too badly.[6] At night slept in my own tent, but the blankets were very damp.

June 6th, 1862

Upon getting up this morning felt sick enough to go to bed. At noon the regiment was ordered on to open platform cars and was carried back to Portsmouth in a hard rain. On arriving, I went, by the advice of the officer, to the Naval Hospital, but it was so full I could not get in. On my way back to camp, met Captain Tom O'Hare, of the 16th Mass., an old Lowell friend, who is Assistant Provost Marshal, and he seeing I was ill, took me into his quarters and gave me a good bed for the night. Tomorrow I shall go to Fort Monroe and try to get into the General Hospital.

June 7th, 1862

This morning took the boat for the Fort and on arriving went to the Hygeia Hotel, now used as General Hospital; found there Harlan Goodale of my old company, who is acting Hospital Steward. He took me in his

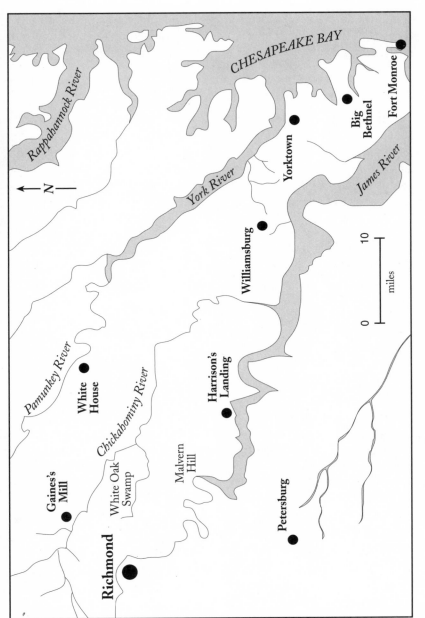

The peninsula of Virginia, 1862.

room and made me as comfortable as possible. Felt very poor and have a bad cough. This morning the regiment left Norfolk by steamer for White House Landing on the Pamunkey River. Wish I was with them!

June 8th, 1862

Felt somewhat better this morning and wanted to go to the regiment, but Dr. Cuyler, the U.S. Surgeon in charge, says no, and that I would better stay here until entirely well. Don't see what the trouble is with me. I don't feel sick enough to go to bed, so wander around without life or energy. Guess it is the combined effects of sun and damp blankets. My cough is bad and spoils my rest at night.

June 10th, 1862

Felt too sick to leave my room today. Am disgusted with myself.

June 14th, 1862

Am feeling better today. Only the cough hangs on still. Shall join the regiment tomorrow, if possible.

June 15th, 1862

In the morning went bidding my friends at the Fort goodbye and at ten o'clock took the boat for White House Landing. Felt rather "blue", homesick and generally miserable, although the sail was very pleasant. We went up Chesapeake Bay to the York River and up that river to the Pamunkey and to the White House. Had a good view of the fortifications at Yorktown as we passed. The Pamunkey is said to be the crookedest river in the world, and I believe it. Was really surprised at its amazing crooks and turns. I arrived at the landing in the early evening and learned the regiment was at the front about twenty miles up the railroad and that I could not reach it that night, so concluded to remain on the boat for the night. Spread my blanket on the floor in the saloon and slept fairly well.

June 16th, 1862

At five o'clock this morning took the train, which consisted of freight cars, on the military railroad and started for the regiment. Captain Pray of "ours" was aboard and on arriving at the end of the railroad piloted me to the camp of the 29th.[7] All hands seemed glad to see me, and I found my dog and contraband all right. Lieut. Brooks has been assigned to the Company as First Lieutenant to fill the vacancy caused by Kern's resignation, and I am much pleased, as I like him, although I feel that I should have had the promotion.[8] The regiment is at Fair Oaks station on the Richmond and York River railroad, and we are in the Second Corps (Sumner's),[9] Richardson's Division,[10] and Meagher's Brigade.[11] The latter is, with the exception of the 29th, composed entirely of Irish regiments, the 63rd, 69th and 88th New York, and is known as the "Irish Brigade". The commander, Thomas Francis Meagher, is an Irish patriot of considerable note. I found the regiment in the front line quite near the enemy. The pickets are in close contact, and there is almost continual firing. The tents issued to us are queer; they are in halves, each about six feet long and three wide, made to button together, forming a tent supposed to be big enough for two men. There are no ends, and are called "shelter" tents, which is all they are. Captain Brady has gone in with Captain Leach, and Brooks and I occupy our "dog kennel" together.

June 17th, 1862

It was quite cold for June last night, and I did not get much sleep. Got up at one o'clock and walked around to keep warm. At three the regiment turned out under arms and stood at the entrenchments in line of battle until sunrise. This I find is the regular thing, and has to be done every morning to prevent surprise, I guess, as our lines are very close to the enemy, the picket lines in some places being only twenty yards apart. By some stupid orders, all overcoats were left with the baggage at White House, and the men suffer some as the nights are cold and damp. Turned in early, but was too cold to sleep. There were several alarms during the night.

June 18th, 1862

Company D on fatigue duty in trenches digging had a pretty hard day. In the afternoon General Hooker on our left advanced his lines, and there was brisk firing over there for an hour or two.[12] The battery where we were at work throwing shells into the woods at the same time made things quite lively. A large body of the enemy came out on the nine mile road, so called, which runs directly through our camp, but were driven back by the artillery fire.

June 19th, 1862

Last night was full of alarms and we spent most of the time in line waiting for an attack. In the morning got a pass and went by train to White House. Took five men with me to get overcoats, blankets, etc., from where the regimental baggage was left. Found we could not get back tonight, so found good quarters for myself and party and had a comfortable night and a good rest and sleep, about the first since leaving Fort Monroe.

June 20th, 1862

Was busy in the morning getting ready to return to the regiment. Met my Lowell friend, Captain Tom O'Hare of the 16th, who gave me a description of the fight of two days ago when we heard so much firing and in which his regiment was engaged. He told me his brother, whom I knew, was killed. Got to camp at noon, found the regiment on fatigue duty in the trenches, and after a hasty dinner, joined it. Our working party was shelled, but no one hurt.

June 21st, 1862

Did not turn out at three this morning, but slept until eight, having a right good rest. Rearranged my tent, fixing things a little more comfortably, and had Bob, my contraband, clean my sword and pistol. Called at hospital to see Lieut. Brooks, who is ill. On return tried to write in diary, but there was heavy firing on the picket line on our front, and we had to form line at the works where we remained most of the afternoon. In the evening tried to write, but it surely is a night of alarms. We were called out fifteen times before morning.

June 22nd, 1862

Was pretty sleepy this morning and after breakfast turned in and slept until noon. An unusually quiet day. Something must be brewing or the rebs would not be so quiet.

June 23rd, 1862

Another quiet day with no firing. The regiment is ordered for picket tonight. Our lines are so near the enemy, the pickets are posted after dark. Our posts are in a dense wood full of undergrowth, and it would be impossible to see anyone a short distance away, even in daylight. We have double pickets, two men on each post, and the posts five paces apart, and are so near the enemy we can hear movements and voices. In the evening Lieut. Col. Barnes, Field Officer of the Day, came out to us and ordered an advance of the whole line, each post to move to the front five paces and halt until aligned on right and left, then five paces more, and keep it up until we struck the enemy. I had no end of trouble keeping my line anywhere near straight in the darkness and thick woods. Had to keep moving the whole length of the Company as deployed, and making as little disturbance as possible. We did not have to go far, however, before we found the enemy all ready for us, as they could not help hearing our movements. Having located them to the satisfaction of the authority ordering the movement, we were ordered to fall back, five paces at a time, to our former position. This was worse than the advance, and I had to repeat the running back and forth to notify my men to fall back slowly and not lose touch. It was a "low down" job and to add to the trouble, it commenced to rain hard with thunder and lightning. In trying to find one of the posts which had probably gotten out of line, I got lost, and completely turned around. I realized I was between the lines, but had lost all sense of direction, and had no idea as to which was north and which south. I could not hear anything to guide me, and felt that I was in a bad situation. If I approached too near either line, I was sure to be fired upon, there being no challenging as with ordinary guards, and I expected the enemy would attack and I should be between two fires. I was pretty nervous, and finally could stand the strain no longer, and made up my mind to find a picket line somewhere. I moved a few paces at a time, and as quietly as possible, and after a time, which seemed ages to me, I heard the unmistakable click, click of a rifle being cocked. I dropped to the ground and kept still, expecting a shot, but none came, and I heard two men talking very softly. From what little I could hear, I thought the voices sounded northern, rather than southern; at any rate, I was determined to end my horrible suspense, so called in a low tone, "For heaven's sake, don't shoot!" and very much to my surprise and relief a voice replied, "Is that you Lieutenant Ayling?" I immediately advanced and found I had wandered off to the left, past the posts of my Company, and had come out on the posts of Company E. I soon got back to my own command; the rest of the night passed without incident, although off to the left the pickets were busy. It was a mighty bad night for me, and I feel as if I should always look back at my experience between the picket lines of two armies as a horrible nightmare.

June 24th, 1862

Did not feel well today, and after being relieved from picket, laid around quietly to recover from the nerve racking of last night. Several alarms, but nothing serious.

June 25th, 1862

Felt poor. Have some of the prevailing camp disorder, diarrhea. Luckily there was not much to do until night, when six companies, including D, were ordered to go out and cut down some trees on our left and front, to clear away shelter from some of the sharpshooters who have been annoying us. We had to go outside the pickets and within a few yards of the enemy, who soon found out what we were doing and attacked us, driving us in. We were then sent to the right, where we were better protected. This whole movement was a farce. The men were furnished with axes and helves, and told to put them together, something very few knew how to do, and the night was so dark a man could hardly see the tree he was at work upon, and everybody was rather nervously expecting another attack. Mighty little chopping was done, but we were out until three o'clock in the morning and tired enough when we struck camp. General Sumner, our Corps Commander, is expecting an attack in force today and advanced his left, having quite a sharp fight. It did not reach our immediate front, although our batteries shelled the woods for several hours.

June 26th, 1862

Contrary to our expectations, we were not attacked today. The pickets kept up a lively rattle and we could hear heavy firing away off to the right, in the direction of General Porter's Corps.[13] We were under arms all day. In the evening, we formed line and General Meagher rode up and made a rousing speech, telling us General Porter had whipped the enemy in his fight on the right, and we all felt first rate and cheered ourselves hoarse. We had our contrabands out dancing and singing. My Bob is quite an artist in that line.

June 27th, 1862

Very heavy firing on the right again this morning and nearer than it was yesterday. We learned that instead of a victory yesterday, it was a bad defeat for our side. We were much disgusted after our "jubilation" of last night, and there is a feeling in the regiment that the next time the 29th cheers for a victory, it will be for a "sure one". We were under arms all day until about five o'clock, when our brigade and French's were ordered to march with blankets and three days' rations, to reinforce the right, which we heard had been badly whipped again today.[14] It was a very hot day and the roads were rough and dusty. After going about five miles, mostly at "double quick", we reached the vicinity of the battlefield too late to do anything but help cover the retreat of the right wing of the army. We moved to the front, meeting stragglers who told terrible tales of the fight—wounded men lying beside the road, and crippled men hobbling to the rear, using rifles as crutches. As we came over the brow of the hill and looked down upon the little valley and the mill which I suppose gives the name "Gaines's Mill" to the battle, we saw a sight never to be forgotten. The whole valley seemed filled with one mass of men, or disorganized mob, parts of various regiments of infantry, dismounted cavalry, and artillery men without guns, all passing not hurriedly, but steadily, to the rear; and in the midst, ambulances filled with wounded, trying to work their way through. Many officers were trying to rally the men, but the tide was setting too strongly to the rear. We were the leading regiment of the brigade and formed in "double column at half distance", which brought our colors in the first division, and we moved steadily down the hill, parting the crowd from right to left as water is parted by the bows of a ship. The enemy seeing the arrival of fresh troops, fell back, and the steady advance of our two brigades gave courage to the dispirited, tired and retreating men, and they began to rally, members of different regiments standing shoulder to shoulder, trying to form a line of defense. Some fell in with our regiment, and one man of a Pennsylvania regiment with his left hand hurt and wrapped in a dirty, bloody rag, came beside me, in the line of file closers, with the remark that he "reckoned he was good for another shot at the Rebs." We moved slowly forward and halted at the foot of the hill, formed line, and the men laid down. The enemy was not far away and occasionally threw shells in our direction. Only three came near the regiment; one went over us, the second struck the remains of a fence, and the third struck Lieut. Mayo, whose Company was next on the left to mine, in the neck, tearing away his throat and killing him almost instantly.[15] I was talking with him at the time and his death was a great shock to me. He was a fine man and I liked him very much. It seemed like a fatality, as no other shots came near us. We had to leave him unburied where he fell, as we were ordered to move at once, and started back for our camp, arriving about sunrise, pretty well used up.

Chapter 4

McClellan's Retreat and the
Hospitalization of Lieutenant Ayling

General McClellan's attempt to take Richmond was stalled by encounters at Oak Grove, Mechanicsville, and finally at the Battle of Gaines's Mill. Thereafter the Army of the Potomac was in retreat. General Robert E. Lee had become, in effect, the leader of the Confederate forces. However, the Federal retreat was well executed, and Sumner's Corps, to which Ayling belonged, played an important part as the rear guard delaying the Confederate pursuit. The climax came at the Battle of Malvern Hill, where a strong Federal defensive position and superior artillery inflicted heavy losses on the Confederates. Thereafter McClellan withdrew safely to a base at Harrison's Landing on the James River with gunboat support.

Ayling participated at Malvern Hill, but weakened by illness, he was eventually hospitalized and nearly died of typhoid fever. He was sent to the military hospital at Bedloe's Island in New York harbor and then given sick-leave to return home.[1]

June 28th, 1862

After breakfast, we were ordered to move our camp about one hundred paces to the rear and while pitching our tents, orders came for Company D to go on picket at once. This was a little rough as we had a hard day yesterday and a hard march last night. Capt. Brady and Lieut. Brooks are both off duty, sick, so I had to go in command, although I am far from well myself. We were posted without much difficulty, and the day passed very quietly, but we could hear sounds back in camp that told us something unusual was going on. After dark, an aide came out and ordered me to hold the line, no matter what happened, until relieved, and impressed it upon me strongly that the line must be held. All night we could hear the rattling of artillery and wagon wheels and other sounds which indicated the movement of the army. My men were getting to be somewhat anxious, and so was I. We felt we were left to be sacrificed and fully expected to be killed or captured. Why the enemy did not attack, I don't understand. They must have heard the same sounds that we did, and known the army was falling back.

June 29th, 1862

Just before daylight orders came to get my pickets out as quickly and quietly as possible, without letting the enemy know. I notified my men

Battle of Savage's Station, Virginia, 1862.
From *Battles and Leaders of the Civil War,* vol. 2, 1884.

and we crawled out as carefully as we could and had almost reached our works when the rebel pickets appeared at the edge of the woods and opened fire. We had to run, but got in all right and started to find the regiment, which we did about four miles away on the railroad. We were kept moving about, from one place to another nearly all day. Made a hurried march to a place called "Peach Orchard", to repel a threatened attack, then moved to Savage's Station on the Richmond and York River Railroad, taking a position on a hill to protect from a flank attack.[2] While lying here some of the wounded were brought up and laid in rows just in our rear, where the surgeons attended them. It was a sad sight. The day was very hot and our hurried movements used up a lot of officers and men, some of whom fell senseless. Everything seems to be going wrong with our side, an immense amount of stores being burned, and ammunition destroyed. A long train of box cars was loaded with shells, cartridges and all kinds of combustible things, and the engine fired up, the cars set on fire and the train started full speed down the road toward a burned bridge over the Chickahominy River, where it plunged off. We could see

Destroying ammunition train, Chickahominy River, 1862.
From *Battles and Leaders of the Civil War*, vol. 2, 1884.

the start very clearly from our position, a great sight. We seem to be a part of the rear guard, and are to wait until the army has a good start for the rear. Started at nine o'clock and marched all night over very rough roads and in a hard rain. Have felt quite sick today, and weak; the diarrhea has troubled me badly, but I managed to keep with the regiment.

June 30th, 1862

About four o'clock this morning, we crossed the bridge at White Oak Swamp, destroying it after us.[3] Here we are to wait until the wagon trains get away, and defend the crossing. We had a few hours before the enemy came up, and took all the rest we could. Along in the forenoon the rebels brought up two batteries, and suddenly opened up on us, without warning, across the swamp. I was fast asleep but I jumped to my feet at the sound of firing. I carried away a half of a shelter tent which some of my men had put over me to keep off the sun. They had made a very good shelter by snapping the four corners of the tent in the locks of rifles and sticking the bayonets in the ground. This act of thoughtful kindness touched me deeply. All was not excitement. A part of the wagons had not started and several hundred mules were unhitched and being watered. When the shells began to strike among them, there was a stampede in all directions and we had to look out both ways, being bombarded by Rebs in front and crazy mules in the rear. Our line was soon formed and we moved up to a little hill to support a battery which had just arrived. Here Col. Pierce made a bad blunder. Instead of forming his line below the hill and then moving up to the proper position, he marched us by the flank along the crest, in plain sight of the enemy and under heavy fire. In the movement Col. Pierce lost an arm, several officers were wounded and four or five men killed. Among the latter, was Sergeant Kellam of Company H, who had both legs taken off, and fell directly under my feet so that I had to step over him.[4] We were marching quite fast, as troops do when under fire, and had I been one step further forward, I should have been killed instead of poor Kellam. It almost completely broke me up. When Col. Pierce was hit, Lieut. Col. Barnes, a soldier every inch, took command, and soon put us in position, behind the battery we were supporting, but under the crest of the hill, where we were as well protected as possible, under the circumstances. We laid down and remained here until nearly dark, under a horrible fire of shell, grape, canister, and apparently every known artillery projectile.

The rise of ground, behind which we were lying, was very slight, and we had to hug the ground very closely. Shots would frequently strike a few feet in front, covering us with turf and dirt, and others seemed to just skim over us. Two officers and several men were wounded here, among the latter, Corporal Darby of my Company.[5] A lead ball, probably from a spherical case shot, struck me on the left arm, inside the elbow, but it was nearly spent and did not penetrate, although it numbed my arm so that at first I thought my arm was gone. A black bruise as large as a silver dollar and a slight lameness was all, but I was surely scared. My First Sergeant, Hamlin, lying beside me, picked the ball from the fold of my blouse, and gave it to me.[6] Shall keep it as a souvenir of White Oak Swamp, and a hard, nerve racking afternoon. About dark there was heavy firing off to the left, and we were ordered to move in that direction, reaching the battlefield about eight o'clock. There was not much firing when we arrived, but plenty of signs that there had been a fight. Broken and disabled artillery carriages, discarded knapsacks, blankets, rifles, etc., and a lot of dead, who would probably never be buried. After remaining here for an hour

Destroyed bridge, White Oak Swamp, Virginia, 1862.
Mathew Brady photo, from *Mr. Lincoln's Camera Man,* 1946.
Reprinted by permission of Russell & Volkening.

or so, we started once more on the retreat, still the rear guard.
Marched all night over very hard, rough roads. Fires had been built
at intervals to light our way, and men stood with axes at partly cut
trees, ready to fell them as soon as we passed, to obstruct the enemy.
It was a very unpleasant night march. Felt really very ill, diarrhea bad
and bowels so sore I had to hold my belt up with my hands. Thought
several times I should drop, but managed to keep up.

July 1st, 1862

After an all night march, we reached and joined the main army,
and were halted on a hill near where General McClellan's headquarters were said to be.[7] We got a pretty good shelling, and after a time
were moved down the hill and stood in line, awaiting and expecting
an attack, most of the forenoon. There was a lively fight going on, but,
with our usual good luck, it did not reach our front. General Meagher,
our Brigade Commander, got a lot of sheep somewhere, or somehow,
and had killed and distributed them to the different regiments of the
brigade, cut up into all sorts of chunks, and the men made little fires
and tried to cook them on sharpened sticks held over the flames. This
is the first thing I have had to eat, with the exception of a few pieces
of hard bread, for three days, and none of us got much good from our
meat, for before it was half cooked, we were ordered to "fall in". Some
of the men stuck their half raw chunks on their bayonets, determined
not to lose their meat. I was toasting my piece on the point of my
sword, and when the order came to move, I marched with sword in
one hand and the bloody, greasy chunk of mutton in the other, occasionally trying to gnaw off a mouthful, but without much success,
except that I got a little of the blood and juice, which helped some.
All the afternoon the fight raged furiously, but we were left in the second line, in reserve, probably on account of our hard service in the
rear guard. We were, however, near enough to the fighting line to get
some of the shots. About the middle of the afternoon we were ordered
on the "double quick" to a position nearer the front. The heat was
terrible and many fell out, overcome and used up. I suffered much from
my sore bowels and had to support the weight of my belt with both
hands. Some of the men were hit here. Towards dark we were ordered
to the left to support a battery and laid here all night, but got no sleep.
During the excitement of the fight all my pain left me, or I forgot it,
but when the reaction came, I was a wreck, so weak I could hardly

stand. We learned the place where the fight was is called "Malvern Hill".

July 2nd, 1862

At three o'clock in the morning we started, again on the retreat, with the rest of the army, for the James River at Harrison's Landing, where we can have the help of the navy and where we hope to have a rest. It rained hard and the roads were very bad—mud half way to our knees in places. I never suffered so much in my life as on this march. Was very weak and in much pain. Could hardly walk and it was only by the strongest effort that I could keep up with the regiment. We all suffered for want of water, and I had to drink from mud puddles to keep from fainting. When we reached our destination, I went, with Captain Richardson, to a building used for a hospital, but it was crowded full, and hundreds were lying in the mud without covering.[8] We sat in the rain a while, when Lieut. Ripley of "ours" came along, and seeing our condition, got us into a house nearby with several other officers of the 29th.[9] We were all in one room and very much crowded, but managed to get a place to lie down on the floor, and after a while, someone brought us a little beef tea, which revived us somewhat. It was the first thing I have had to eat for two days, with the exception of the piece of half raw mutton at Malvern Hill. I got a little sleep during the day, but was cold and very uncomfortable, my clothing being soaking wet.

July 3rd, 1862

Still raining. Was very sore and in much pain. A most miserable day. We had a little more beef tea, and Lieut. Ripley tried to look after us as well as he could. At night our Chaplain, Mr. Hempstead, got us a little better room.[10] There are six of us 29th officers here: Captains Leach and Richardson, and Lieutenants Whitman, Adams, Brooks and myself.[11] We spread some bedding on the floor and made ourselves as comfortable as we could. I have not washed or had my boots off for a week, and there is no chance now to get clean as water is scarce, and guards have been placed over each well. I have not strength to get to the river. It is reported we whipped the rebels badly at Malvern Hill, and I hope the retreat is over and we can get some rest, for we are all worn out. I am feeling quite ill.

July 4th, 1862

Had a fairly good sleep last night, and am feeling a little better, except for weakness and the pain in my bowels, which is bad. We, of this room, are about half starved, so clubbed together and sent to the landing for some soft bread and butter, and made a good meal. Was very "blue" all day. Rather a different "Fourth" from some I have had. Hope to get to the regiment in a few days.

July 5th, 1862

Felt somewhat better today, and in better spirits. Am troubled with the miserable diarrhea, or dysentery, or whatever it is, and it uses up my strength. Walked out a little, but am quite weak. Shall try to go to the regiment tomorrow.

July 6th, 1862

After breakfast Captain Richardson and I walked to the landing, with some difficulty, and bought some necessary articles, and I then reported to the regiment, which was pleasantly encamped in some woods. There were no tents, but during the day some were issued to us, and with the help of some of my "boys" I got mine pitched. Have no blankets or overcoats, so at night, covered myself with a piece of tent, and slept quite comfortably. Am very weak.

July 7th, 1862

Felt a little better today. Went to the landing and bought some food and to the Quartermaster's for coffee and sugar, so guess I shall be all right in a day or two. Captain Brady is on sick list, and I am in command of the Company. The day was hot and we suffered much from the heat. There is a good deal of sickness in the regiment and we can report only a small number for duty.

July 8th, 1862

Another hot day, and couldn't do much but try to keep cool. Toward evening President Lincoln visited the army and rode along our lines twice. This is the first time I have seen him. He looked sad and careworn. Captain Brady still off duty, leaving everything to fall on me. Don't believe he is any sicker than I.

July 9th, 1862

Early this morning went to the river to get a bath, and on coming back, found the regiment had been ordered on fatigue duty, and all the companies in line except mine. I had thought the Captain would be on duty today and look after things, but he went on the sick list again today, leaving me in command. He should have told me and I would have stayed in camp and got my breakfast, which I did not get. The Major spoke very sharply to me for keeping the regiment waiting, and my anger at the Captain for not informing me that he was off duty, so I could have been ready with the Company, and in my indignation at my undeserved reprimand, together with the disgust at losing my breakfast, I ripped out some remarks which were very unmilitary and insubordinate, winding up damning the service and everybody and everything connected with it. I was certainly liable to court martial, and might have been dismissed from the service, had not Major Chipman, in the goodness of his heart, ignored, or pretended not to hear my language, which he, and most of the regiment, surely did.[12] I got my Company into its place in line, and we started off—I breakfastless, and pretty mad. We marched out two or three miles and worked throwing up entrenchments and burying dead mules, until about three o'clock in the afternoon, when the fallen timber outside our works caught fire, and we returned to camp. A very hot day and I suffered badly from the heat and from my old trouble. We had dress parade tonight, the first for a long time.

July 10th, 1862

Rainy and cold and as my tent leaked, was not very comfortable. Had neither overcoat nor blanket, and would have laid without anything to cover me, if one of my boys had not loaned me a blanket. The Company was on camp guard today, but I did not go. Remained quietly in my tent. Am in much pain, blue and homesick.

July 11th, 1862

The wretched diarrhea and accompanying pain is using me up.

Laid in tent all day. It rained and I got pretty wet through my leaky tent. A most miserable day.

July 12th, 1862

A fine day, which cheered me up some and I felt in better spirits. Kept quiet in my tent. The past week has been a hard one for me. I have felt so poor.

July 13th, 1862

Brigade inspection this forenoon and we all suffered from the heat, standing so long in the sun. In afternoon quiet in tent. The bowel trouble and pain seem to grow worse rather than better, and I am getting discouraged, but am going to keep on duty as long as possible.

July 14th, 1862

Took the Company out for drill in the morning, but was not able to go on battalion drill later. In the afternoon we had to move our camp a short distance. The Captain, as usual, was off duty and I had everything to do, which was pretty rough in my condition.

July 15th, 1862

The regiment ordered on fatigue duty today, burying dead horses and mules which had become badly decayed. A very disagreeable and sickening job. At noon, I found I could keep up no longer and was relieved, and went back to camp. It rained hard in the night and I got quite wet.

July 21st, 1862

Was carried to the regimental hospital today, having laid in my tent since the 15th very weak, sick, and a good part of the time unconscious of what was going on.

July 30th, 1862

The past nine or ten days have been blanks to me, and all I know about them is what I have been told by the doctor and nurses. On the

28th, they tell me, (my birthday) I was put into an ambulance and brought to this place, which is the General Hospital, sick with typhoid fever and "crazy as a loon". Today I began to know something, and as I became conscious, saw bending over me, a sweet, womanly face, felt a cool hand on my forehead, and heard a voice saying, "You poor boy." As I looked up into her kind, pitying eyes, it seemed as if she were an angel, and she was to me, for I shall always believe her care and nursing saved my life. I learned she was a volunteer nurse belonging to one of the Roman Catholic sisterhoods, although what order, or where she came from I never knew, but I shall never forget sweet "Sister Agnes". The doctor told me today he did not think I could live through last night, but now the danger was past, and I was going to get well.

August 6th, 1862

The past week has been quietly passed in bed, but I am beginning to have a ravenous appetite, but the doctor says I must keep to a "farinaceous diet". I don't like it and would give something for a big beefsteak. I find myself in a very pleasant room in the General, or Brick House Hospital, as it is called, and in the room are our Adjutant, Collingwood, Captain Tomlinson, and Lieutenant White of Baker's California Regiment, and Doctor Hayes of the 72nd Pennsylvania.[13] It looks as if we will have an agreeable set in this room, when we get acquainted and have a little more strength. I am having trouble with my right leg. Something, I fancy, like sciatica, or rheumatism, but the doctor does not seem to know what it is. It pains me nights and I cannot use it to go out of the room, as I would like to, for my strength is coming back, and I want to get about.

August 7th, 1862

Was allowed a very small bit of meat today. My leg is very painful.

August 8th, 1862

Am getting stronger quite fast, but suffer a good deal from the pain in my leg. It is drawn up and stiffened so that my knee is kept bent and the only way I can get a little sleep is to prop and support the leg with pillows, so that the hip, knee and ankle joints are exactly in line, otherwise the pain is horrible.

August 10th, 1862

Am getting stronger quite fast, and if it were not for my leg, should feel much encouraged, but I cannot straighten my knee, or walk a step, and do not get much sleep.

August 11th, 1862

This afternoon the Ward Master told us that "all who could walk" were to be sent down the river this evening. As I cannot walk, was much worried, fearing I would be left here, but when the ambulance came, I managed, with help, to crawl in, and we were taken to the landing to the steamer "Vanderbilt". Lieutenant White was the only one of our room with me, and without his help I never should have been able to get on the boat. After getting on board, and rested a little, felt better, and enjoyed the cool breeze from the river.

August 12th, 1862

About four o'clock this morning, we started and steamed down the James River to Fort Monroe, where we laid at the dock for some hours. Tried to find a familiar face in the crowd, but saw none. After a tedious wait in the hot sun, we got away, but upon getting outside, ran into a gale and had to put back for the night. Learned we were to go to New York, which pleased us.

August 13th, 1862

Early in the morning, we started again, but found head winds and a rough sea outside, so put back. We went up to Norfolk for coal and while there got some peaches, which tasted mighty good. Anchored off Fort Monroe for the night.

August 14th, 1862

Started once more this morning and at night reached the Delaware Breakwater, and anchored for the night. The "Vanderbilt" is a very poor sea boat, evidently.

Left our anchorage early this morning and reached New York in the early evening. It has been a hard, painful trip, and anything but cheerful.

The main saloon of the boat is crowded with cots, all occupied by sick soldiers, some of whom are delirious. Several died on the passage, one on the cot next to mine. One of the men nurses who was at the Brick House Hospital at Harrison's Landing while I was there, told me the doctor then said there was no hope of my living through the night of July 30th. I seem to have had chronic diarrhea and typhoid fever, combined, so I guess I was pretty sick. We remained on the boat all night.

August 16th, 1862

A very nice breakfast was sent to us this morning from the city, the first we have had since leaving the hospital. They about starved us on the boat, and some of the nurses (men) were saucy and independent. We were glad when on the forenoon a steamer came alongside and took most of the officers and some of the enlisted men to this place, Bedloe's Island, a short distance from the harbor. It is cool and pleasant, and I like the looks of things here.[14]

August 17th, 1862

Am getting settled down here and am greatly pleased with my quarters. The surgeon in charge, Dr. Brown, U.S.A., seems to be a fine man, and everything is clean and neat. The only thing that troubles me is my leg, which aches so, and pains me so badly I get very little sleep nights, and it is drawn up at the knee and stiff so I can not bend it at all. Have been given a pair of hospital crutches, of pine, with no padding for the arm. Rather crude, but I manage to hobble around on them.

August 18th, 1862

Was very lame today. Could not go down to meals. Wrote Mother at Albany, where she is now living, and to Uncle Henry, telling him where I am. It was hard work, I am so weak and in such pain. Quite a lot of visitors came today with fruit and sympathy.

August 19th, 1862

Same old story! Same, and "blue". If I could get a real good night's sleep, would feel much better. Am afraid my leg will be permanently drawn up, and stiff, and I shall be a cripple.

August 20th, 1862

Received a letter from sister Mary saying Mother is ill, but would come to me just as soon as she was able. At noon, was surprised to see Uncle Henry, Aunt Martha and Bertie, with a friend of theirs from New York, a Mrs. Furber. Was awfully glad to see them, and the visit cheered me up quite a little. Uncle Henry loaned me twenty dollars, which will come in very handy, as I have had no pay for a long time and am "broke".

August 22nd, 1862

Yesterday and today have been about alike. Have kept very quiet. In pain all the time and my leg seems to be getting worse all the time. I can see the doctor is puzzled and does not seem to understand the case. Get very little sleep and am getting worn out.

August 23rd, 1862

Mrs. Furber, Aunt Martha's friend from New York, visited the hospital today, and brought flowers and peaches for Lieut. Collins and me. Tried to write some letters, but had to give it up.

August 24th, 1862

Felt a little better today and wrote one or two letters.

August 25th, 1862

Chaplain Yard of the 1st New Jersey, who is in our room, very kindly assisted me in preparing an application for leave of absence, which the doctor endorsed with a strong certification, and sent to Washington. Everybody says I ought to go home.

August 26th, 1862

Mother, having written that she would try to come today, I was on the look-out for her all the morning. She came about eleven o'clock, and I was mighty glad to see her once more. She was not looking well, and has a bad, deep cough, which I do not like. When she first came into the room, she did not know me, and passed by my bed, until I spoke to her. We had a real nice time together, until she left. I wanted to go to New York with her, but found myself too weak and lame.

August 27th, 1862

Very lame and sore—could hardly move. A cold east wind which may affect my wretched leg. Mother sent a basket of peaches.

August 28th, 1862

Another day of cold and east wind and rain. Was worse than yesterday, and could not get down to meals. At night, took a good big drink of wine and got several naps before morning.

August 29th, 1862

My good friend, Chaplain Yard, was discharged from the hospital today and left to join his regiment. I shall miss him badly. He has been very kind to me. He is an ideal Chaplain. He is going to try to get my pay for me.

August 30th, 1862

Had a note from Chaplain Yard this morning. He thinks he can get my pay in Washington. Am growing worse all the time and want to get to Mother, but the cruel orders of the War Department keep me here.

August 31st, 1862

My leg is worse and swelling more and more. I believe the doctor thinks I shall never be able to straighten it again, or walk without a crutch, although he does not say so in so many words. Received a letter today from my old friend, Frank Owen, of Lowell, who says my friends there all thought I was dead and it was so reported in the Lowell papers.

September 1st, 1862

Could not get down to breakfast this morning; started, but was so weak I came near falling. Oh, if I could only get to Mother's, I think I could get well. We heard that there was a U.S. Surgeon over in New

York (Dr. Sloan) who had authority to give leaves of absence. Wrote a note to a Mrs. Davis, who has been very kind, asking her to see Dr. Sloan in my behalf.

September 2nd, 1862

Felt in better spirits today as we heard there was a chance for us to get away. When the visitors came, Lieut. Marston's sister brought me a box from Mrs. Davis with some underclothing, which I need badly, and a bottle of sherry. The ladies in the city have been very kind to us since we came. It was so cold tonight we had a fire in the open grate, which was cheerful.

September 3rd, 1862

My leave of absence came today. Thank goodness! Shall go to New York tomorrow on the eleven thirty boat and take the night boat for Albany. Quite cold tonight and we had a fire again in the grate. A number of officers came in during the evening to say goodbye.

September 4th, 1862

At half past eleven bid goodbye to the hospital and to Bedloe's Island, I hope, and started for the landing with several other officers who are going home, to take the boat for New York. Had a hard time getting on board, the tide being low, and had it not been for the help of my brother officers, could not have gone down the steep gang plank. Upon arriving at New York, took a carriage, and with Lieut. White, who said he was going to see me safely on the boat, drove to the Albany pier. The ride was a hard one; the jolting was terribly painful for my leg. When we reached the pier, I was quite used up. We got a little lunch and went on the boat, White staying with me until time to start, then left to go to Philadelphia. Hope I shall see him again sometime. He was very kind to me and I shall always remember Lieut. White of Baker's California regiment. Had a very uncomfortable night, was in so much pain. The boat was crowded. Most of the passengers were very kind, but some bored me a little as I did not feel much like talking or being talked to.

Chapter 5

LIEUTENANT AYLING ON SICK LEAVE

Ayling left Bedloe's Island Hospital to visit with his mother and sister in Albany, with other relatives in and near Boston, and with friends in Lowell. After recovery from his illness, he rejoined his regiment near Warrenton, Virginia, on November 12, 1862.

While Ayling was on leave, his regiment as part of McClellan's army met Lee's army at Antietam and stopped the Confederate penetration into Maryland. Although not a decisive victory, the Federal forces had checked Lee's advance, and this encouraged President Lincoln to announce the Emancipation Proclamation on September 22, 1862. These events put an end to the Confederate hope that England or France might interfere on behalf of the South.

September 5th, 1862

Arrived at Albany very early and reached the house before the folks were up. Soon "routed them out" and a warm welcome from Mother and Mary. After breakfast, Mother sent for her doctor, who, when he came and looked me over, said he thought he could help me. He gave me some medicine, which made me quite sick for a while, but by night I felt some relief from pain, and was able to get some sleep by supporting my leg with pillows against the back of a lounge.

September 6th, 1862

Felt a little better today, but was very nervous. Passed the day lying on the lounge, talking with Mother and Mary. Had a fairly good night.

September 7th, 1862

I can see some improvement. I do not have so much pain and get more sleep nights.

September 11th, 1862

The last three days have been passed quietly. Am having a nice time with Mother and Mary, who are fine nurses. Am improving fast. This Albany doctor surely does know his business, and what the trouble with me is, and how to treat it. It seems very strange that the doctors in the hospital did not understand my case, but they evidently did not. Felt quite strong today, so after dinner, went out for a little walk with Mother, but the Albany hills are pretty steep, and my leg pained me so, we soon had to turn back. Was obliged to use both crutches.

September 12th, 1862

Was quite sore and lame from my exertion of yesterday, but think the exercise, and getting out in the air did me good.

September 13th, 1862

A rainy, cold, and disagreeable day, which affected my leg some. Shall try to go East tomorrow if able. Want to try in Boston to get the several months' pay due me and which I need. Also want to see my old Lowell friends. Shall come back here before going to the regiment.

September 14th, 1862

Felt pretty well today. Took the night boat for New York. Left one crutch and think I can get along without it, although still quite lame. There were a lot of recruits aboard who over-ran the boat, but I got a very good amount of sleep.

September 15th, 1862

Arrived at New York early in the morning and had breakfast on the boat, where I remained most of the day. Was too lame to venture very far up town. At four o'clock, took a carriage and drove to the Norwich boat. Met some agreeable people and had a pleasant evening. Did not sleep much.

September 16th, 1862

On arriving in Boston, went to the Hancock House for breakfast, and then to Uncle Henry's office. After a chat, we visited numerous headquarters and offices, trying to find some way for me to get my pay but without success. Went to Uncle Henry's home to see Aunt Martha, and she insisted upon my lying down, which I was glad to do, being pretty well exhausted. Aunt Rebecca came in, and, after I was rested, took me to call on Aunt Sarah. In the evening, Mr. Phillips and Aunt Rebecca called and Mrs. Demeritt, Aunt Martha's sister, who invited me to dinner tomorrow.

September 17th, 1862

Went in town with Uncle Henry and then to the Hancock House, where I met Captain Doten and Lieuts. Braden and Corlew, all of the 29th, home on sick leave.[1] Was very glad to see them. Went to the Demeritt's to dinner, after which Mr. Demeritt took me for a drive and then back to Uncle Henry's. Went to bed early after playing a while with Bertie.

September 18th, 1862

Went in town after breakfast and looked in at the Hancock House and Parker House, both the usual headquarters for officers when in town, but saw no one I knew. Took the afternoon train for Lowell, and on arriving went to Ayer's Building, where I met a hearty welcome from my former fellow clerks and employees.[2] Mr. Hills, the head accountant, invited me to supper. Later in evening, went to the Washington House, which I shall make headquarters while here. Afterwards met the old crowd and had a very pleasant time. Stayed with Ed Hardy tonight.

September 19th, 1862

Went out to Middlesex in the morning and spent the day with Grandmother and Aunt Abby, and had a good visit. In the evening was with "the boys" and spent a night with Ed.

September 29th, 1862

My ten days' stay in Lowell has been very enjoyable. It was mighty pleasant being again with old friends and acquaintances. While there, was invited by Fred Ayer to tea and to spend the evening, where I had a delightful time with Mrs. Ayer, who is charming, and her young sister who is also. Was also entertained by Mr. Ely, Cashier at Ayer's, and Mr. Mansfield, head of the forwarding department, and other friends. Went several times to visit my Grandmother and Aunt at Middlesex, and had a good time all around. Went to Boston this morning for a medical examination to find whether or not I am to go with the regiment when my leave expires. If not, shall have to get an extension. At the State House, met Dr. Wheelwright, a sort of State Agent to look after soldiers, who introduced me to Dr. Dale, Surgeon General, who extended my leave twenty days. He did not tell me what my disability is. I am feeling pretty well, but have not much strength or much flesh. My leg troubles me some, but the stiffness has gone and I can bend it all right without much pain, and have discarded the crutch. However, am glad to have a little more time here. Went to Uncle Henry's office and home with him for the night.

September 30th, 1862

Went down town with Uncle Henry this morning and to the Hancock and Parker Houses; saw a lot of officers but no one I knew. Went back to Uncle's and passed the afternoon very quietly. Went to bed early after a play with Bertie.

October 1st, 1862

Rainy and cold, so did not go to town. Read and talked with Aunt Martha. Uncle Charles called in the afternoon. In evening Bertie took me to Aunt Rebecca's, where I spent the night. Had a nice time with Henry and Winnie.

October 2nd, 1862

Another rainy day, cold and disagreeable. This wretched weather does not help my lameness any. Went in town for a short time and then back to Aunt Rebecca's. In evening played Kentucky Loo with Mr. Phillips.

October 3rd, 1862

Visited the Aquarium in the forenoon. In the afternoon Uncle Charles took me out to his home in Grantville. A very pleasant place, adjoining Uncle Isaac's, which is also very nice. Was back and forth between the two houses during the day. In evening, played Loo with Uncle Charles, Aunt Ann and a Mr. Sawyer, cousin Maria's fiance.

October 4th, 1862

Went to ride with Uncle Charles and Aunt Ann in the forenoon. In afternoon was around this place and Uncle Isaac's, at both of which there are plenty of fine pears and grapes. In evening was at Uncle Isaac's. Mr. Phillips and family and Bertie came and we had a jolly time.

October 5th, 1862

Went to church in the morning with Uncle Charles' family. A very prosy sermon and poor singing. After dinner went for a drive. Went to bed early.

October 6th, 1862

This morning rode horseback on a beautiful horse of Uncle Isaac's. Enjoyed the ride very much. Weather fine and scenery beautiful. I like Grantville and have a real good time with both Uncles and their families.

October 7th, 1862

Went in town this morning and then up to Lowell. I found that since I was here last week the boys have formed a club, and engaged and fitted up nice quarters. A few of the right kind have been taken in and we now can have a regular place for meeting evenings. It will be fine for me while here. The girls have named the club "The Wild Animals" and I guess the name will stick.

October 18th, 1862

After a week in Lowell came back to Boston. This morning went to the State House and the Surgeon General told me to take ten days more and then report to him. I am feeling all right and don't see why I am not fit for duty at the front. Don't think I will report to State House any more. Went out to Grantville for the night with Uncle Isaac. Could not get my pay here and have had to borrow from relatives and friends. Pretty rough, with six months pay due me.

October 19th, 1862

Went to church with Uncle Isaac's family in A.M. After dinner we all went to Mount Auburn with Mr. Shaw and his wife and daughter, Miss Georgie. She is a very beautiful girl, and just suits me every way, but "Ephesians 2–12" for me.[3] Had a delightful time. In evening cousin Maria and her fiance called.

October 20th, 1862

Went in town with Uncle Isaac this morning and at the station met Miss Georgie. She certainly is a most attractive girl. On arriving in Boston, went around bidding my Aunts and Uncles goodbye. Was intending to go to Albany tonight, but Aunt Rebecca said if I would wait until tomorrow she would take me out to Jamaica Plain to see Grandfather Ayling, so I decided to wait. Had a very pleasant visit with the old gentleman and am glad I went. Stayed in Aunt Rebecca's tonight. In evening read and talked politics with Mr. Phillips, who is a Democrat.

October 21st, 1862

Went down town in the morning and to the Hancock House, but saw no familiar faces, then to the State House, where I met Dr. Wheelwright, who spoke encouragingly of my speedy promotion, but I cannot get my pay here, which is *not* encouraging. Went to the railroad station with Mr. Phillips, who gave me a pass as far as Worcester, and at half past two started for Albany, where I arrived at about nine after a tedious ride. When I reached the house, everybody was abed.

October 22nd, 1862

Was glad to be with Mother and Mary again. Was in the house all day, and in the evening Mary and I had a good time singing the old songs we used to sing from the "Jubilee" at singing school.[4] It seemed like old times.

October 28th, 1862

The week has been spent quietly and very enjoyably with Mother and Mary. We have taken nice walks together, visited various places of interest, and returned calls. Have made the acquaintance of Mary's beau! He is a Rutgers College fellow and I like him. He seems to be all right. In the morning was busy getting ready to start for New York, where I am to report *en route* to the regiment. We took our last drive in the afternoon, and after supper, Mother and Mary went to the boat with me to say goodbye. It was mighty hard for us all. I am anxious about Mother, whose health is far from good, and she has a hard cough which sounds bad to me. We both felt it would be very doubtful that we should ever see each other again. It was a hard parting, and I felt it deeply.

October 29th, 1862

Arrived in New York early and after breakfast reported to General Brown, who sent me to Fort Hamilton for orders.[5] Upon reporting at the Fort, Colonel Burke, Commandant, informed me I am to go to Washington with a lot of recruits and convalescents, probably tomorrow, but possibly not for several days.[6] He also said the Fort was so crowded he could not offer me quarters and I might go to the city and stay and report to him in the morning. I had been told, and was sure I could get my pay here, and left Albany with only enough money to take me to New York, and now I find I can get nothing here. Returned to the city feeling pretty blue. Went to the Eastern Hotel and engaged a room for the night, but haven't money enough to pay for it, and many meals. Don't know what to do. There is not time to send for funds as I may have to leave tomorrow, and besides am too proud to borrow now, as I have been living on money borrowed from my uncles and other friends. After dark, took my overcoat and went out hunting for pawn shops to see if I could "put it up", but no one dared to take it, as it is the regulation light blue coat issued to enlisted men, and the brokers feared it was government property and would get them into trouble, so gave it up for the night and went to the hotel and to bed, feeling blue and miserable.

October 30th, 1862

Went out early this morning to try again to sell my overcoat and after some trouble found a man who gave me a dollar for it. After paying for my lodging, reported at the Fort, and found the detachment with which I am to go. One of the officers in charge is to leave this afternoon. The other two officers are acquaintances. Captain Hertzog was at Bedloe's and Lieutenant Hagadorn, 1st New York, was at Newport News. This is very pleasant for me. At three o'clock, we left the Fort on a steamer for New York with 150 recruits and convalescents of various regiments. We transferred to another steamer for Amboy, where we took cars for Philadelphia, arriving at midnight and remaining the rest of the night. We, with our men, were quartered in barracks provided by the ladies of the city, and given a good supper, which I certainly appreciated.

October 31st, 1862

Early this morning, went out with the other officers to see what we could of Philadelphia. After breakfast, got our men on train and started for Washington. At Havre de Grace, met Lieutenant Middleton, who commanded the guard on the "Adelaide" when I was Provost Marshall on that boat. Our train was delayed at Baltimore and we did not reach Washington until midnight. We quartered our men at the Soldier's Home, and then Middleton and I went to the St. Charles Hotel for the night. Was very tired and my leg troubles me. Hope I can get my pay here or find someone from whom I can borrow, for I am broke.

November 1st, 1862

In the morning we turned our men over to the proper officer, and the rest of the day I spent trying to find where my regiment is, and how to reach it, and also to find someone who will lend me a little money. I am told I cannot get the pay due me until I am with my regiment, and the Lord knows that is just where I want to be, when I can find it. The War Department either cannot, or will not give me information as to where the 29th is. Am quite lame in hip and knee, and as I have no money for a hotel, went to the Georgetown Seminary, which has been made a military hospital, where I can stay until my lameness is better, and I can get some information as to the location of the regiment. Left my bag at the hotel. Can't call for it until I get money to pay my bill.

November 2nd, 1862

Kept quiet in my room all day. The surgeons are treating me for the lameness, but seem to be puzzled. Wonder if I shall ever be all right again.

November 3rd, 1862

Felt a little better today. Went to headquarters with another appeal for pay, but got no satisfaction. Heard the regiment was somewhere near Harper's Ferry. Shall try to get to it tomorrow if possible.

November 4th, 1862

Found, on going to the depot, that no "Soldier's train" was going to Harper's Ferry today, and if I took the regular train it would cost me four dollars, which I do not possess. Went back to the hospital and will try again tomorrow. Heard today that my sword, which was left in the hospital at Harrison's Landing when I was sent north, is with my friend, Lieutenant Devoll, at Fort Monroe. Am glad it is safe. Saw a lot of paroled prisoners from Richmond today, and some 29th men among them. A hard-looking lot.

November 5th, 1862

Went to the depot in the morning and found that a train would run to Harper's Ferry later in the day, but no one seemed to know just when. Went to the wharf to try to get to Alexandria by boat, as I heard some of our officers are on duty there; but the boat was not running, so returned to wait for the train to start for the Ferry, which it finally did about dark. The train was made up of boxcars with sides knocked out and without seats. Good enough for soldiers, I suppose. The night was cold and I was chilled and hungry. Managed to get a little sleep on the floor of the car, but it was a miserable, uncomfortable night.

November 6th, 1862

Arrived at Harper's Ferry a little before noon, lame, hungry and half sick. Was wandering around, trying to learn something of the regiment when I met our surgeon, Dr. Coggswell, who told me the 29th was forty miles from the Ferry and ordered me to the Post Hospital, of which he is in charge.[7] One of our men, Charles Walker, is on duty here and took good care of me, gave me hot coffee and something to eat, and I felt somewhat better.[8] Remained at the hospital the rest of the day and had a good sleep at night. The only worry I have is how to get to the regiment.

November 7th, 1862

This morning, with an officer of the 61st Tennessee, Captain Humphrey, started out to go over the mountains to find the army.[9] Soon after starting, it commenced to rain, but we kept on for about six miles when we were halted at the cavalry outpost and informed that we could not be allowed to go any farther for the roads were full of guerillas and entirely unsafe. So, wet, cold and disgusted, we tramped back to the Ferry. Went to the hospital and stayed for the night.

November 8th, 1862

After a good breakfast, thanks to Charlie Walker, who also let me have his overcoat which I badly need, the weather being quite cold, I went to the depot to take train for Washington, as I find I must reach the army by way of Manassas. Officers not being allowed to ride on trains carrying troops, unless so ordered, I tried to get a pass, which would have entitled me to a free ride, but could not as I was not under orders. Was wondering what to do next, when I saw a lot of soldiers lined up to board a train, so I quietly mixed in with them, and having on a private's overcoat, was not recognized as an officer, and marched aboard the train with the others. We were nearly all night on the cars, and being quite sick with a severe cold, the ride was not a pleasant one.

November 9th, 1862

Reached Washington at four o'clock this morning after a cold, tiresome ride. Went to the St. Charles and slept until eight. After breakfast, got a pass from the Provost Marshall for Alexandria, where I heard some of our officers are stationed. On arriving went to Marshall House, and was rejoiced to find there Captain Leach of the 29th, who loaned me ten dollars, the most money I have had for a long time, and I feel rich. Went to the camp of paroled prisoners, where Captain Leach is on duty, and met there several of our officers and also some who were at Bedloe's Island Hospital with me.[10] Stayed at the Marshall House with Captain Leach and slept in the room in which Colonel Ellsworth of the New York Zouaves died. He was shot by the proprietor of this house for hauling down a rebel flag. Have a very bad cold and am rather "used up".

November 10th, 1862

Remained at Camp Parole today, and at night went to the Marshall House with Captain Leach. I have at last authentic information that the regiment is at Warrenton, and shall start for that place tomorrow, although quite used up with a severe cold, the result of the tramp out from Harper's Ferry in the rain and sleet with no overcoat.

November 11th, 1862

Went back to Washington this morning, paid my hotel bill and got my bag, and about noon took train for Warrenton. General Burnside, the new commander of the army, was on the same train, and was cheered and saluted by artillery all along the way. At Manassas Junction, we were sidetracked to allow the passage of a train with General McClellan, who was also cheered and saluted.[11] On arrival at Warrenton about nine o'clock, found the hotel and most of the houses crowded full and no chance to get anything to eat, but after a time, three of us managed by showing considerable nerve, to get into a private house, where we had a fair supper. Slept on the floor of the living room with a lot of other officers, who like me, were trying to get to their commands.

November 12th, 1862

After breakfast, started with some other officers of our brigade, and after going a mile or two, I found the camp of the 29th, and at last, after considerable "trial and tribulation" am "home" again. Reported to the Colonel, and then went to see "my boys". All seemed glad to see me and I certainly was glad to get back. At dress parade, orders were read assigning me to Company G (Pawtucket) commanded by First Lieutenant Charles Browne.[12] I like him very much, but would much rather be with my old company, D. Got my tent up and began to make myself comfortable. Am to mess with Lieutenants Browne and Carpenter. The weather is quite cold and I have not gotten quite used to camp life yet after my long absence. My cold is better, but am still lame.

Chapter 6

THE FREDERICKSBURG CAMPAIGN

After sick leave, Lieutenant Ayling rejoined his regiment on November 12, 1862. General Burnside, after taking command of the Army of the Potomac, planned to attack Lee's forces at Fredericksburg. However, the slowness of preparation for this campaign alerted Lee, who brought Stonewall Jackson's 2nd Corps from the Shenandoah Valley and prepared a strong defensive position on high ground across the Rappahannock from Burnside's army. Although the Federal troops greatly outnumbered the Confederates, the necessity of crossing the river on pontoon bridges and charging well-fortified heights spelled near disaster for Burnside's forces. The crossing and attack was made but with such heavy losses that a retreat back across the river was necessary. After this abortive attempt, Burnside's army settled into winter quarters. As the year ended, Ayling received word of his promotion to first lieutenant.[1]

November 14th, 1862

The past two days have been very quiet. This evening, we had orders to get ready to move in the morning. We had a jolly time in our quarters tonight.

November 15th, 1862

After breakfast we started and with the rest of the army marched all day. It was a little hard for me, as I have not had practice enough to get hardened. Camped at night in a large open field. No tents, so spread our blankets on the ground and with feet to a fire, slept fairly well, although it was a very cold night.

November 16th, 1862

When I awoke this morning, my blanket, near my face, was stiff with congealed breath. We started quite early, the regiment being ordered ahead as skirmishers, and we had a hard time of it, through thick undergrowth, over rocks and in and out of ravines. At noon, we were relieved, and returned to the column. Had a long, hard march today, nearly twenty miles. Camped at night in thick woods without tents. During the night it rained hard, and we were soaked.

November 17th, 1862

The regiment was rear guard today, and had to wait until the wagon train passed. As the train was several miles long, and did not start until noon, we had a good rest. My feet are quite sore, but I am beginning to get into "form" again. Toward night we reached Falmouth and found our brigade, from which we had been separated all day, as it had been ordered to cross the Rappahannock to capture one of the enemies batteries, so without stopping to rest, we hurried toward the river to join the brigade, which we soon met returning, the orders having been countermanded. Camped in a big cornfield. Had our tents tonight. Expect we shall have a fight tomorrow.

November 18th, 1862

We were routed out early this morning, and then waited two hours before the orders came to march, when we moved out a couple of miles and went into camp in some woods. A nice place, not far from Falmouth, the steeples of which we can see over the hills. When the regiment halted, Lieutenant Carpenter and I started for a house we could see through the trees, and bought a pair of chickens, some soft bread and some persimmons.[2] Got our tents up and made things comfortable, but don't think we will stay here long. The rebs are too near to allow us to remain quiet very long. Our mess lived high today, fried chicken and soft bread!

November 19th, 1862

No orders to move yet, but all kinds of rumors are heard. Our mess sent out some of the colored boys foraging for eatables, but they were not so successful as we were yesterday. All they could get were pies, so-called. It rained hard all day. Wrote a number of letters, and sent to Alexandria for my sword by one of Captain Wilson's men, who was going there on a pass.[3] Colonel Pierce left today to go home for recruits to fill up the regiment. Am glad he has gone, and if he never returns, I, and most of the regiment, will be quite reconciled.

November 20th, 1862

Cold and rainy. In forenoon wrote letters, and in afternoon and evening played poker with Browne and Carpenter. Our tent leaked badly tonight.

November 21st, 1862

Another cold, rainy, disagreeable day. In the evening a lot of the officers came in, and we had a good time singing. At eleven o'clock after we had turned in, the Sergeant Major woke us up with orders to be in line, ready to move, at daybreak, and told us the army was going over the river to attack Fredericksburg. After getting things in shape to obey the orders, turned in to get what sleep we could. A couple of hours later we were again awakened and told the orders to move at daybreak had been countermanded.

November 22nd, 1862

This morning was detached from Company G and assigned as 2nd Lieutenant to Company I, the Lynn company. Was very sorry, as Browne and I had fixed up our quarters very cozily, and then too, while the company is all right, I very much dislike Captain Tripp and 1st Lieutenant Husband, who are temporarily with it.[4] They are not my kind at all. The regiment was ordered on picket today, some two miles out on the bank of the Rappahannock. We were in plain sight of the rebels all the time, and in some places our men could talk with them across the river. Had a cold, disagreeable day. Very cold at night, and as we were without blankets, did not get much sleep.

November 23rd, 1862

We were relieved from picket about noon, and on coming in, found the brigade had moved to get out of range of the enemy's guns to a nice place in the woods. First Lieutenant "Gus" Oliver has come back to Company I, his old company, and I am very glad, as he is a fine officer and a good fellow all round.[5] At night Lieutenant Browne invited me to bunk with him, as he was alone, which I am glad to do. In the evening the Chaplain had a meeting. Browne and I attended, and then turned in. It was so cold we did not sleep much.

November 24th, 1862

Quiet today in camp. Browne and I were busy making a corduroy bed and fixing things so we can sleep a little more comfortably.

November 25th, 1862

Today, for some unknown reason, we had to move our camp; only a short distance, but just far enough to make it necessary to re-arrange everything. We are hourly expecting to hear heavy firing as it is reported the town of Fredericksburg, across the river, is to be shelled today or tomorrow. We are under orders to be ready to move in fighting trim at a moment's notice.

November 26th, 1862

Am mighty glad that Lieutenant Oliver is with Company I, as I enjoy being with him. He was Officer of the Day, which leaves me in command of the Company. We were ordered out several times to receive General Sumner, but he did not get around to us until nearly night.

November 27th, 1862

This is Thanksgiving Day in "God's Country", and we were able to celebrate in pretty good style. A lot of good things in the way of eatables had been sent to us by our friends at home, and we had a great dinner. Turkey, chicken, ham, etc., which we enjoyed immensely. General Meagher, our brigade commander, with the officers of the 63rd, 69th and 83rd New York, the other regiments of the brigade, had caused a fine silk Irish flag to be made in New York for our regiment, and had arranged for its presentation by General Sumner. It was intended to be a surprise, but by some means it came to the knowledge of our Colonel Barnes, who also learned it was the wish of General Meagher that the flag be carried by the regiment. While we would have been proud to receive the flag as a token of respect from our Irish comrades, and fully appreciated the spirit in which the gift was to be offered, we felt that not being an Irish regiment, we could not carry it. This being explained to General Meagher, the matter was dropped, but it was a very kind thing on the part of the officers.

November 29th, 1862

This morning I was ordered to move from Lieutenant Browne's tent in Company G to Company I, where I now belong. This is all right, I suppose, as I should properly be quartered with my company, but Browne and I were much disappointed, as we had fixed up our tent quite nicely, and hoped to take some comfort while we remained here. Late in the day the order was revoked, much to our delight. In the evening a lot of officers came to our tent and we had a very convivial time and "sing". Received orders today appointing me Judge Advocate of a General Court Martial.

November 30th, 1862

Passed the day quietly reading and writing letters. In evening attended services by the Chaplain. We learned today we are to leave the Irish brigade, and are much pleased, for while we like the officers and men well enough, we feel somewhat out of place, the 29th not being in any way an Irish regiment. This change will vacate the order detailing me as Judge Advocate and I am glad, as I rather dreaded the duty.

December 1st, 1862

In the forenoon we broke camp and marched about five miles to the right, to the Ninth Corps, to which we have been assigned, and pitched camp in an open field, not so pleasant a place as the camp we left. We are now in the Second Brigade, First Division of the Ninth Corps. This corps was formerly commanded by General Burnside, who now is in command of the Army of the Potomac. General Orlando B. Willcox now commands the Corps; General William W. Burns the Division, and

Colonel B. C. Christ (pronounced Krist) of the 50th Pennsylvania, the Brigade.[6] This last name struck our Massachusetts ears as very peculiar, and almost sacrilegious, until we learned that it was not at all uncommon among the Pennsylvania Dutch. We are brigaded with the 50th Pennsylvania, 9th Michigan, 27th New Jersey, and 46th New York. After getting the company streets laid out and tents up, Browne and I fixed our quarters, but no one knows how long we shall stay here to occupy them. Had a severe toothache today, the first for a long time. Lieutenant Oliver has been promoted to Captain. Am glad as he is fine officer and I like him.

December 2nd, 1862

The regiment was busy today policing camp and getting accustomed to the new surroundings. We had company drills, Captain Oliver taking the company out in the morning, and I, in the afternoon. I don't believe I am going to fancy the makeup of this brigade.

December 3rd, 1862

Was officer of the Brigade Guard today, and had a very easy time. After going the rounds occasionally to see that everything was all right, could also get some sleep at night. The regiment was on picket and I had a much easier time.

December 4th, 1862

Upon being relieved from guard, Browne and I went over to the 36th Massachusetts, in the 2nd Division, to call on friends. Then we visited all the camps around to see if we could get some tobacco, but could not find any; everybody is out of it, and I don't believe there is a pipeful in the whole brigade. Our tent has a turf fireplace and a pork barrel chimney, and they work first rate.

December 10th, 1862

The past week was uneventful, the weather very cold, and two inches of snow. Captain Richardson, Browne's captain, has returned from leave, and as I have been occupying his quarters during his absence, with Lieutenant Browne, I am obliged to vacate and go to my own company. I am very fond of my captain, but I did hate to leave the cozy quarters Browne and I have fixed up with so much care. None of us get much sleep nights, the weather is so cold. Tents are not so warm and comfortable in winter as they might be! We have for some time been hearing rumors that we were going to have a fight soon, but considered them only "cook house yarns". Today, however, the brigade commander told us at inspection that we would probably have a fight tomorrow, over the river.

December 11th, 1862

Just after midnight this morning, we were called up to issue clothing, etc. to the men, after which, turned in again until reveille sounded, an hour before daybreak. After breakfast, we broke camp and formed line. We did not move, however, but stood under arms until early night, when we went out about a mile and then came back and pitched camp for the night. It has been quite an exciting day. All kinds of rumors are passing around, and a heavy cannonading, commencing at daylight. Eighty guns are pounding away from the bluff, a short distance from where we stood in line, shelling the houses on the river bank in Fredericksburg to drive out the rebel sharpshooters so our men could lay pontoons for the army to cross. I walked over to the batteries with some of our officers and could plainly see the shells crash into the houses and burst, in some cases starting fires, our pontooneers, all the while, doing their best to get boats laid for a bridge and losing many men.

December 12th, 1862

We were under arms early this morning and moved with the brigade to the river, crossing the pontoon bridge at "double quick", and formed our line in the city near and along the river bank. Here we remained all day, getting, once in a while, a shell from the rebel batteries on the heights back of the city. Lieutenant Carpenter was hit in the shoulder by a piece of shell, but not seriously wounded. We were also kept uneasy by one of our own batteries firing over us from across the river. The fuses were cut too short, or were imperfect, for the shells frequently burst over and around us. At night, we were ordered into line and thought we were to make a night attack, but after moving around a little, were ordered to lie on our arms all night, which we did, and a most uncomfortable night it was. There was a dense fog, and it was extremely cold. We had only one

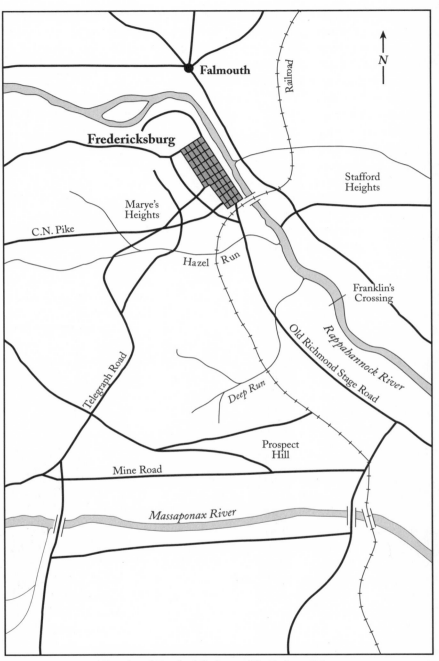

Battle of Fredericksburg, Virginia, 1862.

light blanket apiece, and passed the long, dreary night, half paralyzed with cold, waiting for daybreak, which we felt would bring the opening of a terrible battle in which we would have a part.

December 13th, 1862

At daylight we moved back to the city and stood expecting every moment, as the day advanced, to be rushed into the fight, which we could see plainly, and a most discouraging sight it was. We could see the lines of our men making charge after charge against the hill where the rebels were, only to fall back, shattered and torn, leaving rows of their dead behind.[7] In the afternoon, we were ordered to the left to support Franklin's Corps, and as we moved, were exposed to the enemy's artillery, which opened on us.[8] The proverbial good luck of the 29th stood by us, and we had few casualties, but the regiment next to us, 27th New Jersey, lost seventeen men in the few minutes we were under fire. At night, we advanced through the city and formed in the outskirts facing the enemy, evidently to repel a night attack, should one be made. While we laid here, some of the shattered regiments which had been at the front all day passed us on their way to the rear and told sad tales of disaster and loss.

Ruins of Fredericksburg, Virginia, 1862. Mathew Brady photo, from *Mr. Lincoln's Camera Man*, 1946. Reprinted by permission of Russell & Volkening.

Fredericksburg, as we marched through, was a hard sight, the houses, of course, deserted, and many of them ruined by our artillery fire. Many dead lay in the streets and gardens. I noticed, particularly, in the garden of one house, the body of a boy not more than fourteen or fifteen years old, lying with his face to the sky. He was a very fine looking boy and no doubt was "somebody's darling", poor fellow. It was against orders to loot the houses, but some of the men managed to get flour, cornmeal, tobacco, etc. undetected.

December 14th, 1862

Early in the morning, we fell back from our advanced position to the bank of the river, near the Gas Works, expecting all the time to be sent into the fight. We were troubled a good deal, as we were day before yesterday, by the shell fire of one of our batteries, firing over us with fuses cut too short. Many of the shells burst around and near us, which with every now and then a shell from the enemy, together with the fact that we had been under quite a strain for several days, with little sleep, made us all somewhat nervous. I was smoking a new meerschaum pipe I had bought of our Assistant Surgeon and must have pulled 120 puffs to the minute. This is the first time the regiment ever remained in the reserve all day in full view of the battle which raged and roared yesterday and today from sunrise until into the night. We heard tonight that our side had been badly whipped with terrible loss, and that our old brigade (Irish Brigade) had been cut to pieces and practically wiped out. It is mighty lucky for us that we were detached from it when we were, otherwise many of us would not now be alive. We remained near the river all night, getting "cat naps" and shivering with the cold.

December 15th, 1862

We remained in the same position as yesterday under the familiar order to be ready to move at a moment's notice. After dark, we were ordered to have the men arrange their equipments so there would be no rattling, to make no noise of any kind, and to allow no pipes or fires to be lighted. All orders were to be passed along the line in a low tone and every precaution taken to prevent the enemy hearing us. We felt confident that we were to make a night attack upon the enemy's batteries, but soon learned that our army was retreating back across the river and we were to take up some pontoon bridges over a creek between us and the enemy's position. A mighty risky thing to do under the circumstances, for had the rebels known what we were up to, they could easily have driven those of us not killed or captured into the Rappahannock. After the rest of the 9th Corps had crossed the river, we followed, making as little noise as possible, the bridge having been covered with earth to deaden all sound, and reached our old camp at about three o'clock in the morning. While we did not get into the thick of the fight, we were all very tired and used up from the nervous strain of the past three days. It is as wearing to lie watching a battle, expecting every minute to be ordered in, as it is to jump into the thick of a fight.

December 16th, 1862

When we reached camp last night, or rather this morning, we were too tired to put up tents, so Captain Oliver and I spread our blankets on the ground. Soon after getting asleep it commenced to rain hard and before we could put up any kind of a shelter, we were wet through blankets and all. After a time, we got a tent up and laid down in our wet blankets in the mud, too cold and wet to sleep much, but thankful to be back alive. Two incidents connected with the battle of Fredericksburg made a deep impression on me. When we marched down to cross the river, we passed under some large trees, and the following from Byron's poem "Childe Harold's Pilgrimage", referring to Waterloo came to me:

> Ardennes waves above them her green leaves,
>   Dewey with nature's tear drops, as they pass;
> Grieving, if aught inanimate e'er grieves,
>   Over the unreturning brave.

These lines haunted me all day and seemed to be ominous. After we had crossed the pontoon, my captain, Oliver, one of the coolest and bravest officers in the regiment, told me he felt that he would be killed in the coming fight, and giving me his watch and money, asked that I would send them to his wife in Lynn. We both came back all right, which goes to prove that omens and premonitions do not always materialize, but they affected me quite a little.

December 17th, 1862

Woke up sore and stiff. After breakfast, commenced cleaning and
drying blankets, fixing our tent, and washing and changing clothing,
when an order came to fall in for picket. Rather unwelcome orders,
just at this time. We marched some distance before reaching the place
we were to picket on the bank of the Rappahannock, less than one
hundred yards from the enemy's pickets on the opposite side. It was
very cold, and we had no rations but hard bread and coffee. Heard
today I am to be promoted, but don't take much stock in the report.

December 18th, 1862

Had a hard, cold, disagreeable day. We should have been relieved
this morning, but for some reason were kept on picket until night and
did not get back to camp until nine o'clock. Found our mess had gotten up a pretty good supper for me, and I saw a "Boston Journal"
which had a notice that I had been commissioned First Lieutenant, so
I felt in very good spirits when I turned in.

Meeting of Union and Confederate pickets on Rappahannock River, 1862.
From *Harper's Weekly,* Feb. 7, 1863.

December 19th, 1862

Another cold day. Must say I don't fancy winter campaigning. Passed the day writing and playing cards, as usual, when off duty.

December 20th, 1862

Still bitterly cold. It is hard to keep comfortable day or night. Had an attack of diarrhea today which took my strength away and made me feel poor. Lieutenant Corlew of the Charlestown Company (H) was dismissed the service today. We do not understand why and think he has been wronged. We are ordered for picket again tomorrow.

December 21st, 1862

This morning the regiment was on picket at our old place on the bank of the river. I went out in command of Company H, a fine lot of fellows. Our position is very good, and the rebels on the opposite bank are quite friendly, for enemies, and like to talk across with our men, with a mutual understanding that there shall be no firing. Everything would be quiet for a time, when a voice over the river would call, "Say, Yank, want to talk?" "Yes, Johnny," our men would reply, and then the pickets of both armies would come out into the open, without rifles, and a good natured talk would follow, until the approach of some officer of high rank, on either side, would cause the warning cry, "Get to cover, boys, we've got to shoot!" This talking across, was not supposed to be allowed, but there are some things that it is better for an officer not to notice. When the men of two armies are talking in this way, there is none of the miserable picket firing, which really does no good, and helps neither side.

December 23rd, 1862

General Sumner's Grand Division, composed of the 2nd and 9th Corps, was reviewed today by the General. It was a long, cold job, and we did not get back to camp until in the afternoon—tired, cold and hungry. The army is now preparing to go into winter quarters, and we are all trying our best to make ourselves comfortable for the winter. Each company was divided into squads, and each squad built its own hut. Trees were cut in the woods and then into proper lengths for the

walls and tents used for the roof. Inside, fireplaces were built of turf
and mud, with pork barrels for chimneys. These latter work all right,
until they become thoroughly dry, when the occupants of a tent having an unusually hot fire, one will blaze up, and there will be a cry of
"Fire!" and a little excitement for a time. Officers' houses were built
in the same way and were really very cozy and comfortable. The country around the little village of Falmouth has become a city of huts with
a population of over one hundred thousand veteran soldiers.

December 25th, 1862

Christmas! And what a Christmas. No celebration or excitement
of any kind. Not even any intoxication in the regiment. Nothing to
indicate the day as a holiday.

December 26th, 1862

Expected to go on picket today, but was agreeably disappointed.
Our mess is broken up as none of us has any money to buy supplies
from the Commissary or sutler. We have not been paid for a long time,
and most of the officers are decidedly "short". Don't know what I am
to do. There is a rumor that the regiment is to be paid soon, and I trust
it is true.

December 27th, 1862

Was feeling quite disturbed today regarding mess arrangements,
but was much relieved when Captain Taylor of Company A invited
me to join his mess, which is, I reckon, the only one having funds
enough to keep alive. It was mighty kind of Taylor and I appreciate
the invitation.[9]

December 28th, 1862

Our division was reviewed by General Burns.[10] I went out in command of Company I, Captain Oliver being ill.

December 29th, 1862

Passed the day quietly reading and writing letters, together with the inevitable card playing which is going on most of the time when we are at leisure.

December 30th, 1862

This morning I was detached from Company I, and assigned to Company H. Like my new assignment very much. A fine lot of Charlestown boys in the Company, and my quarters are very comfortable. Have a feather bed, which one of the men brought from Fredericksburg on his back when we retreated. We are ordered to make out payrolls, which looks as if we are to get our long deferred pay, and is encouraging. Was busy all day with rolls and returns, and straightening out things.

December 31st, 1862

Everything is now settled down for the rest of the winter, and the army is comfortably housed. Worked all the forenoon finishing the payrolls of my Company, and after dinner, the regiment was mustered for pay. In the evening, Taylor, Braden and Windsor were in my tent and we concocted a very stimulating beverage, known in the regiment as "Whiskey Chowder", to celebrate not only New Year's Eve, but also my promotion, my commission as First Lieutenant having arrived today.[11] About midnight, we started out "serenading", routed out such of the officers as had turned in and made them join us, then went to the sutler's, made him get up, and then come down with crackers, cheese and canned lobster. Had a somewhat heated argument with the Dutch Officer of the Brigade, Gerard, who thought we were making too much noise, and who threatened to report us. We realized we might get into trouble, so went at once to the quarters of the Brigade Commander, who fortunately had not gone to bed, wished him a "Happy New Year", and said we had been seeing the old year out, and celebrating, perhaps a little too loudly. While we were chatting, the angry Officer of the Guard came in to report us, but the Commander smoothed matters over, saying some allowance may be made on such occasions, and advising us to go to our quarters. We all drank to the coming year, shook hands all around, and went back to the regiment. We were lucky to get off so easily; "monkeying" with an Officer of the Guard is a pretty serious matter. Goodbye '62! Wonder what '63 has in store for us?

Chapter 7

❧❦❧

WINTER CAMP AND TRANSFER
TO NEWPORT NEWS

After the failure of the Fredericksburg offensive, Lincoln replaced Burnside with General Hooker as commander of the Army of the Potomac. However, the army remained settled in winter quarters awaiting better weather. Lieutenant Ayling's regiment was transferred to Newport News in mid-February and prepared there for further transfer to the Western Theater of War.

January 1st, 1863

Felt a little "rocky" this morning, the effects of last night's celebration. We did, surely, have a great time, and ushered in the New Year with the proper formalities. Worked all day and until ten in the evening, making payrolls and the numerous copies required, and at last finished them ready for the Paymaster, who is expected before long.

January 2nd, 1863

Went to General Wilcox's headquarters this morning with my new commission, and was mustered as First Lieutenant. Kept very quiet all day and went to bed early.

January 7th, 1863

The past four days have been quiet and uneventful, passed in the usual way when in camp, reading, letter writing and card playing. Four or five of the officers gather almost every evening in my tent for "a sing", which we enjoy very much. Yesterday there was a grand review by General Burnside, which we did not enjoy as it was cold and rainy. This morning it was beautiful, and I borrowed the Quartermaster Sergeant's horse and rode over to the Eleventh Corps to visit the 33rd Massachusetts in which I have many friends and acquaintances. Had a delightful time, and saw Lieutenants Peabody, Prescott, Philbrick and Thompson, Hospital Steward Shedd, Sergeant Bailey and other Lowell boys.[1] Got back to camp in time for dress parade and to hear an order read detailing me for picket duty tomorrow.

January 8th, 1863

On picket at the old place on the bank of the Rappahannock. Was in command of the detail from the 29th. There was no firing and everything was quiet.

January 9th, 1863

On coming off picket this morning, found a ripple of excitement in the regiment caused by a pedlar who had been robbed of some of his goods, as he claimed, in my Company street. I was ordered to find the thief, or thieves, but could not, and did not expect to.

January 16th, 1863

The past week has been uneventful and without anything happening out of the usual routine of camp life. The weather cold, foggy and disagreeable, with occasionally rain and snow. I was detailed for picket today, but did not go out, as we received orders to get ready to move at short notice tomorrow morning, with three days rations. Where we are going, we have no idea, but it may be to cross the river again for another try at the rebels.

January 17th, 1863

Clear and cold. Everybody was out bright and early making preparations to break camp, which is quite a little job when troops have been in camp for some time. Everything was soon all ready but striking tents, and we were anxiously waiting for the word, when the order of yesterday was countermanded.

January 18th, 1863

We passed the day much as we did yesterday, waiting and wondering what was up. Considerable excitement was caused when Franklin's Grand Division passed, moving up the river. This gave force to the rumor that there was to be a forward movement, which rumor was confirmed, when at dress parade, General Burnside's order was read announcing that the army was "again to meet the enemy". Was Officer of the Brigade Guard today.

January 19th, 1863

Still waiting for the order to move. We issued sixty rounds of ammunition to each man, which looks like business, but were directed not to strike tents until further orders, which is wise, as it looks as if we are to get a big storm.

January 20th, 1863

We got the big storm today, sure enough, the worst yet. Wind blowing a gale and rain in torrents. Troops have been passing all day, and the forward movement, whatever it may be, has evidently commenced. After I had turned in at night, and was fast asleep, the Adjutant came around with orders for us to march at eleven o'clock tomorrow, and later told us the orders were countermanded. Issuing orders and then countermanding them seems to have become chronic with someone. However, I am mighty glad, in this instance, that we do not move tomorrow. I am not anxious to tramp through Virginia mud ankle deep in the rain.

January 21st, 1863

The storm is worse, if possible. Passed the day in a very uncomfortable state of mind, expecting the order to march and dreading to start out in the storm. Fortunately, no order came, and we remained in our tents, and out of the wet, so far as we could.

Major General Joseph Hooker. From *Harper's Weekly,* Feb. 7, 1863.

January 22nd, 1863

The storm is not quite so bad, but bad enough. We learned that in consequence of the pontoon trains and some of the artillery being stuck in the mud, the proposed movement has been abandoned. I am glad! I have no desire to march in the mud if I can help it, nor am I exactly spoiling for a fight.

January 23rd, 1863

Today the report that the forward movement had been given up was confirmed, and the troops who went out a few days since began to return to their old camps. The movement is called by the men "The Mud Expedition", and it is said, although I did not see it, that on the other side of the river, the Rebs had a large sign with the words "Burnside's Army Stuck in the Mud", and it surely was. I am sorry for the General; he is popular with the army, but all his plans since he took command have failed.

January 24th, 1863

The storm has finally passed, but the mud is still with us, and awful, almost ankle deep everywhere, and very sticky. Virginia mud is all that has ever been said about it, and it is not surprising that pontoon trains and artillery were stuck. The army is now settling down into winter quarters again, and it looks as if we would stay here until Spring.

January 26th, 1863

Sergeant George Long of my Company has been promoted to Second Lieutenant and assigned to Company H with me.[2] This is very satisfactory to me, as he is a fine fellow and a gentleman. We shall get on nicely together. We heard today that Burnside had been relieved from command of the Army of the Potomac, and is to be succeeded by General Hooker.[3] Was on picket. Everything quiet.

January 27th, 1863

Came off picket about noon, and after dinner laid down and slept until night.

January 28th, 1863

When I awoke this morning, found it had been snowing all night, and snow had drifted into the tent, all over our blankets and into our boots, and to add to our troubles, we are short of wood. The storm continued all day, most of the snow melting and making travelling around camp anything but pleasant.

January 29th, 1863

Snowed hard all day, and everybody not obliged to be out on duty kept in quarters.

January 31st, 1863

The quiet and rather monotonous life of the past week was agreeably brightened by the arrival this evening of Major Stone, the Paymaster, who comes to give us our long overdue pay. Was busy all the evening having my men sign the payrolls and getting things ready for tomorrow.

February 1st, 1863

The regiment was paid this morning, but for some reason, which we could not learn, was not paid the full amount due. I received pay only to October 31st, when I should have at least two months more. Uncle Sam has a queer way of doing business with his boys, it seems to me. Lieutenants Thompson and Prescott of the 33rd Massachusetts called to see me and dined at our mess. In the afternoon there was a very serious row between the 50th Pennsylvania (the dirty half hundred, as we call it) and our boys; starting in a drunken fight between two or three men and finally taking in most of the men of both regiments. Stones, sticks, and clubbed rifles were used, and the officers had to go in with swords out and revolvers drawn, before we could quell the riot. One of the 50th men aimed a rifle at our Adjutant, not ten feet away, and pulled the trigger, but fortunately, the rifle was not loaded, or was perhaps not capped, for there was no explosion, and the man was knocked down. This whole business was a new experience to us, and quite exciting. We never had anything like it before, not even when in the pugnacious Irish Brigade.

February 2nd, 1863

Was detailed today to take charge of a fatigue party with five wagons, and go to Falmouth to get bricks from the chimneys of the houses with which ovens are to be built to bake bread for the brigade. Soft bread sounds good to us, and it looks as if we were to stay here a while. We were directed tonight to prepare for inspection tomorrow by a regular inspecting officer.

February 3rd, 1863

A bitter cold day, so cold the inspector did not appear. At dress parade, orders were read announcing that a limited number of men in each regiment would be furloughed, and my tent was besieged all the evening by men anxious to be of the favored ones to go home for thirty days. Only a very few can go, and it is hard to make the selection.

February 4th, 1863

Another cold day. Expect to give up command of Company H. Lieutenant Carpenter, who has been on leave, is soon to return, and this is really his command, and I belong with another company. I shall be sorry to leave, as I have become attached to Lieutenant Long and to the men of H.

February 5th, 1863

Snowing hard today. Orders have come to prepare to leave for Fort Monroe. Wonder what this move means. Goodbye to visions of winter camp and soft bread. However, the change suits me all right. and I may have a chance to see some of my old friends at the Fort and at Suffolk.

February 6th, 1863

Rained hard until nearly night. Was detailed on extra picket duty and got wet through going out, but had nice comfortable quarters when I reached the post in an old stone house. The Officer of the Day, a stranger, took me for a Captain, my overcoat hiding my shoulder straps, and put me in command of the post. I must have looked "bigger" than I felt, but I said nothing, attended strictly to business, and none, save my own men, were any wiser. Part of our division broke camp and started off today, and we will probably follow soon.

February 9th, 1863

The past three days have been very pleasant. Good weather for marching, but we don't go. Every night we are told to be ready to move early the next morning, and then a little later the order will be countermanded, as usual, and so it goes!

February 10th, 1863

A lovely day, more like May than February. In the morning, Long and I went to the depot to get some things we needed. There was a lively whiskey row, as sometimes occurs after pay day, this afternoon, mostly in Company B. I had a little trouble with one of my men, who was just drunk enough to be impudent. It was nothing very serious and I got him into his tent and quieted down, saving him from the guard house and punishment. This same man, whose name is Gear, gave me quite a scare this evening.[4] I was sitting alone in my tent, when someone scratched at the door, the camp way of knocking, and when I said, "Come in," saw it was Gear, who, when he entered, had his hand in the breast of his blouse, and as he withdrew it, I saw the butt of a pistol. For a moment I was startled, thinking he was going to shoot, and was just going to jump for him when he handed me the weapon, saying he didn't think he was a safe man to carry it. He also said he was sorry he was saucy to me, and thanked me for not turning him over to the guard. I gave him a little good advice and the matter is dropped, but he did scare me! During the night we had the usual orders to be ready to move, and the usual countermanding.

February 11th, 1863

We received orders today requiring all officers and men to wear on their caps a small, blue, diamond shaped badge. The badge to indicate the corps, and the color, the division. Red for the first division, white for second, and blue for third. We have also orders to move at six o'clock tomorrow morning, which for wonder, have not been countermanded. I am directed to report to Colonel Barnes at the same hour, but for what, I have no idea. Have been assigned to Company E, but think and hope it is only temporarily. E is all right, but I like H better.

February 12th, 1863

Reveille sounded at four, and we at once got breakfast, struck tents, and prepared to leave. I reported to the Colonel as directed, and was put in charge of a detail to load and unload the brigade baggage. Don't fancy this kind of duty, but "orders is orders". We marched to Falmouth station, and as soon as the baggage was unloaded from the wagons and into cars, we took the train for Acquia Creek. On arriving, the regiment went on board the steamer "Hero", and I had to hustle to get everything from the cars to the boat and loaded, as the captain was anxious to start. Lieutenant Deane was sent to assist me, and we finally finished the job, and the "Hero" pulled out into Chesapeake Bay, towing a schooner loaded with mules and army wagons.[5] We had on board with us a company of the 27th New Jersey, a detachment of the 103rd New York, some officers from Corps headquarters, fifty horses and a number of tons of baggage. After getting out into the bay, it was blowing so hard and the seas so heavy, we had to anchor for the night. The officers had the ladies' cabin and we had a very jolly time singing, playing cards, etc.

February 13th, 1863

We had a nice little voyage down the bay, although the wind blew hard and the sea was rough; a good many officers and men were seasick, but I was all right and enjoyed being on the water, as I always do. We managed to get some very bad meals on the boat, by paying a price which should have brought us decent food, but didn't. We arrived in Hampton Roads in the late afternoon and anchored for the night off Fort Monroe, whose gray walls looked familiar enough. Colonel Barnes went ashore for orders, but could get none, so we must wait until tomorrow before we can find out where we are to go.

February 14th, 1863

In the morning, our steamer took us up the James River to Newport News, where we anchored and laid off in the stream until afternoon, when we landed and marched out about two miles outside the earthworks and camped. Here we are back to the "News" again, and it almost seems like home to us. When the baggage was unloaded, I discovered that my valise was missing, and could not be found. This is pretty bad, as it holds everything I own, except the clothing I have on. All my underwear, and what is more important, letters and official papers. Possibly it may turn up, but I have my doubts. Long and I got our tent up just before supper, after which we spread our blankets on the ground and had a good night's sleep.

February 15th, 1863

A cold, disagreeable day. We are to change the location of our camp soon, so did not attempt to fix up much. I was very much pleased to have a visit today from my first commander, with whom I enlisted and left Lowell, almost two years ago, Captain Davis. Was mighty glad to see him. He is a fine officer, and I always liked him. We had a nice long chat over old times, and about the company, which has been turned into light artillery, and is now the 7th Massachusetts Battery, and stationed at Suffolk. Walked to the landing with the Captain, when he left, and promised to try to get over to Suffolk to see him and my old comrades.

February 16th, 1863

Borrowed a horse and rode all around to the places where we camped, drilled and did picket duty here two years ago. There are some changes, but I found things looked quite natural and familiar, and I enjoyed my ride. It was very cold at night and as we are not allowed fires, and have no tent stoves, we had rather an uncomfortable time.

February 17th, 1863

A cold, rainy and windy day. Our old tent, full of holes, let the water and wind in freely, making things very unpleasant. Long made a stiff punch, but it failed to bring any warmth to our benumbed bodies.

February 19th, 1863

Yesterday and today, the same cold, wet weather. We drew "A" tents for the men, but the officers have to keep the old, worn out leaky canvas. We moved our camp today on to the division line, and it is a beautiful sight, looking along the color line, to see the tents in perfect alignment, on a level plain, for several miles. It is the prettiest camp I have ever seen. Am detailed for Officer of the Day, tomorrow.

February 20th, 1863

Was very busy all day, having the camp thoroughly policed and everything put in shape to compare favorably with the other regiments of our brigade and division, which are in fine condition. Was quite tired out at night.

February 21st, 1863

The officers got up a game of baseball today and I enjoyed it very much. We had quite an exciting game. We are having no end of drills now, company, regimental and brigade, which the men dislike very much, as they naturally feel that they are up in drill, after two years of it, and they are, but it will not hurt some of the officers to get a good dose of drill.

February 22nd, 1863

Upon awakening this morning, found it had been snowing and raining all night, and the wind was blowing a gale. There were three inches of snow and water in the tent. We got up quickly and while trying to bail out, a gust of wind blew the tent over, leaving us standing in the rain. I managed to rescue my company books from the deluge and put them in one of the officer's tents still standing. A lot of the tents of both officers and men are in the same condition as ours—down flat. It has been a hard day for all. Was detached from Company E, and assigned to Company H, and am much pleased. Hope I may be able to stay here.

February 23rd, 1863

The storm cleared at night, but very cold. I bought a small stove for our tent and am quite comfortable. Had a little talk with Colonel Barnes in regard to my remaining in Company H, and rather think I can stay there, which is what I want. A lot of commissions came today, among them, mine, as First Lieutenant, dated December 6th, 1862. At night a lot of us gathered in Captain Oliver's tent for the purpose of "Pinching" the new commissions, as it is called in the service. The ceremony is largely of a convivial nature and all the party were thoroughly imbued with the "spirit" of the occasion.

February 24th, 1863

Company and battalion drill. Long took the former and I took the latter. Found I was a bit rusty in some of the movements. In the afternoon, borrowed a horse and with two other officers rode over to the 35th Massachusetts, where I met Captain Ned Park, whose father and mine were next door neighbors on Myrtle Street, Boston, when I was a young child.[6] The two families were intimate and close friends. I used to play with Ned when only three or four years old, and until today, we have not met since. We had a very pleasant time talking over old days and of our families, and I am mighty glad that I met him. We went with a party to the "Scotchman's" and had ale and cigars, after which I had a delightful ride home in the moonlight.[7]

February 25th, 1863

Another fine day. We do have them once in a while. At ten o'clock formed line and marched to the old familiar ground where we used to drill last year, and took part in a grand review of the whole Ninth Corps, by that fussy old martinet, General Dix.[8] It was a fine sight. Got back to camp late in the afternoon and in the evening worked making out payrolls. It seems to be generally understood that our Corps, or a part of it, is destined for active service somewhere in the west, and that, I suppose, is why we are getting so much drilling, although why a higher degree of efficiency should be required in the west than in the glorious army of the Potomac, I can't understand. I reckon our Ninth Corps can hold its own with any western corps in drilling and fighting.

February 26th, 1863

Company and battalion drill today as usual, the latter pretty strenuous. We were all tired out when dismissed. Fixed up a corduroy bed and can sleep more comfortably, I guess.

February 27th, 1863

Company and battalion drill in the forenoon and brigade drill for three hours in the afternoon. We are getting drill in big doses. The officers drew new wall tents today and we are delighted, for we have needed them badly for a long time. Now it may rain and blow. I won't care!

February 28th, 1863

Was Officer of the Day, but had little to do. Had our regular monthly inspection and muster for pay. At night a hard storm, wind and rain, but in our new tent, with a good fire, we were warm and dry.

March 1st, 1863

Inspection of quarters, but the regular Sunday inspection was dispensed with. With the exception that we have no drills, Sunday in camp is very little different from other days, and is not much like the New England Sabbath.

March 2nd, 1863

This morning got a pass from the Colonel to go to Suffolk, and took it to brigade headquarters for approval, where I had to leave it, being told it would be sent to the regiment later on. Then walked down to the landing and around, getting back in time for battalion drill under Captain Richardson, who, after drill, invited the company commanders to his quarters for ale and cigars. My pass for Suffolk came tonight, approved for forty-eight hours. Shall start tomorrow by first boat.

March 3rd, 1863

Took the boat for Fort Monroe early, and on arriving, went to a tailor for some clothing I needed, then into the Fort to see some friends, and then took the boat for Norfolk, where after looking about the city a little, I boarded the train for Suffolk, arriving at three o'clock. Had a warm welcome from Captain Davis and his officers, and from my former comrades of his battery. The 6th Massachusetts, in which are a number of Lowell companies, is stationed near the battery, and I met lots of old friends and acquaintances, among them Captain Pinder, who was my chum at home.[9] It was good to see so many "home faces" and I had a delightful evening.

March 4th, 1863

The battery had to drill in the morning, so I went over to the 6th. Was surprised to see how many I knew in the regiment. Visited the Post Hospital to see some fellows who were wounded in the recent fight near here. In the afternoon, Captain Davis gave me a mount and with him and Lieutenant Farrar rode around the town and entrenchments. Called on Colonel Follansbe of the 6th, a Lowell man, and other officers.[10] In evening had a jolly time at the battery headquarters.

March 5th, 1863

Intended to start back to the regiment, but got left by the train. Railroad movements are somewhat erratic. Can't get a boat from Norfolk until tomorrow morning. Was with my friends during the forenoon, and after dinner Lieutenant Farrar and I took the train for Norfolk, arriving about dark. We had supper together and then went to the theater, after which had steamed oysters and fixings, then to a hotel and to bed. It seemed good to get between sheets, even if they are not so awfully clean. I certainly have had a mighty good time, but have some misgivings as to my reception by the Colonel when I get to the regiment. I am overstaying my leave.

March 6th, 1863

Started for the regiment on morning boat for Fort Monroe and from there by first boat to Newport News, arriving about noon. Reported to Colonel Barnes, who, rather contrary to my expectations, did not give me a "raking over" for overstaying. We had a long, hard brigade drill this afternoon.

March 7th, 1863

Was Officer of the Day, and had a busy time looking after the policing of the camp. There seems to be a disposition throughout the brigade, and I presume the whole corps, to have the camps and men as neat and soldierly as possible, and I am glad. I like it. Today, bought blacking and white gloves for my boys, and expect Company H will look fine at Sunday inspection tomorrow.

March 8th, 1863

Rained in the morning and inspection was postponed until afternoon. My boys looked fine with white gloves and shoes blacked, and I was proud of them. After supper, Harry Braden and I borrowed horses and rode to the camp of the 35th to call on friends and the "Scotchman", the latter being out of ale, we did not stay long.

March 9th, 1863

A beautiful day! With our regular allowance of drill. In the evening, there was some "pinching commissions" business, and the usual hilarious time. Too much whiskey to suit me.

March 10th, 1863

Nothing of importance today. Had some pretty hard drills, which I did not enjoy much, as I felt the effects of last night's celebration. Went to bed early.

March 11th, 1863

Weather very bad in forenoon, so no drills. In the afternoon, the skies cleared and we were ordered out with the other regiments of our division to witness the presentation of a stand of colors to the 8th Michigan, a fine regiment. We are ordered to prepare for a grand inspection tomorrow. In evening, Captain Tripp and I rode to the landing, bought a new blouse, hat and other things. Our mess is broken up by the discharge, for disability, of our *chef*, private Molino of Company B.[11] He was a mighty fine cook, and no end of fun. Long and I will have to mess together, I reckon, and do our own cooking until we can make other arrangements.

March 12th, 1863

Was busy all the morning getting everything in proper shape, and at ten o'clock formed for inspection. My company looked first rate and was complimented by the Division Inspector, which made us all feel good. Engaged a colored boy for servant today at five dollars per month. His name is Frank Kemp and he is about sixteen, I guess, but does not know his own age. Am reading "Charles O'Malley" and like it very much.[12] Ordered for picket tomorrow.

March 13th, 1863

Had a pleasant time on picket in pine woods some two miles from camp. The night was cold, but we had a good fire at the reserve.

March 14th, 1863

Came off picket about ten, and as details off picket are relieved from drills for the day, had nothing to do, so passed the day quietly. Attempted to write some letters, but was too sleepy or lazy.

March 15th, 1863

The usual Sunday inspection, after which we drew clothing and ordnance stores to fully equip each man, the issue of the property keeping me busy until evening. This looks as if some kind of a move will be made soon.

March 16th, 1863

Drills, drills, drills! Had a "numb fit" on today and made several mistakes on battalion drills. Was disgusted with myself. A box from home came today, and in it were some books of songs for use when some of us get together for "a sing", and among them the old "Jubilee", which I used at singing school, ages ago, as it seems. It made me a little homesick to think of the good times I had in those days. In the evening the fellows came in and we tried some of the new songs.

March 17th, 1863

Nothing doing today but drills. There was some little excitement at night when we received orders to issue sixty rounds of ammunition to each man; forty rounds to be carried in cartridge boxes and twenty in pockets, and to keep two days' cooked rations on hand, with the usual admonition "be ready to move at a moment's notice". All kinds of stories were flying about camp, one that we are to go up the peninsula again, one that the army is to retreat, and another that we are going to Suffolk. Hope it may be the latter. It would suit me all right.

March 18th, 1863

Inspection but no drills today. We are still here. At night orders came to have five days' cooked rations on hand instead of two, with the usual addenda. In the middle of the night, was awakened and told we are to move in the morning.

March 19th, 1863

A hard storm—rain, snow and sleet. We broke camp at seven o'clock, but did not move until noon. This was tough on the men. We officers managed to crowd into a sutler's tent, but the men had to stand out in the storm. It was all wrong. When we finally started for the landing, the mud was awful. It was intended that we should go on board a steamer at the landing, but for some reason, only a part of the regiment embarked. The rest of us had to crowd into some old log barracks. It was quite cold and we bought some stoves which made things a little more comfortable for us all. In the evening, Colonel Barnes invited me, with several others, to dine with him at "Webster's" and I had a very pleasant time. Several bottles of wine were opened, and I then went to the barracks to get what sleep I could, which wasn't much.

March 20th, 1863

Still storming hard. Remained in the old barracks all day, cold and cross, envying the fellows comfortably fixed on the steamer. It is reported that we are not to embark while the storm continues. A miserable, blue day this!

Chapter 8

A Wartime Love Affair

The IX Corps to which Ayling's regiment belonged was called by William F. Fox "a wandering corps" because of the many states in which it fought.[1] On March 19, 1863, it was ordered to the Department of the Ohio, under General Burnside, leaving Newport News and going to northern Kentucky, where it undertook occupation duties in that divided border state. For Lieutenant Ayling this meant pleasant duty in Paris, Kentucky, where he fell in love with a beautiful girl, Cordelia Kelley. However, within a month the brigade of Ayling's regiment was moved to other stations in Kentucky and, much to his regret, Ayling was parted from his love.[2]

March 21st, 1863

The weather clear, and at noon we joined the rest of the regiment on the steamer "City of Richmond", bound as we are told for Baltimore. The officers had the saloon, but it was quite crowded, and at night the air was pretty bad. I slept on a dinner table. Colonel Pierce joined us today to the regret of a large majority of the regiment. He is neither an officer nor a gentleman. Lieutenant Colonel Barnes is both.

March 22nd, 1863

We had a fine trip down the James River and up the Chesapeake Bay, and I enjoyed it much. Arrived at Baltimore at eleven this forenoon and

hoped we might remain here over night and have a chance to take in some
of the sights, but were disappointed and had to go at once to a train and
get our men on board. We did not start, however, until after dark, and
had some trouble trying to keep the men from straying off to the rum
shops, which are plentiful in the vicinity. Some of the companies succeeded
in getting whiskey, and there were some tough fights but Company H did
not give me much trouble. We travelled all night, the men in freight cars,
and one passenger car for all the officers. We were so crowded that none
of us got any sleep.

March 23rd, 1863

Arrived at Harper's Ferry in the early morning and remained two
hours. Was much interested in seeing this place, made famous by the
"John Brown raid".[3] The scenery is grand. Mountains all around, with
the Shenandoah winding through to join the Potomac. We were on the
road all day and all night. I enjoyed seeing this part of the country,
which is interesting, and new to me, and different from anything I have
ever seen, and the scenery on the Baltimore and Ohio Railroad is certainly magnificent. Our car is the last of the train and I spent the day
on the rear platform, where I could have a good view of the country
and the people. There was a good deal of patriotism and enthusiasm
displayed in the villages through which we passed. The men cheering
and the girls waving flags and handkerchiefs. We responded by cheering the men and throwing kisses to the girls and tossing our cards to
them, with a regimental address and the request "Please write". We
were side-tracked many times to let regular trains pass. At such places
the people would bring nice things to eat and the girls sing patriotic
songs. This part of Virginia is loyal to the old flag, surely.[4]

March 24th, 1863

Another day and night on the road. We are not making much headway, we are side-tracked so often. Evidently there is no hurry to get us to
our destination, wherever that may be; but I don't care, for I am having
a great time. We crossed the Alleghany Mountains on a very steep grade,
117 feet to the mile, they told us. Went through tunnels and saw no end
of grand scenery. At Grafton, we remained long enough for a square meal
at the hotel, the first of the trip. We found the same patriotism among
the people as yesterday and were received just as enthusiastically and

treated as hospitably. Not much sleep at night. Too crowded and too noisy. Some of the officers are inclined to drink too much and get hilarious. It disgusts me. I can take a drink occasionally, when with a crowd, but do not like whiskey and do not want any of it.

March 25th, 1863

We arrived at Parkersburg, West Virginia, early in the morning, and after a good breakfast went on board the steamer "Eclipse", and started down the Ohio. We had fine quarters on this boat, the officers having staterooms. We are not accustomed to such treatment, and hardly know how to behave. I enjoyed the trip immensely. It was a new experience; everything was new and interesting. The same spirit of loyalty, as yesterday, was shown on both the Ohio and West Virginia sides, and at places on the Kentucky shore flags were flying and the people cheered and waved to us. Saw several coal mines in the sides of the Virginia hills along the river, and many other interesting things.

March 26th, 1863

On the river all the forenoon, enjoying, as yesterday, seeing the country and the people. Arrived at Covington on the Kentucky side of the river, opposite Cincinnati, at noon, where we had to wait a while for orders, then our boat took us across to Cincinnati, where we had a magnificent reception. We are the first regiment from the Bay State the city has seen, and our Pine Tree flag was new to most of the people, although quite a number, they told us, were originally from the East. Our coming was expected, and we were given a right royal welcome. The landing was crowded with men and women cheering for Massachusetts and the Union, and waving flags and handkerchiefs. When the regiment landed and marched up from the boat, it was accompanied by a crowd that filled the street and cheered all the way to the Fifth Street Market, where a fine dinner had been prepared for the men, the officers being escorted to the Gibson House and given a banquet. Nothing seems to be too good for us. We found it to be impossible for us to buy anything, and pay for it, anywhere. One could go to a store and select any article desired, but when offering to pay would be politely requested to take the goods and informed that our money was not good here. This spirit prevailed everywhere; not only would our money be refused, but the storekeepers would press all kinds of little gifts upon us. Toward evening, we formed and marched back to the landing escorted by, I should judge, the entire population, cheering and bidding us goodbye, and after we boarded the boat, people came with boxes of oranges and baskets of apples for our men. Cincinnati has certainly treated us royally, and I shall always have a warm place in my heart for the city. At the Gibson House, I met an old friend of father's named Brooks. About dark we crossed the river to Covington, and after some delay, took cars for Paris, Kentucky, eighty miles distant. It is understood that our whole Ninth Corps is being sent to Kentucky, which being a border state, is partly Union and partly "Secesh", to keep it in the Union by preventing its being occupied by the enemy, and to protect the loyal people from guerillas, who have been raiding the country, robbing, and sometimes murdering those who are opposed to secession.[5] We are also to guard a lot of trestle bridges on the railroad. During the night, two companies were detached and left at different places as bridge guards. Company H being one of them, I had to get my men out at three o'clock in a country entirely unknown to me and in almost impenetrable darkness. Did not like the job a bit!

March 27th, 1863

Was dumped with my company at this place at three o'clock this morning with orders to report to the captain commanding the guard. Found no pickets, sentinels or guards anywhere. We were not challenged by anyone and I wondered what kind of an outfit I had come on to. I had considerable difficulty in finding the camp of the guard, it was so dark, and when I finally located it, found everybody, officers and men, asleep. This kind of guard duty is somewhat different from that to which I have been accustomed. Six or eight good men could have captured the whole lot. I went to a tent and pulled a man out, told him who I was and what I was there for, and made him assist me in finding quarters for my men, which he did in a sort of blockhouse. After posting some pickets as well as I could in the darkness, crawled into a tent full of men and slept until morning. Upon awakening, reported to the captain as ordered, and then looked around to see what kind of a place I am in. There is a high trestle over what is called "Stony Creek" with two blockhouses for the protection, if attacked, of the bridge guard, which is a company of the 118th Ohio. They are a fine lot of men, but have had very little experience and are, naturally, rather green. The Captain is a good fellow and quite willing to accept suggestions as to the proper way to guard the bridge, to make camp, etc., and we will get on nicely. Had my boys pitch their shelter tents in the proper way to show the Ohio fellows how to do it. During the day, visited some of the farmers in the vicinity and had a very interesting time. Met one man who told me he used to take cattle to Brighton before the war.

March 28th, 1863

This morning we got up a game of baseball and I was having a good time, when Captain Brooks came marching in with his company to relieve me, and with orders for me to report to the regiment in Paris at once, so we struck camp and started out. Had rather a rough march of four or five miles, reported my arrival to the Colonel, had my company tents pitched and then went to my tent for a nap. Our camp is very pleasantly situated, a short distance from Paris, which is the County Seat of Bourbon County, and a city, although a mighty small one, not really more than a village. A long trestle bridge spans a creek, and I presume this bridge is what we are to protect.

March 29th, 1863

Sunday inspection in the morning, after which, went in town to church with Lieutenants Windsor and Conant, and it seemed good to be a little civilized once more.[6] In the evening, took my company to the Episcopal Church. Captain Tripp was Officer of the Day, and at night went the "Grand Rounds" with him, visiting all the outlying pickets. We had good horses, and the ride, some twelve or fifteen miles, in the moonlight, was quite exciting and I enjoyed it much. I notice there are lots of pretty girls here in Paris.

March 30th, 1863

Was busy with my company most of the day, getting the tents pitched properly, and aligned, also had a table and bed built for my tent. In evening, went in town to look around. Captain Tripp was to take me to call upon some ladies he had become acquainted with, but we missed each other some way. Returned to camp about nine o'clock and was detailed for picket to go on at once. Information had been received that we are to be attacked tonight, and extra pickets are ordered. Went out, with twenty men, about two miles, placed my posts as well as I could and waited, but nothing happened, except during the night four or five negroes came in, one of them riding a fine horse, which I confiscated and kept to use when visiting my pickets.

March 31st, 1863

Was relieved early this morning and rode my captured horse into camp and turned him over to the Quartermaster. Passed the day quietly. It was cold and hard to keep comfortable in the tent, as we have no fireplace or stove. In the evening, went with Captain Tripp to make the call he had promised me, upon some ladies—a Mrs. Kelley and two daughters, Eliza and Cordelia, the former an invalid, but very bright and agreeable, and the latter very attractive and very musical. They have a piano and two guitars and we had some good music, which I always enjoy. The Kelleys are a fine family and intensely loyal, the two sons being in a Union cavalry regiment. Their place borders the creek which runs through Paris, and is appropriately named "Creekside". It is a great pleasure to meet and be with such people. I am much interested in Miss Cordelia, or "Cordie", as the family call her.

April 1st, 1863

We received orders this morning to join our brigade at Lexington and to leave this evening. This made us sorry enough, for although it is what one must expect in the army, we hated to leave the only "soft thing" we have ever had. I was particularly blue to have to leave Paris and the Kelley family! At noon, the 51st New York came in to relieve us. Went in town to dinner and to "Creekside" to say goodbye. Stayed there most of the afternoon. They all seemed as sorry to have me leave, as I do to go. Two very pretty girls were there, Miss Duncan, the Mayor's daughter, and a Miss Ingalls, but they are not so pretty as Miss Cordie. The citizens of Paris have taken quite a liking to the 29th, I reckon because it has behaved better than some regiments that have been here, or passed through, and when it was learned that we were ordered away, telegrams were sent, and a committee of the leading citizens went with a petition to General Burnside at Cincinnati asking that the order be countermanded. When I went to camp to get ready to leave, I was delighted to hear that the order for us to go had been countermanded, and we are to stay in Paris for a time, at least. In the evening, was invited to Mrs. Kelley's for supper. Some of the 51st officers were there, one of them, a typical "Lord Dundreary", and we

General Ambrose E. Burnside. From *Battles and Leaders of the Civil War*, vol. 3, 1884.

had a little quiet fun at his expense.[7] When I left "Creekside" tonight I was surely very much in love with "Cordie".

April 2nd, 1863

We are all getting a little short of money. Hope the Paymaster will show up soon, for being broke is not a pleasant sensation. Captain Tripp has arranged for us two to take our meals at Mrs. Kelley's. This is fine and will give me a chance to get better acquainted with "Cordie". Went there to supper and had a very pleasant evening with lots of music. Am certainly very much taken with "Cordie". She just suits me exactly.

April 3rd, 1863

We had just finished breakfast when we heard the music of a band in the street, and Cordie and I walked over to see what it was, and saw the First Brigade march through on the way to Lexington. When I went to camp, found I was detailed as Officer of the Provost Guard for duty in the city. The regiment moved in town today, seven of the companies being quartered in the Court House and the remaining three in adjoining buildings. The officers have a large room in the Court House to sleep in, and can take their meals at the hotel or where they please. Was invited to a little party at "Creekside" tonight, and wanted to go awfully, but had to remain on duty with my guard, so could not leave. Colonel Pierce is in command of the Post and Lieutenant Colonel Barnes the regiment. Wish he was Colonel instead of that miserable Pierce, for he is a better man every way.

April 4th, 1863

Am getting more and more in love with the young lady at "Creekside", and I notice Tripp seems to be quite interested there too. He has much more "cheek" than I and may succeed in cutting me out, but we will see. Borrowed a guitar from Cordie and took it to the quarters this evening. Have not touched a guitar for two years and my fingers are somewhat stiff, but I managed to play some accompaniments, and we had a good time singing. Captain Brooks has picked up a feather bed somewhere, and invited me to share it with him, tonight, which I was glad to do, as the nights are cold.

April 5th, 1863

In the morning, went to the Dutch Reformed Church, and in afternoon to the Episcopal, where I saw Cordie and a lot of other young ladies. Paris can certainly boast of having a lot of pretty girls, but it is not easy to get acquainted with them. We had our first dress parade in the city this evening, and there was a good crowd of people to see it. We are all looking very anxiously for the Paymaster.

April 6th, 1863

Passed the day quietly reading, playing the guitar and walking around town. Spent as much time as I dared at "Creekside". Am getting better acquainted with the Kelleys and long for meal times to come that I may have an excuse to go there. We had our dress parade this evening in front of the Court House, with a lot of spectators, including a good many young ladies.

April 7th, 1863

Bought a lot of boards for my boys to build bunks. Started Corporal Taylor at work making out Quarterly Returns.[8] In the afternoon, was invited to drive with the Kelleys to the camp of the 45th Pennsylvania to see dress parade. Was to go in the carriage with Cordie, but Tripp played rather a mean game, and got ahead of me, so I went with Miss Elliott and Miss Ford. Had a pleasant time, but didn't like being "euchred". Tonight Colonel Barnes called for volunteers to go with him on a scout to try to capture some guerillas. Wanted to go, awfully, but could not get a good horse, and as the party is to be mounted, had to give it up. We received our long looked for mail which has been held up in Cincinnati, or somewhere. Had a lot of letters.

April 8th, 1863

Was Officer of the Day and had an easy time, no trouble or disturbance anywhere. The weather was fine and there were lots of young ladies out. Cordie was at dress parade and I walked home with her, and played a few games of dominoes. Was on duty at Colonel Barnes' quarters all night, to be handy in case of trouble. Four of my men who were left behind at Baltimore, either by accident, or purposely, reported today. Several of us have answered advertisements in the papers of young ladies desiring to correspond with officers. Expect we will have some fun.

April 9th, 1863

Upon being relieved this morning, was on the street a while and then went to quarters and laid down. I feel as if I had a cold coming on. Was invited to tea by one of the citizens, but felt too poor to go. Have an invitation to a little party at Creekside for tomorrow night, with permission to bring Captain Brooks. Hope I shall feel better.

April 10th, 1863

Was around as usual in the morning, but laid on my bunk all the afternoon. Have a bad cold and sore throat, and feel like the deuce, generally. Took Brooks to supper and we spent the evening there. Captain Tripp and Lieutenants Whitman and Conant were there. We had a nice party, and Mrs. Kelley gave a fine supper. I should have enjoyed the affair very much if I had not felt so miserable.

April 11th, 1863

Felt somewhat better this morning, but not first rate. We had no drills or parade and I kept quietly in quarters until supper time. In the evening, Tripp and I walked with Cordie out to the home of the Honorable Garrett Davis, U.S. Senator from Kentucky, a fine place two or three miles from the city, where we were received by his adopted daughter, Miss Mollie Elliott, and Miss Nicolai Ford. These young ladies and Cordie are very intimate friends. They call themselves "The Sisterhood" and are inseparable, and are all bright, attractive girls. Enjoyed the call very much. When we started to return, it was very dark and the road was rough, and had it not been for a lantern we borrowed, we would have had a pretty hard time. Did not get to my quarters until twelve o'clock.

April 12th, 1863

Inspection and muster in the morning, after which it was too late for church, so read and slept until dinner. In evening, went to the Episcopal Church. Another scouting party went out tonight, but I did not volunteer. They are not to be mounted, and I do not fancy travelling over the rough roads in the dark on foot. There is neither fun nor glory in it.

April 13th, 1863

When I went to breakfast, took writing materials and wrote some letters. Was at Creekside most of the afternoon, also, Cordie singing for me. Miss Elliott and Miss Ford came, and Mrs. Forman, Cordie's married sister, a charming woman. The ladies joked me about looking so serious and dignified when on dress parade, and insisted they could make me smile. I declared nothing could do that, and we made a wager. If I lose, I am to walk blindfolded to Garrett Davis'. If I win, Cordie is to play or sing whenever I ask her. At dress parade this evening, the four were all there and stood on the sidewalk directly opposite me, laughing, making little faces at me and pretending to talk about me, and doing everything they could think of, that did not show too plainly to the public, to get me to smile, but they had to give it up!

April 14th, 1863

Had my men sign the payrolls, but the scouting party has not come in, and we can't be paid until they return. Was at Creekside most of the day, when off duty, and in the evening, Cordie paid the wager of yesterday, and gave me all the songs I asked for. Am certainly in love with that young lady, but whether she is with me, is altogether another thing, and what I would like to know.

April 15th, 1863

No news from the scouting party. We are all impatient for them to come in so we can be paid. This evening, took Sergeant Pippey of my company, a nice gentlemanly fellow, to supper with me, and to have some music, but I left early as I had arranged to make a call at Dr. Dunnington's with Captain Brooks.[9] I found, however, he had gone before I got back from Creekside, so did not go. Tonight I received a bouquet with the compliments of some unknown young lady. Suspect it is from Miss Florence Burr, who lives near the Court House. I have never met her.

April 16th, 1863

The scouting party came in late last night and today we were paid to February 28th. Was Officer of the Day, a job I do not fancy much on pay day when things are usually somewhat lively, and there is more or less intoxication and consequently trouble, not only with our own men, but from the battery and regiments that are camped outside the city. Did not have quite as much trouble as I expected. Had to put several men in the "Cage", and one was pretty ugly, but I got along all right. Sometime about midnight heard shots out on the picket line, and the "assembly" sounded from the battery. Took a patrol of twenty men and went out to see what was up. Found the alarm was caused by some men of the 118th Ohio, who were out stealing chickens and had come on to the pickets, who fired. One of the Ohio men was killed. The poor fellow was disobeying orders, which are very strict against stealing from citizens. While out investigating, Colonel Pierce came and directed me to deploy my patrol and surround and search a house outside the lines, whose owner was suspected of harboring guerillas. I did as ordered, but found nobody and nothing suspicious. Received a fine large apple today, with the compliments of Miss ——, somebody unknown. She is very kind, whoever she may be.

April 17th, 1863

Beautiful weather. Was relieved at eight o'clock, and am off duty for the day. Took Brooks to dinner with me, and spent the afternoon at Creekside. Miss Elliott and Miss Ford came and we had a jolly time. In the evening, with the young ladies and Captain Tripp, called at Mrs. McAboy's, and from there went to Mayor Duncan's, where we met his daughters, Miss Winnie and Miss Kate. Had a pleasant evening, but would have enjoyed much better being with Cordie, alone. Received a newspaper today with a marked notice of a meeting to be held at a church next Sunday evening. Take it as an invitation to be present, and will be there. The notice came from Miss Florence Burr, I learned.

April 18th, 1863

Another warm, beautiful day. In the morning, Tripp and I got a team and took Cordie and Miss Ford for a drive. Called on Miss Elliott, who insisted upon our staying and being put in the "Guard House", which is a circular enclosure on the lawn with walls of high, thick shrubbery, and a single entrance. There are seats and a small table where Miss Elliott reads and writes. It is certainly a charming place, and the girls call it the "Guard House". They say that only their particular friends are allowed to enter, and we must consider ourselves highly honored, which we did. I had the additional honor of dedicating the "Guard Book" which is the name they give to the Guest Book. In the evening was in quarters writing letters. Sent a bouquet today to Miss Florence Burr.

April 19th, 1863

After inspection went with Captain Brooks to the Christian Church, and in the afternoon to the Episcopal. At dress parade, orders were read assigning Captain Lee to Company H.[10] This is all right, I suppose. Lee is entitled to a company, but I have gotten along so nicely with the men of the company, and like them so much, I cannot help feeling bad to have to give up command. I do not fancy Lee much, anyway. In the evening was at Creekside and my friends there all sympathized with me, which helped some, but I can't help feeling blue. Two years ago today I enlisted.

April 20th, 1863

This morning while whittling at the barracks, my knife slipped and the point of the blade struck my knee, and for a time made me quite lame. Went out on company drill in the forenoon, but travelling around on battalion drill in the afternoon was too much for the knee and I was excused and went over to Creekside and remained until dress parade, when I took my company out. I shall not have many more chances to handle Company H, as Captain Lee, who has been on leave, is to return in a day or two to assume command. In the evening, called at Mayor Duncan's. Met there the two Williams girls. Quite a crowd of our officers were there and we had a jolly time.

April 21st, 1863

Was a little lame today, but was out on duty. We had a fine battalion drill in street clearing and firing. Tried to get leave to go to Cincinnati for a few days, but Colonel Barnes desires me to wait until Captain Lee arrives. Spent as much time at Creekside as possible. Am in love with Cordie, more and more every day, but rather think Tripp has the inside and is ahead of me.

April 22nd, 1863

Went fishing this afternoon with Mr. Forman, Cordie's brother-in-law. Had fair luck. In evening at Creekside. Several of the officers came in and we had music and a general good time. Captain Brooks told me tonight of a conversation he had with Cordie, and certain things she said have raised my hopes somewhat.

April 23rd, 1863

A damp, disagreeable day. Have a cold and cough and feel poor. Stayed at Creekside all the afternoon until supper, writing letters and listening to music. In the evening Cordie gave me a guitar lesson, and as I was leaving, saying good night, she put a slip of paper in my hand, which I was not to read until I reached quarters. When I opened and read the paper, she had written, "Tell your sister there is a Kentucky girl who ———". I had just told her that I had written Mary. I would give much to know what the unwritten words would have been had she finished the sentence, but I certainly feel somewhat encouraged.

April 24th, 1863

Was Officer of the Guard and had a very easy time. Wrote a note to Cordie telling her how happy the few words she wrote last night had made me, and inviting her to go to a concert next Monday night. Was on duty all day and night, so could not be with her. When leaving, after supper, she gave me a nice little note accepting my invitation, and saying some things that made me feel very happy. She is a dear girl and I love her. We have arranged to go to Garrett Davis' tomorrow afternoon. One of the prisoners, a deserter, escaped from the Guard House today. Felt bad to have this happen when I was in command of the guard, but no one blamed me as it was the fault of the sentinel on duty over prisoners.

April 25th, 1863

On being relieved this morning, Captain Brooks and I took a walk down town; as we passed Mayor Duncan's place, saw the young ladies, his daughters, who invited us into their garden where we spent most of the forenoon, lying on the grass under the trees, chatting. At dinner Cordie thought it would be better to go to Mr. Davis' after supper instead of in the afternoon, as previously arranged, so we had an early supper and started, Cordie and I and Captain Tripp. Miss Ford was there with Miss Elliott to receive us and we had a delightful time until nearly eleven, when we were interrupted by the appearance of an orderly sent by Colonel Barnes to notify us that marching orders had come and we are to move at an early hour tomorrow. This came like a thunderbolt from a clear sky, and we were stunned. It was a hard blow and we felt bad to think we must leave Paris. The girls felt as sorry as we did and we were a disconsolate party. I cannot tell how disconsolate and unhappy I am to have to leave Cordie just as we are getting to understand each other. It is the fortune of war, I suppose, and I must bear it, and trust to luck for what the future may bring. Said goodbye to Miss Elliott and started back to town, Miss Ford going with us. Cordie held to my arm all the way and we were too sad and sorry to talk. Bid her goodbye at her house and we promised to write each other. Went to the barracks and got everything ready to march in the morning, and then laid down but could not sleep. Was very miserable.

April 26th, 1863

We did not leave as early as was expected, after all, so went to Creekside to breakfast, but had no appetite. All the family felt bad to have us go away. Went back to the regiment and found we were to go at half past ten, and were ordered not to go to church. I was determined to see Cordie once more, so Lieutenant Long and I went to the Episcopal Church nearby, where I knew I would see her. Managed to get seats near her and we exchanged notes. Sat with both ears listening to hear our bugles sound the assembly, but everything was quiet. On returning to the regiment found our departure was again postponed until half past one. Went with Captain Brooks to say goodbye to Mrs. McAboy and the Misses Duncan and Williams and other friends, and then to Creekside, once more, for dinner, but could not eat anything. After dinner went with Cordie to Miss Ford's where we met the other member of the "Sisterhood", Miss Elliott, and stayed until the order came to fall in, and we marched to the railroad. The girls were all there, and Cordie gave me a nice little prayer book from her sister Eliza. The train finally started, carrying away a good many sad hearts, and I think leaving some behind. We arrived at the little village of Nicholasville at six o'clock, left the cars and marched out two miles and camped for the night. No tents were pitched, so laid on the ground looking at the stars and trying to sleep but could not. This has been the bluest, saddest day of my life. It is bad enough to leave Paris, where the citizens did everything possible to make things pleasant for us, and where our stay of a month has been the only bright spot in the history of the regiment, but for those of us, and there are several, who have found attachments for Kentucky girls, it is doubly hard. I am perfectly miserable.

Chapter 9

❧❧❧

OCCUPATION DUTY IN KENTUCKY

After leaving Paris, Ayling's regiment was ordered to various places in Kentucky to protect Union sympathizers and to guard against attack from Confederates beyond the Cumberland River. Ayling keeps in touch by mail with Cordie, but finds the separation painful.[1]

April 27th, 1863

Started early this morning and marched sixteen miles to Camp Dick Robinson, and went into camp.[2] Have not eaten anything today, and was so blue I was not tired on the march. Captain Brooks and I kept together most of the time, consoling each other, and talking of the girls we left behind us. He and I are in the same state of mind and our hearts are in Paris.

April 28th, 1863

Broke camp at half past eight and marched to Lancaster, only eight or nine miles. We are to stay here until tomorrow, so pitched tents in a very pretty place, a mile from town, and made ourselves comfortable. Captain Brooks, my companion in misery, is to tent with me. In evening he and I went to a house nearby and got a very good supper. The young ladies of the family played and sang for us and helped to make the time pass, but it was not Creekside. Commenced a letter to Cordie, but did not finish it. It is a hard letter to write, satisfactorily to myself.

April 29th, 1863

On the road early to join our brigade at Stanford. Passed through several small villages and reached the town at noon. Moved out two miles, found the brigade and went into camp in a hard rain. My tent leaked and made things uncomfortably moist. Wanted to finish letter to Cordie, but the Colonel ordered that muster rolls be made at once. Worked with Corporal Taylor until eleven o'clock, but did not quite finish.

April 30th, 1863

The whole brigade moved today and we marched eighteen miles to Carpenter's Creek, two miles beyond Houston, and had a fine camping place. Our marching in Kentucky has usually been on pike roads, but today we have travelled through a wild mountainous country with very rough roads and with numerous creeks to ford. It has been the hottest day of the season, and we all suffered from the heat. We are more than fifty miles from a railroad. At night my boy Frank, who is a first class forager, got some eggs and butter, and we had a good supper, after which, and a smoke, Brooks and I spread our blankets on the lee of a rail fence and talked until we fell asleep.

May 1st, 1863

Was agreeably surprised that we had no marching orders this morning, and found we are to remain all day. The regiment was mustered for pay, after which I finished a long letter to Cordie. Wrote her as I never have written or spoken to any other girl, and shall look anxiously for her reply. Could get no opportunity to send my letter today and don't know when a mail will go, but her letter in answer will decide everything. We have orders to march at four o'clock tomorrow.

May 2nd, 1863

Was awakened at two this morning to be informed that the order to march had been countermanded. This has a familiar sound, but suits me all right. I am content to remain here a day or two. The weather is very hot and I kept as quiet and cool as possible. A mail was sent today and my letter has gone. Cordie's reply will make me very happy or very unhappy.

May 3rd, 1863

Another scorching day. Tried to write some letters, but it was too hot. Spent the day in my tent, reading, smoking, sleeping and trying to keep cool. No drills or duty and no orders to march, for which I am glad.

May 4th, 1863

Very warm. There being no duty, we are having a lazy time. Laid around reading everything I could get hold of. At night some of the officers got a keg of lager from some sutler and we had a gay time in Captain Oliver's tent. We are ordered to march at four o'clock tomorrow morning.

May 5th, 1863

Reveille sounded at one, and we made coffee, rolled blankets, struck tents and moved promptly at four as ordered. Commenced our march by crossing a mountain and had a long, hard day. Passed through Middletown, and saw there the brigade that was going to take the place of ours in Paris and vicinity last month, but did not, thanks to the citizens who induced General Burnside to keep us there. It rained hard all day and the roads muddy and rough. We forded twenty creeks and climbed many small rugged mountains or knobs, as they are called, and at night camped at Fishing Creek, or as it is called locally "Buncomb", after a pretty hard march of twenty miles. My colored boy, Frank, went out foraging and brought in a chicken and some biscuits, so we had a good supper. Rained hard all night.

May 6th, 1863

Started out as we did yesterday by climbing a high hill, but we did not make much distance today, the travelling is so rough, and the mud so deep, only eight miles, and went into camp four miles from Somerset. Just as we turned into a field to make camp, it began to rain hard and before I could get my tent up, was soaked through. Heard one of the men, wet to the skin, singing "A soldier's life is always gay", which at the time seemed a pretty strong statement, but after some hot coffee and a good smoke, felt that things might be much worse!

May 7th, 1863

Had rather a hard night, wet and cold, and woke up stiff and sore, but soon got limbered up. Rained hard all day, and we did not move. Sent out my two grub scouts, Billy Farnsworth, and my boy Frank, and they came in at night with a ham and a chicken, so we are all right for a while.[3] No mail yet, and I was disappointed, as I hoped to have a letter from Cordie. Turned in early, leaving the two boys cooking the chicken before the fire on two sticks. We go into Somerset tomorrow.

May 8th, 1863

Broke camp in the forenoon and marched to Somerset, arriving at noon. Only four miles but through the stickiest kind of mud, much like that in Virginia, which tires one badly to walk through. Camped in a pleasant place just outside the town and prepared to make ourselves comfortable. It is reported that we may stay here sometime, but we can never count on anything. Captain Brooks will tent with me until Lee comes. After getting things into shape, Brooks and I went to town to look around. Do not fancy the place at all. Although it is the county seat of Pulaski County, and has, it is said, two thousand inhabitants, it seems to be quite dead. There are some fine residences, but there is an air of dreariness that makes the place uninviting. Somerset has been raided and plundered several times. Perhaps that accounts for its desolate appearance. The people are glad to have us come for protection, but it is not much like Paris. Our brigade is camped near us and there are lots of troops stationed throughout this part of Kentucky.

May 9th, 1863

A fine day. Went in town with Brooks, Braden and Goodwin, and had several bottles of Catawba wine, which seems to be quite plentiful and cheap here.[4] We walked all about the place and found it very uninteresting, not to be compared with Paris. Several officers who have been home on leave returned today, among them Captain Lee, who assumes command of Company H, and I am down and out. Well, I am relieved of responsibility for arms and equipments—that's something. In evening

wrote several letters. Am much disappointed that I have no letter from
Cordie.

May 10th, 1863

Was Officer of the Brigade Guard. A pleasant warm day. Had an
easy time. My guard being only for the brigade camp, I was not obliged
to keep up all night, and was able to get some sleep in an old cart which
stood near the reserve. No mail from Paris yet. I hear that the 2nd
Maryland is now stationed there, and perhaps Cordie is too busy entertaining the officers to write or care for me. Can't help feeling blue.

May 11th, 1863

Upon being relieved, passed the day reading and sleeping. Tried to
write some letters, but it was too hot, and besides, I don't feel like doing
anything until I hear from *her!* We are under orders to be ready to move
at short notice, with two days' rations. A large force of the enemy is reported to be on the other side of the Cumberland River, four miles distant, and we are liable to have a brush with them any time. Wish we could,
and then get out of this country, where we are eighty miles from a railroad, and the mails are very irregular, which may account for my not
receiving the anxiously looked for letter from Cordie.

May 12th, 1863

Passed the day in the usual way—reading, writing letters and loung-
ing. Inspection was ordered for seven o'clock this evening, but postponed
until tomorrow. Captain Tripp had a letter from Paris today, but did not
tell me from whom, and I will not ask him. I presume it is from Cordie,
and feel pretty blue, as I get nothing from her in answer to my letter. There
was quite a little excitement in the company today, one of the men getting drunk, making a disturbance, and being impudent to Captain Lee,
who had him tied up. Lee does not know how to get along with the men.
In the evening, I walked into town with Brooks, but came back early and
went to bed, feeling anxious and unhappy.

May 13th, 1863

Rained hard all day, so no inspection. Had letters from Lowell friends, but nothing from the one whose letter I want most. Tripp had a letter from Mollie Elliott, Cordie's most intimate friend, and I would give something to know the contents. I begin to think there is no use to expect any letter from Cordie, anyway. Between eleven and twelve, an orderly came around and woke us up to say an attack was expected, and with the Colonel's orders that we be ready to fall in quickly at the sound of the long roll. Got up and warned the company and fixed things ready for a sudden alarm, but I have heard too many reports of expected attack to be disturbed, so went back to bed and slept peacefully until reveille.

May 14th, 1863

A fine day after the storm. Was busy writing letters most of the day. Was again disappointed when the mail came; no letter from Cordie. Think I will write Mollie Elliott, her chum, and try to find out the cause of Cordie's silence. Made a rough draft of letter and showed it to Brooks, who thought it was just right. In evening, took our usual walk, Brooks and I, consoling with each other. He is not altogether happy in his love affair.

May 15th, 1863

Sent letter to Miss Elliott today and await developments. Am afraid I wrote a little strongly, but can't help feeling hurt when I know the others are getting letters from friends in Paris almost every day, and I get none. My letter to Cordie certainly called for a reply. At night when the mail came there were Paris letters for several of the officers, but nothing for me. I guess it's Ephesians 2–12.[5]

May 16th, 1863

The usual routine today. The air is full of all kinds of rumors—that we are going to Cincinnati, to Vicksburg, back to Paris, and to various other places. There are reports that we are to attack or to be attacked, but nothing happens except letters from Paris for others and none for me. Suppose I am foolish to take it so hard. In fact, I know I am.

May 17th, 1863

Sunday inspection, after which wrote several letters. Received letters and papers from home. Heard we are to go on reconnaissance to the Cumberland River, but nothing came of it. I would be glad to have a fight, or anything to take my mind away from my troubles for a time.

May 18th, 1863

Was Officer of the Brigade Guard again. This detail comes pretty often, but I don't object. It is a cinch compared with picket duty. At night made my headquarters in a house, and with a bottle of Catawba and some cigars, had a comfortable time, although it was quite chilly after sundown. Brooks came over to see me in the evening for a chat. Countersign "Baltimore".

May 19th, 1863

On being relieved, laid around doing nothing. Tried reading, but could not settle down to it. We are having delightful weather, and I wonder why we don't do something in the way of active service. Perhaps we are doing some good by protecting the people from guerilla raids, but I think at the present I would rather be in the field. I hear nothing from Cordie, and the suspense is raising the deuce with me. It keeps me fretful and restless. Wonder if she is offended at anything I said in my letter to her. Surely there was nothing at which a girl could take offense.

May 20th, 1863

Still beautiful weather and still no letter from Cordie. Am getting to feel desperate, and at the same time, am well aware that I am a fool. Tripp had two letters from Paris today, and was careful to let me know it, which does not add to my peace of mind. Had a corduroy bed built in my tent today, and sometime in the night while I was asleep it broke down. I was too much disgusted and too sleepy to try to fix it, and finished the night on two rails.

May 21st, 1863

Woke up a little stiff and sore from my uncomfortable bed, but nothing counts now, for I have the long looked for letter from Cordie, and am happy and feel like myself once more. Her letter is dated May

7th, and why it has been so long delayed, or where, I can't imagine. It is favorable to my hopes, and all I could ask or expect, under the circumstances, and has made me very happy. She is a dear girl. In the evening, Brooks, Braden and I had a sing, and I felt very much more like singing than I have for a good many days. Went to bed in a very pleasant state of mind.

May 22nd, 1863

Went in town in the morning to see Guard Mount in one of the other brigades and then came back and wrote and sent a long letter to Cordie. In the evening received another letter from her, which is even better than the one of last night, and made me very happy. In evening went in town with Brooks and Braden to serenade a lady friend of the latter. Answered the letter from Cordie that I received this evening, and went to bed in a decidedly pleasant state of mind.

May 23rd, 1863

We had orders today to turn in our wall tents and have got to come down to the shelter tents, or dog tents, as the men call them. This looks as if we are to take the field soon. At night another letter from Cordie, the dear girl, enclosing a group of pictures of the "Sisterhood"—Mollie Elliott, Nicolie Ford and Cordie, in the center. In this letter she reproves me a little for not waiting longer before writing Miss Elliott, and feels hurt that I thought she was not going to answer my letter. I sent the letter I wrote her last night by our Quartermaster Sergeant, who is going to Paris, and enclosed my gold chain for her to keep for me.

May 24th, 1863

After Sunday inspection, went to church with Brooks and Braden. In evening Braden and I borrowed horses and rode out into the country as far as was safe, and had a very pleasant time.

May 25th, 1863

At nine o'clock this morning, the alarm sounded and we formed in a hurry and then stood under arms until noon, when we stacked arms and went to quarters. We learned later that Morgan with a thou-

Confederate General John Morgan. From *Harper's Weekly,* Sep. 24, 1864.

sand men had crossed the Cumberland River,[6] and surprised and captured forty pickets of Colonel Wolford's cavalry, a regiment of loyal
Kentuckians, and a most remarkable organization it was—very little
of army discipline and drill, but mighty good fighters in their own irregular way, and they did good service. Their commander, Colonel
Wolford, was a unique character.[7] He did not bother himself about
the phraseology of tactics, and furnished lots of fun for us by his way
of giving orders, one of which became a sort of byword. Instead of
giving the proper command, "Prepare to mount! Mount!" he would
sing out, "Prepare to git onto your critters! Git!" We turned in our
wall tents today and drew the shelters. Captain Lee and I made a very

good substitute for a wall tent by buttoning a number of the shelter halves together. In the evening, took a short walk with Brooks, who is not as happy as I. Went to bed quite early.

May 26th, 1863

Was Officer of the Brigade Guard and had the usual pleasant, easy time. Countersign "Mill Spring". Made quarters in a house, and went to sleep at three, and was awakened at six by my bed collapsing and letting me down. My head struck the hilt of my sword and I got quite a bump. This is the second time a bed has dumped me. Guess the safest place for me to sleep is on the ground.

May 27th, 1863

After coming off guard, went to work on a bed in my tent, and tried to make it strong enough to keep up. In evening went in town with Brooks, then made a call at Brigade Headquarters, then back to camp and after a bottle of sparkling catawba, to bed.

May 28th, 1863

Warm and pleasant. In forenoon read and slept. At noon orders came for everybody to remain in camp and be ready to fall in at a moment's notice. Nothing happened as usual. At night commenced a letter to Cordie but did not finish it.

May 29th, 1863

Rainy, cold and disagreeable. Doctor Wood, our surgeon, who went to Lexington with our sick, returned via Paris tonight, and brought me a letter from Cordie, enclosing a picture of herself and one of Mrs. Kelley, the latter signed "Your Kentucky mother", which is encouraging and pleased me very much.[8] Wrote a long letter to Cordie in the evening. Have the blues badly, and it may be the weather, but I think it is because I want to see a certain "Blue Grass" girl. At night had the familiar orders to be ready to fall in at a moment's notice, as an attack was expected, but the night passed quietly without alarm. I wish we might have a little brush with Morgan. Think we could whip the tar out of him.

May 30th, 1863

Pleasant in the morning. Stayed in quarters reading "Waverley".[9] In the afternoon a sudden and severe storm came up with rain in torrents and raised the dickens with some of the tents. Fortunately, mine was so situated that it escaped the deluge, but some, Lieutenant Taylor's in particular, had a regular Mississippi River flowing through the middle. At night received a letter from Mollie Elliott, which was very unsatisfactory. Tripp had one from Cordie enclosing a message for me on a bit of paper, which read, *"La Patience es amére, mais son fruit est doux"*, and I suppose I must be *patient* and satisfied.[10] In evening, Brooks and Hunting came in the tent and we had a sing from the "Jubilee". Am summoned as witness before a Court Martial for next Monday.

May 31st, 1863

Went to church morning and evening. In afternoon, read. Am blue as can be. Don't feel at all satisfied that things are running smoothly for me in Paris, and wish I could run up there for a day or two, but cannot leave. Wish I had never seen the place, for it's thinking of a certain Kentucky girl there that makes me so uneasy and blue. I doubt my ever seeing her again, but can't help making a fool of myself.

June 1st, 1863

At ten o'clock reported as ordered at the Presbyterian Church, where the Court Martial is in session, and after hanging around for some time, was informed that the case in which I am to be called would probably not come up today, so went back to camp and passed the day reading. At night, Brooks, Braden and I walked to town and had a nice little sing. On return was agreeably surprised to find a sweet letter from Cordie. We received orders tonight to reduce all baggage, officers from the usual allowance of eighty pounds to thirty, and the enlisted men to be allowed only a single change of underwear, and to be ready to move with eight days' rations. This looks as if we are to have some hard marching.

June 2nd, 1863

Reported to the Court Martial in the morning, but was not called as witness. Went to town with Captains Wilson, Richardson and Lee and had some wine. In afternoon went to the court again, but the prisoner having pleaded guilty, I was not called. Wrote a number of letters and sent off my extra baggage and now have but sixteen pounds. One of the General's aids told me today that we would probably go south, but not this week. Received tonight a silver shield that I had ordered with name and regiment on it, to be worn for identification if killed.

June 3rd, 1863

Went in town and had a picture taken, but it was poor. Passed the day in the usual way, reading, smoking and sleeping. Am tired of this inactive life, but suppose I should be thankful we are not fighting every day as we were for a time last summer. In evening went to town with Brooks and Braden to call on some friends of Braden's. Very nice girls and had a pleasant time. After leaving, met Captain Lee, who wanted us to serenade some friends of his, who invited us in and gave us cake and wine. Then went to several other places and had a general good time, winding up with a good night drink of "Bourbon" at brigade headquarters. Got to bed about twelve.

June 4th, 1863

Was just nicely asleep last night, when I was awakened with orders to prepare to move at once. Got up, warned the Sergeant to have the men get breakfast, packed everything ready, got some coffee and waited until half past four, when we started out on the back track to Nicholasville. Had a pretty hard march and kept it up until half past five in the afternoon, but made only eighteen miles. It was hot and dusty and my feet are somewhat sore. Halted for the night at Waynesboro, a village with one tavern, three whiskey shops and five dwelling houses. Letters from Paris came tonight, one very short one for me from Cordie. Don't quite fancy the tone of it, but am tired, jealous and unreasonable, I suppose. Wrote her a short note. Was too tired and dirty to do more.

June 5th, 1863

On the march at half past four. Halted at noon, for the men to get dinner at Hall's Gap, a pass in the mountains, and then went on to

Stanford, where we camped for the night on the same ground we occupied when here in April. The Paymaster joined us here at night and paid the regiment, which took until nine o'clock. Did not get to sleep until two. Have had a hard time today with sore feet. My heels are blistered and the skin has worn off while marching, leaving the flesh raw and sore.

June 6th, 1863

My heels were a little better this morning, but sore enough. We started on the road early this morning, and just before arriving at Lancaster, Company H was detailed as Provost Guard in the village to prevent men straggling or buying whiskey, so we had to hurry ahead and post our sentinels. We had to wait until the whole brigade had passed through, when Captain Lee and I went to the hotel and had a fair dinner, then followed, acting as rear guard. Towards night, my heels got worse, the limestone dust from the road getting into the raw flesh where the blisters had worn off. I suffered so much I feared I could not get to the regiment tonight, but I managed to limp along with the company, and at last reached camp, a mile or two beyond Camp Dick Robinson. As soon as we got in I laid down and at once fell asleep and did not wake for supper or anything. The pain and march had, together, about used me up. My socks were stuck to my feet with blood from the blistered heels, which were in pretty bad shape.

June 7th, 1863

The regiment started early. My heels were in such bad condition that our surgeon, after examining and dressing them, said I could not march and ordered me into an ambulance. It was hot and dusty, but with help of several bottles of native wine, managed to get along. We reached Nicholasville at noon, to remain until tomorrow. Went with several other officers to a house nearby and had a very good supper. No tents pitched. Spread my blankets at the foot of a tree and slept first rate.

Chapter 10

Down the Mississippi and the Siege of Vicksburg

In June of 1863, the IX Corps, which included Ayling's regiment, was sent down the Mississippi River to aid in the siege of Vicksburg under General Grant. General Pemberton surrendered the city to Grant on July 4. On the day before, July 3, the three-day battle of Gettysburg ended, and Lee's forces, having suffered heavy losses, retreated southward. These two crucial Federal victories proved to be a turning point in the war. The Confederacy had been split—east from west—by the Mississippi River campaign and Grant was free to press the campaign in the east. General Sherman took command in Mississippi and pursued Johnston's army, forcing him to evacuate Jackson, an action in which Ayling's regiment participated.

June 8th, 1863

We took cars early this morning for Cincinnati. At Lexington, I telegraphed Mr. Forman telling him when we would reach Paris, and when we arrived there was a big crowd to receive us. Buildings were decorated with flags and bunting, and we were greeted with cheers and handkerchief waving. A collation had been prepared, which we had to hurry, as we were allowed only a short stop. The girls were all out, but I did not get a sight of the one I wanted most to see. Can't understand why she did not appear. When the train started, I threw out a short note to her, tied to a stone, and saw it picked up by a young fellow, who I know will deliver it. As the train passed Creekside, saw

Cordie's mother and sister in the garden. Was disappointed and grieved that I could not see Cordie, as I feel this is a final good bye to Kentucky and to her. Don't believe I shall ever see either again. On arriving at Cincinnati, we had a fine reception, almost as cordial as when here before. We were taken to one of the market buildings and given a good supper, after which we marched to the depot and took cars on the Ohio and Mississippi Railroad bound for Cairo, Illinois. It is generally known that our destination is Vicksburg, which has been besieged by our army for a long time, and much interest was shown by the people, who crowded the street at the market so that it was almost impossible to form our line. It was after dark when we started. The men in box cars, and one passenger car for the officers. It having been ordered that an officer ride in each box car with the men, it was my luck to be one of the victims, so I did not get much sleep. It has been a horribly blue day for me.

June 9th, 1863

On the road all day and night. The cars were poor and it was a pretty rough road, was dusty and dirty, with no chance to wash. We have been travelling through parts of Indiana and Illinois, and have been received and treated, in most places, in the same patriotic way that we were in Ohio and West Virginia. Girls waving handkerchiefs and flags and men cheering. We were told that in certain sections of Indiana there was a copperhead element, and, advised to be careful what we ate or drank at Sandoval.[1] At Washington, Indiana, we were sidetracked at the request of the people and a fine collation served. The ladies who waited upon the tables gave each of the officers and men a bouquet. There are lots of pretty girls here, and just before we started, a party of them came to my car and sang "Brave Boys Are They", very sweetly. Have enjoyed the trip and seeing a new country very much, but am awfully dirty and would like a good bath.

June 10th, 1863

Early in the morning, at Odin, Illinois, changed cars to the Illinois Central. A change very much for the better. The cars are cleaner and the road smoother. Have enjoyed the trip better than yesterday. Like the looks of the country, but it can't come up to the "blue grass" region of Kentucky. Arrived at Cairo at three o'clock in the afternoon,

Clement L. Valladigham, Ohio politician and notorious "Copperhead."
From *Harper's Weekly*, June 6, 1863.

and Company H was detailed for fatigue duty, to transfer the baggage
from the cars to the steamboat "Mariner". Was busy at this work until
six, then went on board the boat, had a bath, put on a clean shirt, and
felt better. Letters from Paris came to us here, and among them was a
very sweet letter for me from Cordie, which I answered and then went
to bed as I am quite tired and my heels are very painful yet. We are

very comfortably fixed on the boat and the officers have staterooms.
We are off for Vicksburg.

June 11th, 1863

On steamer "Mariner" going down the Mississippi. We have
Roemer's New York Light Battery on board with us, and the rest of
the Ninth Corps has either gone ahead or is following closely.[2] At ten
o'clock we put in for a short time at Island No. 10, where there had
been much fighting, earlier.[3] Was rather disappointed in the place; it
does not look very formidable, although it gave our gun boats considerable trouble before it was captured. Passed the day reading, writing
letters and looking at the banks of the river as we passed. About sunset, passed Fort Pillow, where the colored troops, after they had surrendered, were massacred by the rebels.[4] In evening played euchre a
while and then all hands joined in a sing. Am enjoying this trip immensely,
and the rest from marching will get my sore heels in shape again.

June 12th, 1863

When I awoke this morning, found we were tied up at Memphis,
Tennessee, where we arrived sometime in the night. The city is on a
high bluff, and not much of it can be seen from the river. After dinner,
Lieutenant Conant and I went ashore and looked around some, but
as we did not know how long our boat would stay, did not go far. Like
what I saw of the city very much. There are some pretty girls here, but
I fancy they are all "Secesh". At night, we are still here, probably to
remain until tomorrow. In evening played euchre. Two dead men
floated by us on the river today.

June 13th, 1863

Still lying here at Memphis, waiting for orders it is reported.
Conant and I, finding there was no probability of the boat leaving
today, went on shore and pretty much all over the city. Looked in at
the Gayoso House, the principal hotel, went to a photographers for
pictures, indulged in sundry ice creams and iced drinks, and had a very
pleasant day. Got back to the boat about three in the afternoon and
found an old schoolmate, Newell Cram, waiting to see me, and we had
a good time talking over old school days. After supper, went ashore

again with a lot of officers and after various "juleps" and "cobblers", went to the theater, and saw "The Drunkard".[5] Not very interesting! After the theater, went with the crowd around town and did not get to bed until about two.

June 14th, 1863

Laid at Memphis all day. Did not go ashore. It is so hot, one can keep cooler on the boat. In the afternoon wrote Cordie. At five o'clock the "Mariner" cast off, and, with a lot of other transports, we started our four hundred mile trip down the Mississippi. There have been reports that the orders sending us south were countermanded, and that we are to go back to Kentucky, but now there is no doubt that our destination is Vicksburg. Not a very pleasant prospect at this time of year, but to obey orders and go where we are sent, is what we are here for. As we are now going into the danger zone, we are convoyed by two gun boats, "tin-clads" as they are called, because they are armored to resist rifle fire only, not artillery, one going ahead of us and the other keeping about a mile astern to protect the transports from guerillas, who hide behind the levees and fire on passing boats. Everything was quiet today and we had a pleasant time. In the evening, some of the officers went on quite a "bat", and after getting to bed, one of them fell out of his berth and broke a collar bone. I was not in that crowd. I like a good time, but not that kind.

June 15th, 1863

Beautiful, but lazy, weather. Lounged, read and played euchre. Captain Clarke is reading aloud to us "Les Miserables", and I think it intensely interesting.[6] At night we tied up at White River Cut Off, and posted pickets. During the night our pickets were attacked and there was quite a little skirmish, with lots of noise and excitement. My company and three others were ordered out as reserve, and I was on duty all night.

June 16th, 1863

When we started out this morning, our convoy drew up quite close to us, evidently looking for trouble, which came as we were passing Roddy's Bend, when we got a volley from the shore. The gun boats opened at once with shell, and our men with rifles. No one hurt on our side, but some excitement for an hour. It is a wonder that nobody was hit, as our men were exposed all over the boat. We had received shots occasionally on our way down from individual guerillas, but this time there was a party of them. All the damage we received was broken windows and holes in the woodwork. Some bullets came through into the saloon where some of us were sitting when the firing commenced. Late in the afternoon a heavy squall struck us and blew our boat and one other on a sandbar near a place called Providence, where we remained all night. Was officer of the boat guard and on duty all night, which I did not fancy as I had no sleep at all last night. This place, Providence, is most desolate and forsaken.

June 17th, 1863

A fine day for the last one of our voyage. At noon we left the Mississippi and turned into the Yazoo, up which we steamed for two hours, and landed at Snyder's Bluff, or Milldale, as it is called, about ten miles by land from Vicksburg. We waited here, for orders I suppose, three hours nearly, and then marched four miles into the country and went into camp with our Ninth Corps. There are lots of troops all about, and we are told this is the extreme right flank of Grant's army besieging Vicksburg. All the regiments here are from the west, and when we landed a crowd of western fellows came down to look us over. Our uniforms being comparatively new and clean, they took us for new troops and began to quiz, and make fun of us, until they found we were veterans from the Army of the Potomac. Then they good-naturedly wanted to know "why in ———— we did not stay there and capture Richmond." To this, our fellows retorted that "we had come down to take Vicksburg for them" and lots of other good-natured bantering. We are camped in a very pleasant place and I am agreeably disappointed in the country, so far. It is hilly and wooded, not so swampy as I thought it might be. I notice some entrenchments near us.

June 18th, 1863

Have not felt well today, a touch of diarrhea, so kept quiet. Don't fancy my captain, Lee, much. He is inclined to be very disagreeable. I do not like the prospect of living with him all summer. Had nothing to eat except "hard tack", and guess we will get only army rations here, but I can stand that kind of grub all right.

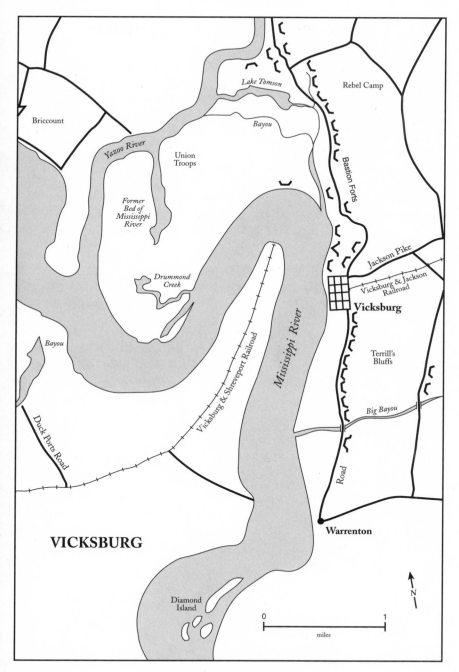

Vicksburg, Mississippi, 1863.

June 19th, 1863

Felt better today. This morning, the Adjutant asked me if I would like to take command of Company D in place of Lieutenant Carpenter, who, Colonel Barnes thinks cannot get along with the men there as well as I. This is quite a compliment, as Carpenter ranks me. Company D is the company I was first assigned to when I joined the regiment, and is a pretty tough lot in some ways, but I never had any trouble with the men. I told the Adjutant I would be glad to go to D. Shall be glad to get away from Captain Lee, although I like the men of H very much. At dress parade, orders were read transferring Carpenter to H and me to D. Thought I would not move my quarters tonight so remained in H, and went to bed early. Could hear all night the booming of big guns at the front. Wrote Cordie today.

June 20th, 1863

In the morning, moved from Company H and assumed command of my old company. The boys seemed glad to have me with them, and those of Company H seemed sorry to have me go. I was greatly pleased to see I was so well liked by both companies. Lieutenant Pope is assigned to me temporarily as my Second Lieutenant.[7]

June 21st, 1863

Inspection today, after which, laid off reading "No Name", which I liked and trying to keep cool.[8] In the evening made a fine corduroy bed of cane poles, which are plentiful about here, and are nice and springy. Wrote to Captain Brooks, who is absent on leave, and made requisitions for ordnance stores and clothing for the company. Our duty here, for the present at least, seems to be pretty easy, but the fellows at the front must be busy, I fancy, by the heavy firing we hear most of the time night and day.

June 22nd, 1863

A bit cooler than yesterday. Had little to do but read and lounge. We have orders to keep on hand three days' rations. This looks as if we may be moved in a hurry, but I hope not, while it is so awfully hot. Our corps, since arriving here, has done some work strengthening the old entrenchments and building new, but the details for fatigue duty do not come to us very often and the men are not worked very hard in this weather and climate. It is reported that a rebel army under General Johnston is quite near us, threatening Grant's rear, and that our Ninth Corps is here to watch out for him and to help whip him if he attacks.[9]

June 23rd, 1863

Hot and sticky. Tried to write some letters, but did not finish them. Have no life or energy for anything. Don't see how any white people can live in this climate, anyway.

June 24th, 1863

Finished the letters I started on yesterday. The payrolls for the regiment came today, but I can't make mine until Captain Brooks returns as, for some reason, he has taken the company records with him. Will be glad when he gets back. We get on finely together, and are congenial. This would not be so bad a place to camp in were it not for the mosquitoes, gallinippers, ticks, rattle snakes and a few other unpleasant "natives". The mosquitoes, particularly, are simply awful.

June 25th, 1863

The hottest yet. They can get up a pretty good heat down here, surely. At four o'clock in the afternoon was detailed for picket. My post was in a beautiful, romantic place in deep dark woods, and the duty would not have been at all bad, if the mosquitoes and nippers had not almost eaten me alive. The countersign was "Town Creek". We heard today that Banks had captured Port Hudson and that Farragut's fleet was up to Vicksburg.[10] This may be true for there is a tremendous cannonading over there tonight. There have been some promotions recently in the regiment which may cause my again being transferred to some other company.

June 26th, 1863

Was not relieved until six o'clock this evening. Had a pleasant tour of duty. No alarms on my front. Passed the day fighting "skeeters" and "nippers". Am badly bitten all over. My boy Billy brought out to me some blackberries, and we found some green corn, so managed to have one pretty good meal. Was somewhat tired when I got in. It's quite a tramp from the picket line to camp.

June 27th, 1863

Worked some on the payrolls, but can't do much until Captain Brooks comes. I hear he is on the way, and may be here tomorrow. Passed the day taking it easy, and trying to keep cool. Would like a tub of ice cream and several gallons of ice water.

June 28th, 1863

Worked a little on payrolls, and laid off, taking it as easily and coolly as possible in this awful hot weather. A great objection to this Mississippi climate is that the nights are about as bad as the day and don't let up any on heat. So different from up north where after sundown it is almost always cooler.

June 29th, 1863

Was at work on the rolls this forenoon when orders came to break camp and prepare to move at once. Did not fancy this at all, but it is all right, I guess. We started at ten and only marched six or eight miles, but it was enough. The air was like heat from a furnace, and thick with dust. Four officers and a number of the men were prostrated and fell out. I managed to keep along but it was hard work. We camped in a beautiful place, in thick woods, and after a supper of "hard tack", spread my rubber coat at the foot of a tree and had a good sleep. This locality is called Oak Ridge, so they say, and it is well named.

June 30th, 1863

The regiment was mustered for pay today, although Company D rolls are not completed and cannot be until Captain Brooks comes. It is rumored we are to stay here a while and I hope it is true. This is surely a lovely spot, with trees that are large, and the branches hung with long gray moss. The quiet and shade are delightful. No baggage has been allowed to come up and we cannot change underclothes, so remain dirty and uncomfortable. Food is somewhat scarce. It is only possible to get a little hard bread, but I fortunately have some coffee in my haversack, and can get along pretty well. At night Captain Brooks, who has arrived at our last camp at Milldale, sent up a letter to me from Cordie, which he brought from Paris, and which I was glad to get. Lieutenant Long, who has had a half interest in the colored boy, Frank, we hired, gave up his share today, and the boy is to be my servant only, which suits me better.

July 1st, 1863

Was lying on the grass smoking after a very frugal breakfast of hard tack and coffee when a party of axemen came to cut down the trees where we were camped to clear a range for artillery, so we had to move camp a short distance to the rear, which was easily done having neither tents nor baggage. It seemed too bad to cut down all those beautiful old trees. Our new camp is as nice as the one we were ousted from, in a grove of oaks and beeches. Lieutenant Windsor and I made a corduroy bed and we will bunk together. We have no covering, and need none, but the bed will keep us from the ground and away from ticks and snakes, both of which are plentiful. The men killed two rattlesnakes today, each nearly five feet in length. Snakes, however, do not trouble me as much as does the desire to get into clean clothes once more, and have something to eat besides hard bread.

July 2nd, 1863

The sutler of the 46th New York came in today and we got some canned stuff, but had to pay a big price for it. In the afternoon Captain Brooks joined, and I was glad to see him. We at once went to work completing company payrolls, making the necessary additions and corrections. After supper we took a walk off into the woods, and he gave me all the news from Paris.

July 3rd, 1863

Every day seems hotter than the day before. Tried to write some letters, but the weather was too much for me, so gave it up. We have had no mail from home for a long time, but hear we may get one tomorrow. Hope so!

July 4th, 1863

At noon the long looked for mail came and the regiment rejoiced. I had a lot of letters, including two from Cordie, and papers, all of which I enjoyed much. After dinner, wrote a long letter to Cordie in answer to hers, and had just finished it, when we were ordered to fall in, in a hurry. We marched a few miles toward the front and were halted a short distance from Vicksburg, and told that the city had been surrendered.[11] This was great news to us for it was generally understood that our corps would join the other troops here in a general assault upon the rebel works, tomorrow morning, if Vicksburg was not surrendered today. It would be a hard job and cost lots of lives, and I am glad we haven't got it to do. Everybody went to bed happy tonight.

July 5th, 1863

We started out early, but did not have a hard march, halting long and often. At night turned off into some woods and went into camp, a few miles from the Big Black River, and near a stream called Bear Creek. We hear our corps and two western corps, all under General Sherman, are to start in pursuit of General Johnston, who retreated when Vicksburg fell, and has gone into the interior somewhere.[12] Almost everybody in the regiment is half sick with diarrhea, due probably to the bad water we have to drink, and everybody is badly bitten by mosquitoes and vermin, so it is one continual scratch. I wouldn't care to live in this country.

July 6th, 1863

Contrary to our expectations, we did not get orders to move this morning, so remained quietly in camp all day. Lieutenant Windsor, who has resigned, started for home this morning, and I sent some letters by him to mail, including one to Cordie. Am sorry he is leaving, for he is a fine fellow and I like him. We have some trouble in getting enough to eat. Had hard bread for breakfast, and no dinner, but at night my boy, Frank, who had managed some way or some how, to get a little poor flour, made flapjacks for supper; not very tender or palatable, but better than nothing, and a change. Had a hard thunderstorm tonight. As I have nothing to shelter me but a rubber coat, I could only wrap it about me and "lie down to pleasant dreams". We are under orders to be ready to move upon the enemy at short notice.

July 7th, 1863

No orders to move this morning, but at noon, just as I was sitting down to my dinner of boiled cabbage, without vinegar, and hard bread, we were ordered to fall in quickly and started on what surely proved to be a very hard exhausting march. The heat was awful. Several officers and a large number of the men were overcome, and left on the road. I came pretty close to giving out, but managed to keep along. We halted at sundown for the men to get their supper, and then started again. Crossed the Big Black on a floating bridge and moved on as rapidly as possible. Soon after dark we had a fearful thunderstorm, with torrents of rain like a cloudburst, and the most vivid, dazzling lightning I have ever seen. It seemed to play on the butts of the rifles, which the men carried at "Secure Arms", and blinded us so that we ran against each other as we stumbled along the road in the dark, ankle deep in water. It certainly was a pretty tough march. We dragged along through mud and water until nearly twelve, when we turned into a piece of woods and halted for the rest of the night. The rain had stopped and we soon had fires going to dry off a little and make coffee. I sat down in my rubber coat with my back to a tree and soon fell asleep, quite tired out, but had not slept long when awakened by a stream of water running down my back. Found another storm had struck us and it was raining hard. Stood up against a tree until the rain let up a little and then laid down and slept until reveille. A mighty unpleasant night.

July 8th, 1863

Laid around in the shade all the forenoon expecting orders to move, but was agreeably disappointed. Went to a mud hole nearby and took off and washed my only suit of underclothing and while that was drying on a bush washed myself as well as I could. Went back to camp and tried to get a nap, but it was too noisy. At four in the afternoon we started and kept marching all night long, and it was a very tiresome march. Was mighty glad when we halted for the night. Laid down just where I stopped and was asleep in no time. Bill of fare today. Breakfast: fried pig. Dinner: tea and molasses. Supper: "nix".

July 9th, 1863

Commenced our march for the day at six o'clock and kept it up

until eight at night, with occasional halts. Extremely hot and everyone suffered. My feet are getting quite tender and hurt me a good deal.
When we turned into some woods to camp for the night, I found my
boy, Frank, and Sergeant Kern had come in with some flour and bacon.[13] They had looted, and they at once started to get me some supper. We were just sitting down on a log to enjoy bacon and flapjacks
when the regiment was ordered to fall in for picket duty. I was hungry and disgusted, but had to go. Managed to bolt a few flapjacks
before we started, but had no time for the bacon. When we reached
the line we were to picket, Company D was in the reserve, so had a
chance to get a little sleep. We are near the house of Jeff Davis, and a
part of the regiment is on guard there.[14]

July 10th, 1863

Started on the march early in the morning, and kept it up until
nearly night. About two o'clock we struck the rear guard of the enemy, and formed line of battle, but there was only a slight skirmish
and the enemy retired. We halted for the night in a large corn field on
the plantation of a Mr. Hardman, on the line of the Mississippi Central
Railroad, and were allowed to sleep undisturbed all night, which we
appreciated, having had very little sleep for three days. The heat has
been terrible and a good many were overcome. I was nearly knocked
out, and thought at one time I would have to take an ambulance, but
hated to give up, and kept along.

July 11th, 1863

This morning we were ordered to the front where the firing had commenced, and marched and countermarched until noon, most of the time
being under the fire of shot and shell, the latter bursting over and around
us, and the former shrieking overhead, and occasionally tearing off limbs
of the trees under which we were passing. We finally took position on a
hill to support Edward's Rhode Island Battery. Don't like this business,
supporting batteries; have to lie taking the enemy's fire, without being able
to return it. We remained here until about seven in the evening, and then
moved to a position near the Insane Asylum, a fine large building five miles
from the city of Jackson. Here our whole brigade was supplied with shov-
els and picks, and kept at work all night throwing up entrenchments and

digging rifle pits. The particular job of the 29th was building a place for a battery. While on the march today, I ran across Lieutenant Colonel John Hudson of the 35th Massachusetts, who was a roommate at Lawrence Academy, Groton. A mighty fine fellow and I was glad to meet him, although we could exchange but a few words. The regiment had a mail in the evening and I received a nice letter from the Illinois soldier that I smuggled into the car with my company while on the way from Baltimore to Cairo. The poor fellow had been on furlough to see some member of his family who was sick, and was trying to get back to his regiment, and had little or no money. I took him along with Company D and the boys shared their rations with him. I had forgotten about it until his letter came. He was very grateful to me and to the company, writing from his regiment, the 66th Illinois, stationed near Corinth. We had another Mississippi deluge this afternoon.

July 12th, 1863

The first thing in the morning, we moved to the front to support the skirmish line, our position being at the edge of some thick woods, and we laid here all day, most of the time under fire, jumping into line several times ready to repel a charge, if the skirmishers fell back, but they held the line finely. The rebels threw lots of grape and canister, but we escaped by lying down and hugging the ground. Bullets fell around us pretty freely. I picked up two that struck just in front of my head. The proverbial good luck of the 29th stuck by us, and while the other regiments of the brigade suffered some, we escaped. It has been rather a hard day, very hot and little to eat.

July 13th, 1863

Today has been a second edition of yesterday. We occupied the same position and laid under the same fire. The colonel of the 50th Pennsylvania was hit and a number of men of our brigade. The enemy charged our rifle pits, but were driven back. At night I was on guard duty, and had to go out to the advanced line of pickets with orders. On my way back I got lost, and wandered around in the thick dark woods sometime before getting my bearings. Was relieved from guard at one o'clock and slept the rest of the night, until daylight. An attack was expected tonight, and we were prepared and ready, but none came.

July 14th, 1863

Just after daylight we were relieved, and moved back some distance to our former position near the Insane Asylum. I managed to get a good wash, and then laid down and slept a while. Rather quiet all day. We had evening parade to hear orders read, and later were sent forward to support the same Rhode Island battery we were with before, and they kept firing most of the night. We laid just behind the guns but the noise did not prevent my getting some sleep. My captain, Brooks, is sick and discouraged and I fear he will be obliged to give up and go home. Received a first rate letter from Cordie today.

July 15th, 1863

Early in the morning my company was sent out on picket on the left flank of the battery. Captain Brooks was too sick to go, and I went in command of Company D. After I had established my line and posted my men and returned to the reserve, an Aide came with orders to be extremely careful and watchful as an attack on my front was expected; so I went out to each of my posts and cautioned them to keep a good lookout and be ready if attacked. We were not disturbed, however, and the day passed quietly. At dark we were relieved and went back to the regiment. Learned that we are to take the front line tomorrow morning at one o'clock. Laid down to try to get some sleep, but the mosquitoes were so ravenous I did not get much.

July 16th, 1863

We were roused up at one o'clock this morning and started for the front, passing under a heavy fire to within forty rods of the enemy's works, the right wing of the regiment going into some rifle pits, and the left wing, to which my company belonged, taking position in some woods. During the forenoon things were comparatively quiet, but at noon, orders came for a simultaneous advance of the whole line until the enemy is found. The signal for the movement was to be two guns from the twenty pounder battery. When the signal was given, we on the left started, deployed as skirmishers, through dense woods with thick undergrowth crossed by ravines, making it difficult to keep the line at all straight, or the men in sight or touch of each other. We advanced about half a mile before we struck the rebels, and when we did wake them up, it was like a hornet's nest, and we soon had orders to fall back to the former picket line. Bullets flew around pretty thick for a while, but we got out all right and the rest of the afternoon was quiet with only a little picket firing. The night was very still and we could hear plainly, from the front, the rattle of wagons and artillery moving, sounds that indicated the falling back of the enemy.

July 17th, 1863

We were relieved from picket at one o'clock this morning and moved back to the rear to act as reserve. Slept until nearly day break and was just going to eat my breakfast, such as it was, when we had to fall in and start for Jackson, the enemy having evacuated.[15] We passed the deserted rifle pits and entrenchments that had held us in check, and saw that they were very strong and could not have been taken by assault without heavy loss to us. We entered the city about seven, and halted in front of the capitol. Our men at once went to work putting out fires, which had been started in the depot and other buildings, undoubtedly saving a portion of the city from burning. The regiment was then given liberty for two hours and allowed to forage for food and fruit, but there was not much of either. The place appeared to be almost deserted, most of the white people having left with Johnston's retreating army, taking what valuables they could. There were some of the colored population left, however, and they were glad to see us, and anxious to be of service. At noon we marched a short distance out from the city and halted for dinner near a fine mansion, belonging the negroes told us, to a doctor who was a surgeon in the rebel army. Some of us officers made the house our headquarters for the time. It was richly and elegantly furnished and evidently the owner was wealthy. We went into the parlor in which there was a fine piano, and a very large music box, the largest I ever saw, nearly four feet long. We wound it up and started it, drew easy chairs around a beautiful center table and drank our tin cups of tea and nibbled our hard bread. I do not think much, if anything, was looted from the house, nor was anything destroyed or injured. If the ladies of the family had remained, they would have been perfectly safe from annoyance or insult, and we would not have entered the house without permission. If the southern women had not been so thoroughly impressed with the idea that we yankees are worse than barbarians, and stayed at home instead of running away, their property would have been safer and they saved much hardship. In the afternoon, we marched back to our old camping ground in the woods and remained all night. I am quite used up by the heat and diarrhea, and feel, as all do, anxious to get away from this wretched climate. It is a camp rumor, however, that we are to remain here with Grant.

July 18th, 1863

Agreeably disappointed at not receiving marching orders this morning. Kept quiet all day. Am sick with the same trouble that has knocked out most of the regiment. Captain Brooks being very sick leaves me in command of the company, and I don't want to give it up. We received copies of the *New York Herald,* the first we have had for a long time. Was glad to see it.

July 19th, 1863

Laid around all day, expecting orders to fall in. At night we were told to be ready to start at short notice. The regiment has been detailed as Provost Guard for the whole division, and Colonel Barnes appointed Division Provost Marshal. This is intended to be a compliment to the regiment, but it is a hard, disagreeable job, and we don't fancy it much. Captain Brooks was taken to the hospital today. Hope I shall not have to follow him. Commenced a letter to Cordie, but did not finish it. Felt too miserable.

Chapter 11

Occupation in Mississippi and Return to Kentucky

After the fall of Vicksburg and the evacuation of Jackson by Johnston's army, the IX Corps under General Parke entered the city briefly and then returned to Vicksburg as an occupation force. Federal troops suffered much from the climate and malaria. Ayling contracted malaria and was seriously ill. In August of 1863 the IX Corps was sent back to Kentucky. Ayling is granted sick leave to return home to convalesce.

July 20th, 1863

Reveille at four o'clock roused us this morning and we started for the Big Black, marching all day, with a halt of two hours at noon, and until eleven at night. No one knows why such a forced march is necessary in such terribly hot weather. There is no enemy anywhere near, and we are simply returning to Vicksburg, so it would seem this hurry is entirely unnecessary. There is much feeling in the regiment, and there is a story around that General Parke, commanding our corps, has a bet with the commander of a western corps that he would reach Vicksburg first.[1] Don't know how true this is, but if true, he should be shot. We had a hard time of it, as provost guard, marching in the rear of the column, getting all the dust, and trying to keep the poor exhausted fellows from falling out and straggling, when we had all we could do to keep from falling out ourselves. So many men from the different commands were used up by the excessive heat that regiments almost lost their identity. The roads were lined with exhausted men, and we had to use every effort and sometimes threats to keep them moving. If left behind, they were liable to be captured and perhaps killed by guerillas. I got a touch of the sun myself, and fell, and was insensible for a time, but after treatment by our surgeon, kept along, but it was hard work. There was very little water to be had and what we found was bad. One small mud hole of a pond had dead mules lying partly in the water on the opposite side, but we had to wet our lips just the same.

July 21st, 1863

We were started off at half past three this morning, after a pretty short ration of sleep, and kept going all day, with a halt of two hours at noon. Today has been a repetition of yesterday. Awfully hot, no shade, no water. So many men were unable to travel that the ambulances were full and we took all the old carts and wagons and disabled horses and mules left behind by Johnston to transport them. I don't know how I kept along, but I did, and was thankful enough when we halted for the night, a few miles from the Big Black. We camped in a big corn field, and made soft and sweet beds by cutting off the tops of the corn and filling the furrows between the rows. Slept splendidly. We hear that protests have been made to General Parke by the subordinate commanders against this unnecessary forced marching. If he is the one responsible, and I don't see who else can be, he should be court martialed. If there was any need of this hurry, no one would object, but we all know there is no occasion to so use up men.

July 22nd, 1863

Evidently someone has awakened to the fact that the forced marching under present conditions is all wrong, for today we had an easier time. Started at nine and marched a few miles to some woods, where we remained until four in the afternoon, when we again started out. Just as we reached the Big Black, one of the regular Mississippi showers came up with the usual deluge, and in ten minutes the mud in the fields was six inches deep, and the roads full of water. We crossed the river on pontoons in the midst of the shower, and the rest of our march was pretty tough, the mud deep and slippery. Had hard work to keep along, but did not want Company D to go without an officer, so stumbled on, until we halted at half past nine for the night in a large field. Had nothing to eat but hard bread, but my boy, Frank, came in a little later with a piece of cow that someone had killed, which I roasted over the coals, and then put some fence rails down to keep me out of the mud, spread my blanket on them, and fell asleep at once.

July 23rd, 1863

Moved out at four o'clock, and after a short and easy march, comparatively, came in sight of Milldale, our old camp ground, to which we went. Our baggage is here and I got my tent up, found my valise, and after a good wash and change of underclothes, felt better. Went to the hospital to see Captain Brooks, who is quite sick. My feet have troubled me a good deal, and when I examined them, I found two large sores which accounts for the fact that every step for several days has been torture. Heard that we are to remain here, instead of going north, which made me deucedly blue.

July 24th, 1863

My feet are so swollen and sore that I can hardly step with them. Captain Brooks hobbled over from the hospital, but is too weak to go on duty. Kept quiet all day, nursing my feet and reading. Tried to write some letters, but felt too poor. The old trouble, diarrhea, is taking my strength away pretty fast. The report that we are to remain here seems to be believed by the regiment. Not very encouraging to us poor devils who are sick. When we were in Jackson, one of my men took a guitar from a house that was burning and has brought it to me, saying he got it for me. How he managed to tote it along I don't know, but he did and kept it from the wet when it rained by rolling it in his blanket. It is a very fine instrument and in excellent condition. I judge from its make it is a lady's guitar and imported. Am very glad to have it and will send it home by express at the first opportunity.

July 25th, 1863

Felt quite sick and have no strength. Wrote a short note to Cordie and read a little in "Les Miserables". Appropriate reading for me in my present state of mind.

July 26th, 1863

We were to have inspection today, but it was rainy—one shower after another. The thunder and lightning were simply awful. A tree a short distance in front of my tent was struck and the shock, or my jump, or something, sent me away out into the rain. Am feeling very sick and the surgeon says I have malaria as well as diarrhea—encouraging, very. Lieutenant Jenks of Company E died last night of malaria and exhaustion and was buried today.[2] The poor fellow had just been promoted from Sergeant, and would have been a good officer, and was a fine man everyway. Lieutenant Ripley of B Company is seriously ill and has been sent north. Most of the officers are about as badly off, and a number of the men have died.

July 27th, 1863

Think I am feeling a little better today. Am taking quinine and capsicum powders alternately every hour.[3] Don't get the taste of quinine out of my mouth before I have to take capsicum, and the taste of that holds on until time for quinine again. We hear now that we are to go north after all, and the reason we are left here is because as Provost Guard, we were in the rear of everything on the march here. The other regiments, on arriving, filled all the transports there were, and we, with one or two other regiments, must wait the arrival of steamers to take us away.

July 28th, 1863

My birthday. Twenty-three years old. Hope when the next one comes I shall be home. Attempted to do some writing, but a violent tempest struck us, and I had to give it up. I never saw anything like this for a storm. We have had some pretty tough ones, but this beats everything so far. The thunder and lightning were frightful and the wind a hurricane. It was all that four of us could do to hold down my tent. Just before dusk it cleared off, and we got things straightened out, but everything was soaking wet, except the guitar which I had protected by rolling it up in my blanket and a piece of tent, but I had to sleep in wet blankets.

July 29th, 1863

Wrote several letters and laid on my bed, keeping very quiet. Read a little in "Rob Roy".[4] My trouble is better, and I feel encouraged, but have not much strength.

July 30th, 1863

Very warm. We have nothing to do but take things easy, and keep as cool as possible, while we wait for a steamer to take us out of this miserable country. The negroes tell us that the white folks do not stay here, around the Yazoo River, but go away up north. If the southerners can't stand this sickly climate in summer, no wonder it has laid out so many of our men. Deaths are very frequent in the regiments here, and we hear very often, the too familiar sound of fifes and drums playing the dead march as the burial parties go out. The surgeons say that many of the deaths are the result of the hard and exhausting marching in the hot sun, together with the bad water we were obliged to drink.

July 31st, 1863

Hotter than the deuce, but managed to finish some letters. We had an inspection, and as the captain is not on duty, was obliged to go out in command of the company. In evening played Kentucky Loo. Heard we will have to stay here ten days longer, before we get away. It's too bad. The men are sickening and dying in this swamp hole. Three men from our little brigade were buried today.

August 1st, 1863

Hotter than yesterday, if possible. Each day seems worse than the day before. Had a shower in the afternoon, not so bad as some we have had, but bad enough. Showers here don't cool the air as they do at home. Received several letters tonight, including one from Cordie, which was "affirmative" and splendid.

August 2nd, 1863

Wrote letters in the morning, and kept quiet and as cool as I could the rest of the day. Another shower in the afternoon. They come so often I have to keep busy looking after my guitar, and keeping it out of the wet. My leg that troubled me so much a year ago started trouble again tonight, and the pain was so severe I could not sleep, so got up and did some writing. We received today a copy of an order from General Grant, returning our corps to its former command, expressing his thanks for our services in holding Johnston at bay before Vicksburg, and for our assistance in driving him from Jackson. The General praises "the endurance, valor and general good conduct of the Ninth Corps", and directs General Parke to cause the several regiments and batteries of his command to inscribe upon their colors and guidons "Vicksburg and Jackson".[5] This is quite a feather in our caps.

August 3rd, 1863

The usual routine of camp. Wrote a long letter to Cordie. Certain things she has said in her letters rather confirm the suspicion I have that Captain Tripp has not been quite square with me in regard to Paris matters, and I went to him today and asked an explanation of some things he has said or written. He said if I would give him three days time he would give me an explanation in writing which would be satisfactory.

August 4th, 1863

It is reported we may get away the first of next week, and I sincerely hope we may. Lieutenant Conant came in this evening and asked me to try to get a horse and ride into Vicksburg with him tomorrow. This will suit me first rate, although perhaps I should not go in my present condition, but I want to see the city very much, and will try to get some kind of a mount in the morning.

August 5th, 1863

Started out at daylight to hunt up a horse so I can ride into Vicksburg with Conant. It's too much of a trip to go on foot in this weather. Could not get a horse anywhere but succeeded in chartering a mule and we started at six o'clock for the city. I had rather a hard looking mount, but it was much better than walking. About a mile out the saddle girth broke, and we had to stop for repairs. We reached the city about ten, riding through some of the parallels, zig-zags and approaches of our engineers in their siege operations. On the way almost fainted from heat and weakness, but after resting a little, kept on. We went pretty much all over the place, seeing the effects of the long siege and bombardment. Visited some

Vicksburg after the surrender, 1863. From *Battles and Leaders of the Civil War,* vol. 3, 1884.

of the caves the people had dug in the high bluffs, to live in and be safe from shells. Some of the caves were quite large with two or more adjoining rooms. Nearly all had board floors and were well furnished with all the necessaries for cooking, eating and sleeping. The people said they were not only safe, but very comfortable in their "dugouts". We tried to find something to eat, but as Vicksburg has been starved into surrender, there was nothing for us; water was scarce too, and hard to get. Both Conant and I were pretty well "done up" and had to go into a barber shop for a rest. We then went out to look at the engineering work of the defense, going into some of the parallels and trenches which were very strong. Rested in the shade until three and then started for camp, but got lost, and wandered some five miles out of our way, part of the time through almost impassable paths, before we struck the right road, reaching camp at half past nine, having ridden between thirty and thirty-five miles. I was completely used up, and realize what an absolute fool thing it was to undertake so long and exhausting a trip, but I did want to see the famous city of Vicksburg and I did.

August 6th, 1863

Was lame, stiff and sore this morning, but was in better shape than I expected I would be. Guess I will come out all right. Received a letter from home telling of the death of Grandma. Captain Tripp sent me the written explanation he had promised, and it was satisfactory, and he wrote a pleasant letter. Am detailed for picket tomorrow. Don't feel much like it now, but may feel better in the morning.

August 7th, 1863

Started about six this morning with the picket guard. It was five miles out to the line I was to picket, and ten o'clock by the time I had my men posted. Had my old trouble, diarrhea, but after getting things fixed, and the men in position, felt better. We had the bank of the Yazoo, where it is marshy, but I found a pretty good place for my reserve, only the mosquitoes were too plentiful and too hungry. Colonel Barnes, who is Field Officer of the Day, made his headquarters with me, and asked me to share his dinner and supper, which I was glad to do, as I had only hard bread. During the night, I went the rounds with him, and we were bitten all over by the infernal mosquitoes. They bite through clothing easily, and the colonel declared they bit him through his heavy riding boots, and I believe it.

August 8th, 1863

Was relieved at nine o'clock, but did not get back to camp until noon. Felt pretty well used up, but after washing, eating and a nap, felt better, but kept very quiet all day. Have not gotten over my Vicksburg trip.

August 9th, 1863

The old trouble has me again today in spite of capsicum powders, so did not feel like moving around much, but at noon orders came to break camp and march to the landing. We had nearly all the tents down and everything packed to go, when the order was countermanded, as usual. Was greatly disappointed. The colonel sent for me today and gave me a raking over on account of two of my men, who had been drunk and raising the deuce. In the evening Captain Tripp came to my tent and we talked over Paris affairs. Sometime in the middle of the night, orders came to be ready to go to the landing in the morning.

August 10th, 1863

Broke camp at six o'clock with the rest of the brigade. Only one boat was there, and not room on her for all, so we have to remain on shore. Were told to make ourselves as comfortable as possible, which is not much, there being no shade, little to eat, and the mosquitoes, like the poor, being always with us. We are informed there will be a boat for us tomorrow.

August 11th, 1863

Hot as blazes, and we all suffered. In the afternoon a steamer came up and we loaded our wagons and mules and supposed, of course, we were to go on board at once, but we had to wait all the afternoon in the sun until nine at night, when finally we embarked on the "Catahoula". She is a fine boat, and we got a pretty decent supper. Brooks and I have a stateroom together. We remained at the landing all night, and the mosquitoes remained with us. Am glad I am going to say good bye to Mississippi.

August 12th, 1863

Woke up this morning just as we were leaving the landing, and after a good wash and breakfast, felt first rate. Arranged with the Adjutant to go on guard today, so as not to be on duty when we get to Memphis. The day passed very pleasantly. At night we tied up at an island just above Providence. Was up and on duty all night, and so were the mosquitoes.

August 13th, 1863

Nothing of importance today. After being relieved from guard duty, kept pretty quiet, playing the guitar, reading and sleeping. Have a touch of the old trouble and it takes away my strength. We are not making much headway, as the boat is not fast and we are going against the current.

August 14th, 1863

A pleasant, quiet day. Played the guitar and cards and read. Am enjoying the trip, but will be glad when we get to Memphis, where I can have a bath, and a hotel dinner with white table cloth, napkins and other articles of luxury.

August 15th, 1863

The usual routine of duty when *en route* on a steamer, which is easy guard duty and occasional inspections. We pass the time pleasantly, reading and card playing. We are getting on rather slowly and stop often to "wood up".

August 16th, 1863

Had a severe attack of diarrhea and felt miserable, but kept around. We expect to reach Memphis tonight, and to lie there all day tomorrow. If we do, I have received permission to spend the day ashore. Hope I will feel better than I do this evening. A later report. We expect to get to Memphis tomorrow early to stay all day. If we do, will try to take advantage of the permission I have from Colonel Barnes to go ashore.

August 17th, 1863

Our boat arrived at Memphis some time during the night, and after breakfast I went ashore although feeling weak. It was a change, however, and I did not go back to the boat until late in the afternoon. Spent the evening around the city, resting occasionally in hotels, restaurants and stores. Had some ice cream which tasted mighty good, but perhaps is not very good for my trouble. The city is, of course, under military control and is garrisoned by colored troops. Saw some of them on guard and patrol duty, and they are a fine, clean soldierly lot of men, but it must gall the "rebs" awfully. I bought some new strings for the guitar some of my boys found at Jackson and in the evening tried to have a little music, but was too used up. Many of the officers are sick, and those of us who can stand, have a lot of extra guard and other duty to do. We received a mail here which had been held for us and I had a letter from Cordie and several from home.

August 18th, 1863

Was quite ill today, but was detailed for officer of the guard, and went on duty. Am bound to keep up as long as possible. Did not have a very hard time. We stopped to "Wood up" several times when I had to have my guard out, but I managed to get a little sleep.

August 19th, 1863

Was really quite ill today and after being relieved from guard, laid in my berth all day. In evening got my things ready to leave the boat, as we are due to arrive in Cairo early tomorrow morning. Wrapped up and packed my guitar to send home by express when we arrive. Have taken so much opium or morphine that I am stupid and dazed.

August 20th, 1863

We did not reach Cairo until noon. It has taken us eight days to make the trip from Milldale, Mississippi, to this place, including one day in Memphis. We remained on the boat until dark and then had to wait until midnight before our train was ready. Did not get any sleep to speak of and was so sick and weak I had to go off duty. Was so weak I could hardly drag one foot after the other.

August 21st, 1863

Felt a little better and have rather enjoyed the ride in the cars as a change. At noon, stopped at Centralia, Illinois, for dinner, and they gave us a fine one, which tasted good. In the early evening, reached Sandoval where we changed cars to the Ohio and Mississippi Railroad, but did not get away until midnight. This is a broad gauge road and the officers have a nice passenger car, so we are as comfortable as possible.

August 22nd, 1863

Was detailed for guard and although in pretty bad shape, went on duty. Had to ride with the guard in a baggage car. It was rough riding and I was badly shaken up, which is bad for my complaint. In the afternoon we stopped at Washington, Indiana, where we met the same big crowd, including lots of pretty girls, that greeted and fed us when we passed through here in June last on our way south. This time we were treated in the same royal way. All kinds of nice things to eat were brought for officers and men and the girls sang patriotic songs as our train moved off. Truly Washington, Indiana, is a fine town.

August 23rd, 1863

Arrived in Cincinnati about noon and marched to the familiar Fifth Street Market, where the regiment was given a good dinner. This is the third time we have passed through this city, and each time have been treated splendidly. After dinner we crossed the river to Covington and marched out three miles to a large field where camp was pitched. I was quite weak and just before reaching the field, had to fall out and lie down. After lying on the ground a while and having a chill, managed to get to the regiment. Was feverish all night with bad diarrhea. Am afraid I am going to be sick. Over half the regiment is sick and off duty. Chills and fever from the malarial swamps and bayous of the Yazoo.

August 24th, 1863

Was worse this morning, burning with fever and very weak. Have done my best to keep on duty but have to give it up at last as the doctor has put me on the sick list and talks of sending me to a hospital. There are but three captains and three lieutenants able to perform duty, only six officers in the whole regiment. I made the seventh, until today, and now I am out. The weather has been rainy and quite cold for August, which has not helped us any, coming as we have from the torrid heat of Mississippi.

August 25th, 1863

Was about the same today. Laid wrapped in my blankets feeling pretty well used up. Have not much confidence in the doctor who is quite young and inexperienced. Don't believe he can cure me.

August 26th, 1863

No better this morning. Lieutenant Long joined the regiment today from leave of absence. He loaned me five dollars which is the first money I have seen for a long time. No paymaster has visited us for many moons. Towards night I seemed to feel a little better and stronger. Think if I could get something relishing to eat I might gain a little strength, but nothing tastes good.

August 27th, 1863

Was worse this morning and could not get up. At nine o'clock orders came to be ready to move, so tents were struck at once, but we did not move for some time, and I with other sick ones laid on the ground waiting for an ambulance which came at last and we were loaded in and taken to a place where we were to take cars for Nicholasville. No cars were there and we were dumped on the ground where we laid without any shelter for nearly seven hours. Was deathly sick, head burning with fever and body shivering with chill. After we were put on the train, I was on fire all over, and from what they told me, must have been out of my head a part of the time. We passed through Paris at midnight. Of course, seeing no one.

August 28th, 1863

Arrived at Nicholasville about noon in a hard rain and were crowded under an old orchard shed where we remained for several hours and then learned that the regiment would be here all night. We sick officers went to the hotel which was crowded full. After a lot of trouble, we finally succeeded in getting a room in the garret with three beds, and we turned in, glad to get any shelter. Was quite used up and miserable. Colonel Pierce and one of his satellites, Lieutenant Pippey, joined today from recruiting duty in Boston.[6] We were not overjoyed to see Pierce. He is an incubus on the regiment, and neither officer nor gentleman.

August 29th, 1863

Cloudy and cold. After breakfast a baggage wagon drove to the hotel and those of us who had not strength to walk were loaded in and started after the regiment, which had gone on. The ride was a hard one for me. It was quite cold and I had no overcoat. The road was rough, the wagon had no springs and the jolting was bad for diarrhea and sore bowels. When we reached the place where the regiment was to camp on the Lancaster pike, I was in bad shape. Had a chill which lasted over an hour. Laid on the ground until my tent was put up, and then crawled in and burned with fever for several hours.

August 30th, 1863

Felt somewhat better today, but weak, and kept between my blankets. By taking large doses of quinine, managed to keep from having a chill, but my head buzzes some. Hope the worst is over and that I soon will begin to get better. Received a lot of letters from home and Lieutenant Pizer, who has been on a short leave to Paris, brought me a note from Cordie asking that she be released from her engagement to me.[7] This was a complete surprise, and something of a knockout blow, coming just now when I am so sick. Cannot understand it, after her letters and all that has passed between us. I had heard there was a lieutenant of an Ohio regiment who had been very attentive to Cordie before I met her, and I suppose she has gone back to him. I fancy too there has been some underhand work by certain officers of this regiment. Well, I shall release her of course, and there is nothing to do but "grin and bear it"!

August 31st, 1863

The regiment remained in camp today and was mustered for pay. Had a severe chill in the forenoon, and the fever that followed lasted until nearly night. Chills and fever are bad enough, but in addition to have Cordie's note sprung upon me so suddenly makes me feel miserable and unhappy.

September 1st, 1863

The regiment started for Crab Orchard this morning, and the sick were sent in ambulances to a sick camp near here. There were six or seven of us officers and we were dumped out and laid on the ground without any shelter until the surgeon in charge came around and looked us over. He advised us to go back to Nicholasville, and three of us, Captain Tripp, Lieutenant Long and I, chartered a team to take us back to the hotel. We found it crowded full, but by good luck met an old lady who seeing our plight said she would take us in. We went to her house and found things nice and comfortable. Did not have a chill today so felt much better. The surgeon here advises going to Lexington, so will go there tomorrow.

September 2nd, 1863

Felt a chill coming on this morning, so went back to bed and stayed there all day. The fever came on later and I was sick enough. No Lexington for me today. Although we have been mustered for pay, there is no knowing when we will be paid. I am all out of money with a hotel bill to pay in Lexington, if I ever get there. Sent my boy, Frank, out with my revolver to see if he could sell it, and much to my surprise, he got ten dollars for it. This will help some. Wrote a short note home to let Mother know I am still alive and also wrote Uncle Henry for a loan of seventy-five dollars.

September 3rd, 1863

Have felt pretty well today, no chill and no fever. I find that every other day is an off day for chills at the present stage of the disease, and while feeling all right today, expect I will shake tomorrow. Took a short walk before breakfast and met two officers of our brigade, Captains Yeager and Heisinger of the 50th Pennsylvania, and with them went to hunt up the surgeon in charge, but could not find him.[8]

September 4th, 1863

The chill came as I expected, sometime about two or three o'clock this morning, and held on for nearly two hours. Then came the fever and I had to stay in bed until noon, when I attempted to go down to dinner, but had to give it up as I was so dizzy I could hardly stand. Remained in bed all day. Lieutenant Long went back to the regiment, and I am alone with my colored boy, Frank, who still sticks by me faithfully. Gave Long an order on the Paymaster for my pay, if he shows up while I am away. Towards evening felt better and with the two 50th Pennsylvania captains went to a minstrel show.

September 5th, 1863

My good day. No chills! Captain Heisinger and I went to the hospital to see the Surgeon, Dr. Emerson, who proved to be a very good man. He gave me some medicine which he thought would help me. Have felt pretty well all day, but could not sleep much at night, on account of the fever blisters which came out all over my body and are very uncomfortable.

September 6th, 1863

As was to be expected, the miserable chill was on hand today, and struck me sometime in the early morning, and then came the fever, so

I was laid out until afternoon when I got up. My head felt bad and I was quite dizzy, probably from the medicine Dr. Emerson gave me. Am going to Cincinnati tomorrow to try to get my pay.

September 7th, 1863

My good day again and feel pretty well, only not much strength. My box of things I had sent for came from Paris where the regimental baggage is stored, and I am able to put on some decent clothing. Have been rather seedy. The two captains and I took the noon train for Covington, where we arrived late in the afternoon after a tedious ride. As we passed through Paris, saw Nicolai Ford, but no one else I knew. On arriving at Covington, took a bus over the river to Cincinnati. Went to the Hewins House and after supper, we all went to the theater. The play, "Aladdin", was not much and the captains soon left, but I stayed as they were going on "the war path" around the city, and I did not care to travel with them. Could not sleep after going to bed, so got up, dressed and went down and had a sherry cobbler and a cigar, after which I turned in with better success. Expect the chill and fever will be on duty with me again tomorrow.

September 8th, 1863

Much to my surprise and joy have felt first rate today. Don't understand what has sidetracked the chill scheduled for today. Went around with the two captains trying to get our pay, but without success until we ran across an army surgeon, Dr. Heister, who after taking us from one office to another, finally got things straightened out for us.[9] In the evening the party started out to do the town, but I went to my room, laid down and slept until eight o'clock, then got up, had dinner, went to the theater, then after several sherry cobblers, went to bed and had a good night's sleep. I go back to Lexington tomorrow. Wonder if the chills have left me for good. Hope so!

September 9th, 1863

Had a pleasant surprise this morning in meeting Lieutenant Hunting of the Twenty-Ninth and our Surgeon, Dr. Coggswell, both on their way to the regiment from leave.[10] The doctor examined me and told me

I ought to go home and said he would get me a leave of absence for twenty days, which he did. He said the only way to get the malaria out of my system is to go north. I have been feeling pretty "blue" lately, but the prospect of getting home has cheered me up immensely. Will not go until next week, as my leave does not commence until I start from Lexington, for which place we three took the train towards noon. At Paris we saw lots of our lady friends. Mrs. Forman, Cordie's sister, and Miss Ford came to the car and upon hearing that I was going home soon, made me promise to stop over a day or two in Paris. Arrived at Lexington feeling in better spirits than for a long time. In the evening we all went to a "Polyorama", whatever that may be. It was a humbug, anyway.

September 10th, 1863

Have had some letters from home and wrote a few. Feel blue and discouraged. Have had no chills for several days, but don't feel at all well. Reported to the doctor again in the morning and he gave me more medicine. Went to a dentist and had a troublesome tooth fixed. Dr. Coggswell and Lieutenant Hunting started for the regiment today, and I sent my boy, Frank, back with them.

September 11th, 1863

Expected a chill last night, or this morning, but it did not come. The two Pennsylvania officers left for home today and I hope to go tomorrow. Lexington is a nice town, but I know no one and am lonesome.

September 12th, 1863

Reported to Dr. Emerson in the evening, and he endorsed my leave of absence to date from the fifteenth, which gives me three more days. Mighty kind of him. At the hotel, while at dinner, was agreeably surprised to meet Cordie's sister, Mrs. Forman, who is in town for the day. Upon learning that I was to start for home on the next train, insisted that I stop over at Paris, and "ordered" me to report to her husband on arriving, and she would be home later. I obeyed the orders and found Mr. Forman, who seemed very glad to see me, at his store. The Formans have always seemed to be on my side. On Mrs. Forman's return, went to her house for supper. In the evening, Miss Ford and her mother and Miss Elliott were in. We had a very nice time, but no reference was made by anyone to Cordie. Don't know what I am here in Paris for, anyway. The whole situation is peculiar.

September 13th, 1863

After breakfast, went with the Formans over to "Creekside". Found Captain Tripp there. All were, or appeared to be, glad to see me. Have some doubts as to the genuineness of Tripp's friendship, although he claims to be my friend. Cordie was rather embarrassed, but I braced up and acted as if nothing had happened and I was simply making a call. Tripp and I went to the Formans to dinner, and on the way had a confidential talk regarding Cordie and things at "Creekside". In the evening we were there for supper, after which we had music and a general good time. I let myself out and was as gay as if everything was all right. If I was feeling bad, I was bound I would not show it.

September 14th, 1863

Was intending to take the morning train for Cincinnati, but Tripp said if I would wait until the afternoon, he would go with me, so I agreed to wait. In the forenoon we hired a horse and buggy and drove out into the country, and called on Miss Mollie Elliott. She urged me strongly to stay over another day and come to her home for supper, but I had to decline. Just as we were leaving, Cordie's young brother rode up with a note from her, saying she wanted to see me before I left, so when we got back, I went to "Creekside" and we had a long talk. She felt bad, I could see, and her tears almost broke me up, but I feel I have not been treated just right. It is, as I have thought, a young Ohio officer, to whom she was almost engaged before I came, and she finds she loves him, and so good bye. After farewells to our Paris friends, Tripp and I took the afternoon train for Cincinnati, arriving too late for the theater, so turned in. Don't believe I will ever see Paris again, and but for the Formans and some other good friends, I certainly don't want to see it. Have a bet with some of the ladies that they will never see me again.

Chapter 12

Travel to Knoxville on Return from Sick Leave

In November of 1863, when Ayling's sick leave expired, he set out to join his regiment, knowing only that it was somewhere in eastern Tennessee. He was able to travel by rail only as far as Nicholasville, Kentucky. General Longstreet was besieging Burnside's army at Knoxville, Tennessee, and consequently Ayling was cut off from communication with his regiment. He headed for Knoxville in the company of a sutler, a traveling merchant supplying Union troops. Later he continued on foot through mountainous terrain and through Cumberland Gap. On December 19 he finally reached his regiment camped about twenty miles from Knoxville. Longstreet was repulsed at Fort Sanders on November 29 and thereafter abandoned the siege of Knoxville to go into winter quarters at Greenville, Tennessee.[1]

September 15th, 1863

Left Cincinnati at six o'clock in the morning and had a long and tiresome ride to Cleveland, where we did not arrive until four in the afternoon, too late for the train east, for which I had to wait five hours. Went up town to the American House for supper and met there a gentleman who proved to be a friend of Uncle Phillips and had a pleasant chat with him. He told me he was going to put a young lady, a niece, on the train I am to take and asked if I would take charge of her to New York and put her on a train for her home in Connecticut,

which I, of course, was glad to do. We took the night train at nine
o'clock, and as there was a sleeping car, managed to get a little sleep.
Am feeling very poor, one of my ankles is quite sore, is swollen and
aches. Wonder what is going to hit me next.

September 16th, 1863

We arrived at Buffalo early in the morning and changed cars for
New York. Was very tired and feeling wretched. The young lady in
my charge I found to be a school teacher and a very pleasant traveling companion, and if I had only felt well, would have enjoyed the
journey.

September 17th, 1863

We arrived at New York at half past two in the morning. Took a
carriage and went with the young lady to the Metropolitan Hotel,
which I found was full and but two rooms were left, and these part
of a suite. My charge I could see was a bit uncertain as to the conditions, but after a little hesitation took one of the rooms and I the other.
It was a rather peculiar situation, arriving at a hotel in a strange city
with a girl at half past two in the morning. Don't wonder she was a
little uneasy at first, as I was a perfect stranger to her. After breakfast, took a carriage to the depot and put her on a train for her home
in Connecticut, and then went up town to a friend of Mother's where
I expected to find her, but found she had gone east to see Aunt Abby,
and that Mary was in Albany, so took the first train for that city and
found her much surprised and glad to see me. We had a real pleasant
evening. I will take her east with me tomorrow to visit Aunt Abby and
some school friends in Lowell.

September 18th, 1863

Started in the morning with Mary, and had a long, tedious ride
to Lowell with numerous stops and changes. On arriving, sent her in
a carriage to Mr. Searles' house where she is to visit his daughter,
Leora. Went to Washington House for supper and then to the "Wild
Animal Club", where I found the old crowd and had a very pleasant
time.

September 19th, 1863

After breakfast got a team and called for Mary and drove out to Middlesex to see Mother and Aunt Abby and we had a glad reunion. Am feeling tired and weak, probably the result of traveling. Have several sores or abscesses on one of my ankles, which pain me a good deal and are very troublesome. From this time until November 13th, I was on leave, and up and down, part of the time feeling quite decently and able to go around and enjoy things, and part of the time feeling mighty bad. Have a hard cough that keeps me awake nights, and which some of my very considerate friends encourage me by saying, seems much like consumption. The sore ankle has been very painful, and my old enemy, chills and fever, has been with me occasionally. I have lost all the flesh I can spare, and seem to be chock full of malaria, swamp fever and other souvenirs of the Yazoo bayous, and nearly down and out. Aside from the time spent with Mother and Mary, and Aunt Abby, I have had nice visits with Uncles Henry and Phillips in Boston and Uncles Isaac and Charles at Grantville, and their families, and with friends in Lowell. Everybody has been very kind and I have been treated like a son by my Aunts and Uncles, who have done everything possible to make me comfortable. October first, my leave having nearly expired, I went to Boston to be examined for an extension. I had a certificate from Dr. Burnham of Lowell that I was unfit for service, and Dr. Dale, Surgeon General, at the State House, evidently thought the same and gave me an extension of twenty days, and intimated that he thought it was doubtful if I would ever be fit for duty.

October 21st, 1863

I went to Boston again for another examination and both Dr. Dale and Dr. McLaren, the latter a U.S. Army Surgeon, gave me twenty days in which to get well or get out. They did not say so, in just those words, but it was evident that was what they meant. They ordered me to report to them when my leave expired.

November 1st, 1863

I was bearer at the funeral of George Critchett, one of my old comrades, who enlisted at the same time I did in '61, and who died in Virginia. The funeral was at the Kirk Street Church, Lowell, and was very impressive. While in Lowell, I had my meerschaum pipe mounted in silver, with name, regiment and date engraved, and it is a beauty.

November 11th, 1863

I am feeling much better. My ankle is about well. I have had no chills for some time and my trouble is the cough which still hangs on. I have made up my mind that I will not report at the State House when my leave is up, as I was ordered, but to the regiment, which I hear is somewhere in east Tennessee. Feel blue to leave all my friends, but am anxious to get back, so after good byes to those in Lowell and Boston, started for Albany, where I expected to be a few days with Mother and Mary, but found that to reach the regiment in time I must take the night train on the thirteenth, which I did. They went to the depot with me, and it was hard for us all to say good bye, as I left for Cincinnati and the front.

November 14th, 1863

On the train all day and night, a tiresome ride. Am not feeling as well as when I started, and the car dust makes me cough.

November 15th, 1863

Arrived at Cincinnati in the forenoon and went to the Gibson House, where I met Lieutenant Harry Braden of the 29th, who is on his way home on leave. Was quite tired; kept very quiet and went to bed early after seeing Harry off on the evening train. He tells me my getting through to the regiment is very doubtful at present, as it is shut up in Knoxville, which is besieged by Longstreet.[2]

November 16th, 1863

Started on an early train for Nicholasville, Kentucky. Haven't the faintest idea how I am to get to the regiment, but this seems to be the proper starting place. At Paris stepped out on the platform to see if there was any one I knew, and saw Captain Brooks and Lieutenant Darby of the regiment, who urged me to wait here and go on with a party of sutlers who were going to try get through in a day or two, and had wagons, so we could ride over the mountains instead of traveling on

Confederate General James Longstreet.
From *Harper's Weekly*, July 9, 1864.

foot. I decided to go to headquarters at Lexington first, and learn something definite regarding the situation, if possible. Brooks went with me and upon reporting to Colonel King, Commanding the District, we were advised by him to return to Paris and wait until communication with Knoxville had been reopened.[3] On Colonel King's staff, I met Captain Ned Park of the 35th Massachusetts, my boyhood friend and with whom I used to play when a child. I have met him once before in '62. I dined with him and had a chat of old times. Brooks and I returned to Paris, and in the evening called on friends. Mrs. Forman was very cordial.

November 17th, 1863

Nothing in the shape of news from the front today. After dinner went to "Creekside" with Captain Brooks, who is boarding there. It was rather embarrassing all around, but I got through all right. We made some other calls, and in the evening, we're invited to the Forman's to supper. Two members of the "Sisterhood", Mollie Elliott and Nickie Ford, were there, but the third member, Cordie, was absent. We had a nice supper and a good time, and later in the evening, egg-nog.

November 18th, 1863

Tried to get some information as to the condition of affairs at Knoxville, but can learn nothing satisfactory. Was around town all day in an uncomfortable state of mind. My leave has expired, but I can't get to the regiment through Longstreet's besieging army. In the evening went with Captain Brooks to Miss Duncan's where there was a rehearsal for the concert, which was at "Creekside". Did not want to go, but had an invitation and Brooks thought I ought to accept it. Lots of young people there and the music was fine. After the rehearsal there was dancing and I went in for a good time and certainly had one.

November 20th, 1863

Heard today there is a chance to get through to Knoxville with the sutlers of our regiment, Holland, so will take the morning train for Nicholasville, which is as far as the railroad goes, and from there go on with a sutler's party. The rehearsal this evening was at Miss Duncan's and I went and had a good time, as usual.

November 21st, 1863

After more saying good bye to my Paris friends, who certainly have been mighty good to me, Lieutenant Darby and I took the train for Nicholasville. The sutler's party was not ready to start, so we went to the Buford House for the night. All kinds of rumors are flying around, and it is reported that Longstreet has attacked Burnside and all communication with our army is again cut off. Pleasant, very!

November 22nd, 1863

We called on the Quartermaster who gave us an ambulance to go to headquarters at Camp Nelson, six miles out, where we reported to General Fry, the Commandant, and to Colonel Griffin.[4] Both told us that the roads to the front were closed. Went back to town and found the sutlers with whom we are going to travel, and who are going to get through as far as possible. We drove out three miles and camped. With our five wagons and ten horses, together with the outfit of two other sutlers from an Indiana regiment, we made quite a camp. We put up a Sibley tent and as we have plenty of provisions, are all right.[5]

November 23rd, 1863

In the morning went out in a field and practiced pistol shooting. Then rode in to town for newspapers, but there was no news that encouraged us much. I don't quite fancy this sutler crowd to travel with and wish I could get to the regiment.

November 24th, 1863

Rainy and very cold, so we did not start out. All kinds of rumors among them one that Burnside has had a fight with Longstreet and whipped him. Expect our party will start tomorrow, if not, I will go alone.

November 25th, 1863

A nice day, but cold. We started early and made twenty-three miles, going into camp at night at Lancaster. At the hotel, found Lieutenants Darby and Pippey of the 29th on their way to the regiment. They told us they had heard that those of us who had overstayed our leaves were

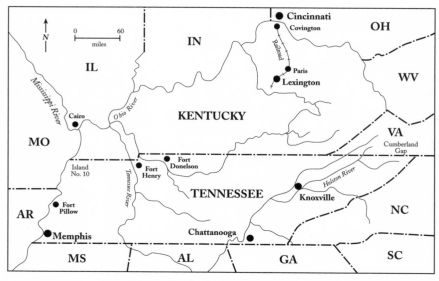

Kentucky and Tennessee, 1864.

to be put under arrest when we reached the regiment. A pleasant prospect for me.

November 26th, 1863

Did not get away until about nine. Reached Crab Orchard at four. The weather was fine, but the roads were horrible, and we made only twelve miles. Found here some of our men in the hospital and some on detached duty. It seemed good to see them once more. At night we moved out of town a mile to the place of Mr. Hains, a Prussian, a very nice man. We had a good supper, and in the evening celebrated the day, Thanksgiving, with a bowl of egg-nog, which we enjoyed much, before a big fireplace with a roaring fire. A mighty pleasant evening. The people of the country through which we are to travel are partly Union and partly "Secesh", some of the latter being "bushwackers", who will take a shot at a Union soldier whenever they get a safe chance.[6] Mr. Hains advised us to be very careful as to where we stopped over night and gave us the name of a Union man, a day's march ahead, and told us we could get names ahead at each place we stayed, which will be better than trusting strangers.

November 27th, 1863

The sutlers decided they would not start today. The roads are very bad. We remained with Mr. Hains and it is a good place to stay.

November 28th, 1863

Raining hard and the wind almost a gale, but we started out in the morning. The roads the worst yet. The mud so deep and sticky, the horses could hardly draw the wagons. We had to give up and stop for the night, after making only four miles. We stayed at a miserable log house, but better than nothing, this weather. We took chances, but the owner proved to be a strong Union man. We found here a woman refugee from Missouri who is trying to get north. Her experience with the "rebs" was very interesting. The people from this section are mostly poor and ignorant, and seem to have barely enough to prevent starvation.

November 29th, 1863

Cold with some snow. The traveling is perfectly awful. Our teams get stuck in the mud a number of times and at night found we had made only four miles and a half. Camped about a mile from Mount Vernon at a Mr. Hunt's. This traveling with the sutlers is too slow and we of the 29th will start on foot. Our party consists of Captain Taylor, Lieutenants Darby, Pippey and Goodwin, and me. There are also two officers of the 46th of New York, a German regiment, who have been with us since leaving Crab Orchard.

November 30th, 1863

This morning bid good bye to the sutlers and started on our march, trusting to luck to take us through and to protect us from "bushwhackers". We took with us only what was absolutely necessary, leaving the rest to follow with the teams. The roads were hilly, rough and the ground partly frozen. We passed Mount Vernon, and at night stopped with a Mr. Roberts, who had been recommended to us as "all right", at the Big Rockville River. A very cold night, but we had a bed and managed to sleep comfortably. Met today a party of the 12th Tennessee out after guerillas and "bushwhackers", which they warned us against. They were a tough looking lot, ragged and apparently half starved, but they have the name of being mighty good fighters. They are very bitter against the rebel guerillas, who have burned their houses and murdered friends and relatives, and when they catch one, they know just what to do with him. We made twelve miles today.

December 1st, 1863

A beautiful day for marching. Crossed the Wild Cat Mountains, and passed the place where there was a fight last year. We were overtaken by a troop of the 6th Indiana Cavalry, and were given a lift of a few miles on their spare horses, which helped some. Stopped for the night with a Mr. Swan where we had been advised to go, two miles from London. This is the best place we have hit since leaving Crab Orchard. Had a fine supper, but had to sleep on the floor before a big fire. Slept very well, but toward morning, it was pretty cold. We marched twelve miles today. Good enough on these roads.

December 2nd, 1863

We started in good season and soon passed through London, a small "no account" place. A beautiful day. Almost too warm for marching. Nothing happened during the day, and after a tiresome march of fourteen and a half miles, reached our destination for the night, the Widow Collins—a very good place, good beds, and we slept first rate. Am getting a little tired and my heels are blistered and sore. Met here a Lieutenant Davis, who is a relative of my old Lowell friend, Billy Davis.[7] The lieutenant belongs to the 11th New Hampshire of our corps.

December 3rd, 1863

We did not get away until nine o'clock and had a hard day. It rained and the roads were muddy and slippery. Reached Barboursville about three and we felt we had gone far enough, so went to Pogue's Hotel for the night. This is a small neglected looking place, about the same as most of the towns in southwestern Kentucky and eastern Tennessee. Not much like the Blue Grass country of Kentucky around Paris. I met at the hotel Colonel Brownlow, son of the famous "Parson" Brownlow of Knoxville, who defied the whole Southern Confederacy.[8] The Colonel is a smart looking young fellow, and mighty strong for the Union. We made only twelve miles today.

Colonel Brownlow on a picket hunt.
From *Harper's Weekly,* Aug. 13, 1864.

December 4th, 1863

A lovely day for this time of the year, and almost too warm for marching. At noon we came to the very small village of Flat Lick, where we stopped for half an hour and got some apples and likewise some apple jack. At half past one we arrived at our intended stopping place, Mr. Tindley's, and tied up. Only ten miles, but quite enough for my blistered heels. In the afternoon had some pistol practice, and made some very good scores.

December 5th, 1863

Raining hard in the morning, so we did not start. At noon the weather cleared and Taylor, Darby and Pippey went on, but I remained with Goodwin, who had a severe chill and was quite sick. Met here Captain Britton of the 15th Kentucky, a very fine fellow. In the evening played a few games of "sixty-six" with him and went to bed about eight thirty.

December 6th, 1863

Goodwin felt a little better this morning and was anxious to get on, so we started about nine towards Cumberland Gap.[9] We crossed the river at Cumberland Ford at eleven, and at half past two reached our designated stopping place, the widow Moore's. A very good place. Goodwin and I had a comfortable bed to ourselves. Met here an officer of the 11th Kentucky, a Lieutenant Williams, and we played "Rounce" in the evening. We have seen some fine scenery today, particularly around the Ford, where it is very beautiful, but the roads are awful. Ten miles was all we could do today.

December 7th, 1863

We left the widow's at nine and at one were at Mr. Campbell's, four miles from the Gap. We had been advised to stay here over night as it is the only safe place where we can lodge or get anything to eat for some distance, and Mr. Campbell advised us not to try to get through the Gap tonight, tired as we were. We were quite willing to stop. It appears that communication with Knoxville is not yet entirely open, but I trust it will be by the time we get over the mountains. Lieutenant Gerhard of the '46th New York joined us here today. This is a very pleasant place to stop, but we had to sleep four in one bed, which is rather "crowding the mourners".

December 8th, 1863

We got away at about eight and at ten after a pretty hard march, over rough and steep roads, were in the celebrated Cumberland Gap. It is certainly a place worth seeing, for anyone. The scenery is magnificent and wild, with rugged mountains all around. The pass, or gap, would seem to be naturally impregnable, without the numerous earth works and other fortifications which have been thrown up all about, and which are now deserted. It is a wonderful place and very interesting. There is a stone which marks the boundaries of Kentucky, Tennessee and West Virginia. I walked around it and set foot in three states. We left the German officer here and continued on our way. My heel is quite sore. I have worn the skin from the blister and the raw flesh bleeds and makes things pretty bad. I was lucky enough today to get a lift for two or three miles in an army wagon, which helped some. Our quarters for the night were at the house of a Mr. Jones, ten or eleven miles from the Gap, and two and a half from Tazewell, the county seat. Mr. Jones is a very strong Union man and bitter enough against the rebels. He was very good to us and did everything in his power to make us comfortable. This is one of the very best places we have struck. Good food and good beds. We made nearly fifteen miles today.

December 9th, 1863

Left Mr. Jones' at half past eight and an hour later passed through Tazewell Court House. This was probably quite a place before the war. We saw the ruins of a number of good sized buildings, both wooden and brick. Evidently the rebels have been here and left their mark. At one o'clock crossed the Clinch River, and at four reached our destination for the night, the house of Mr. Harris. We found here Lieutenants Darby and Pippey, who left us several days ago. They haven't beaten us very badly. Was very tired and lame, and went to bed early. Had a good bed. We made sixteen miles today. The roads this side the Gap are much better than those on the Kentucky side.

December 10th, 1863

A fine day, only rather warm for marching. We got away at eight o'clock, and after a few miles had a chance to put our overcoats and blankets on a wagon and then got along better. At noon we were at Maynardsville, the county seat of this county. It was mostly in ruins, but at one house, we had a very good dinner. At half past three we all felt we had done enough and couldn't go much farther, so decided to take chances and stop at the first decent-looking place we struck. This proved to be the house of Mr. Joel Buckner, who we afterwards heard is a rebel sympathizer. Anyway he used us all right and gave us good beds, only three of us had to sleep together in one bed. Did not rest very well. Fourteen miles was the day's march.

December 11th, 1863

We got an early start this morning and after going about four miles, overtook the sutler of the 36th Massachusetts, who gave us a ride through Knoxville. We could hardly have made it today if we had not been brought along in the sutler's wagon. We wandered around the city trying to find someone from our regiment, or where it is, and finally ran across Lieutenant Pizer, who told us the regiment had gone with the army in pursuit of Longstreet, but was coming back soon. Found my boy, Frank, with the quartermaster's boys, and he was very glad to see me, as I certainly was to see him. Pizer gave us some supper and Taylor and I walked out to the regimental camp where we found Captains Clark and Wilson in charge of the camp guard, the sick, and other men left behind when the regiment went out. Captain Clark gave us a description of the fight at Fort Sanders in which the 29th took part, and told us about the siege.[10] We found an unoccupied shelter tent and took it. We were crowded some, but I slept pretty well. I was tired enough to sleep anyhow or anywhere.

December 12th, 1863

In the morning reported to Captain Clark, who is in command of the camp. Then visited Fort Sanders, the scene of the recent fight, and later went into the city to look around. Knoxville is not a very attractive city to me, but presume it was a little more attractive before the war. It is on the Holston River and is considered an important place from a military standpoint. Longstreet wanted it pretty badly and our fellows put up a

Confederate assault on Fort Sanders, Knoxville, Tennessee, 1863.
From *Battles and Leaders of the Civil War,* vol. 3, 1884.

stiff fight at Fort Sanders, the key of the position, to keep him from getting it. Burnside's army was shut off from the outside very closely during the siege, and provisions and forage were very scarce, and a good many animals were shot to prevent their starving. I counted one hundred and eleven dead horses and mules out on the way to the camp. We are told that our party was lucky to get through when we did, as there has been a lot of Bushwhacking on the roads we traveled. I reckon the activity of the Tennessee and Kentucky cavalry, who do not love "bushwhackers", has kept the roads clear, and then too, our stopping only where we had been advised to stop with Union men made it safe for us. I called on the Paymaster while in the city, and found I could not get my pay as someone had not made the rolls correctly. Slept in Pizer's tent.

December 13th, 1863

Rainy and cold. Have not been able to get any kind of a tent, and have to hang around in the quarters of other officers. Lieutenant Pizer has been very kind and has invited me to sleep in his tent until I can get one. This is a rather blue and discouraging outlook for us, who tramped so many miles to get here. If I can't get a tent very soon, will start for the regiment. In the evening played casino and did not realize it was Sunday until too late. I don't advertise as being very good, but this is the first and only time I ever played cards on the Sabbath.

December 14th, 1863

Cold with snow. We four "refugees" found an old condemned tent and pitched it, then got some boards for a floor and are, at least, housed. Later the weather cleared up and we made a turf fireplace with a chimney of pork barrels. The boy, Frank, managed to get something for us to eat, although where he got it or how I don't know or care. Played casino in the evening. Captain Clark has detailed me for camp guard tomorrow, which is all right. Am glad to have something to do.

December 15th, 1863

A fine winter day. In the morning reported to Captain Clark for guard as ordered, but found I would not be needed. Went to the city and wandered around for a while, and then back to camp. We worked on our old tent in the afternoon, trying to make it a little more live-

able and a little less likely to blow away. I don't like this hanging
around waiting for the regiment, and if it does not come in soon, will
start out to find it, if possible. Wrote home to let the folks know I am
all right and am feeling first rate.

December 16th, 1863

Another beautiful day. Heard that the regiment is only nineteen
miles away and is expecting a fight. Want to get to it just as soon as I
can, but the commanding officer wants to keep us here on detail, but
we "can't see it." A very hard storm during the night, and we feared
our tent would leave us, but we succeeded in holding it down.

December 17th, 1863

A cold disagreeable day. In the morning Captain Taylor and I went
in town and called upon the commanding officer and after a little talk,
he gave us permission to join our regiment, and transportation as far as
we can go by railroad. Then went out to the Quartermaster's corral, where
Lieutenant Pizer is on duty, and took dinner with him. At night it cleared
off cold with a high wind and we found our tent mighty uncertain.

December 18th, 1863

Taylor and I went to the depot early this morning to take the train,
but it had gone. Time tables don't count here. We must wait until tomorrow morning to take the early train in order to reach the regiment by night.
This waiting around is awfully disagreeable. I don't seem to belong anywhere or to anybody. I managed to get a little coffee and sugar today, the
first I have seen since coming here. Anything to eat is scarce and hard to
get. In the afternoon our sutler, Holland, whom we left at Crab Orchard,
came in and we were glad to see him and his supplies. In the evening he
invited us to his room in the city where we had a little spread and some
egg-nog. Had the best time since striking Knoxville.

December 19th, 1863

Taylor and I took cars this morning to ride as far as we could towards
the regiment, which was only ten miles, and then had to get out and foot
it ten miles more. We got something for dinner at a house on the road

and about six o'clock reached camp. Found the 29th encamped at a place called Blain's Cross Roads, situated on a bleak mountainous plain twenty miles from Knoxville. The regiment is in mighty bad shape. The worst I have ever seen. The clothing of officers and men is ragged, torn and patched. Some of the men have no shoes or stockings and many have only one blanket. Tents are very scarce, and the whole command is on quarter rations. Some of the men call this place "Valley Forge", and others call it "Forty miles from the knowledge of God". It looks as if Taylor and I had jumped "out of the frying pan into the fire". The prospect is certainly very blue. Fortunately there is a good supply of wood and Taylor and I had made up our minds to spend the night sitting on a log before a fire, when one of my Company H boys, Dan Perkins, offered to share his shelter and blanket with us, which we gratefully appreciated. Got a little sleep, but was very cold.

Chapter 13

Winter Camp in Eastern Tennessee

In late December of 1863, Ayling rejoined his regiment near Knoxville, Tennessee. Although Longstreet had abandoned the siege of Knoxville, Burnside failed to drive him from Tennessee, and Grant was forced to keep a large force in occupation until April 1864. For the IX Corps and Ayling's regiment, this meant a long cold winter of suffering with a scarcity of food and equipment and the necessity to forage to survive. With enlistments due to expire, a large part of Ayling's regiment was transferred to the 36th Massachusetts Regiment.[1]

December 20th, 1863

Very cold. Reported for duty to Colonel Pierce, who assigned me to the command of Company D and later I took it out for inspection, and a sorry inspection it was. Have joined Lieutenant Long's mess, and when we get anything to eat, will be all right. Lieutenant Atherton has gone to Knoxville, so took his blankets and slept with Long.[2] Have never seen the regiment in anywhere near so bad a condition since I have been with it. The men are not half clothed. There is a shortage of tents, blankets, overcoats and shoes, and the men being on quarter rations, are about half starved. Officers and men alike are equally infested with lice. A pleasant outlook, surely.

December 21st, 1863

Not quite so cold as yesterday, but cold enough. The sutler of another regiment came today, and I went over and bought some butter and cheese, canned butter at one dollar a pound. These are luxuries about here now, but I expect supplies will begin to come soon, now the railroads are open. In the afternoon, was playing Loo, when I was surprised to receive orders detailing me for picket duty at once. Went out with twenty men, but can't see what in the world it is for, or what use there is for pickets with our troops away out ahead of us on all sides. We had no countersign, and nothing to do but take it easy. This is probably Colonel Pierce's idea of the proper way of picketing. There is a rumor that we are to leave this department and go back to the Army of the Potomac, where we belong, and I hope it is true, but don't dare believe it.

December 22nd, 1863

Was relieved about four in the afternoon and returned to camp feeling dirty and disagreeable. Have had my underclothing on for a month, and have no change, as no one seems to know where the baggage is. Am also becoming infested with vermin, but this is only being in the fashion as everybody is in the same condition. Slept in Atherton's tent. He brought some whiskey from Knoxville and we all "warmed up".

December 23rd, 1863

A bitter day and we all suffered much from the cold. Was ordered before a Board of Inquiry at Division Headquarters, having been reported absent without leave, my leave of absence and the extensions I got in Boston having expired before I reported to the regiment. This is all right and proper. Went before the board and showed my papers, and after some explanation think I satisfied the members that I was all right, but will not know the decision for a day or two, probably. Slept in Atherton's tent tonight, but was awfully cold.

December 24th, 1863

Pleasant and not quite so cold, but there is some snow on the ground. Got hold of four pieces of shelter tent this morning, which put together make a very good tent. Frank got a lot of cedar twigs, which make a nice floor for the day and a soft bed at night. By digging a hole a foot square, and as deep in a corner and filling it with coals from the company fire, I can keep the tent very comfortable. It is nice to have

a house of my own. In the afternoon Lieutenant Pizer took two horses
from the Quartermaster's corral and we had a nice ride. Am always
glad to get on horseback. Things are beginning to look a little better
in some ways. We feasted today. One of the men got a sheep somewhere and let our mess have a piece. It surely did taste good. In the
evening played Casino with Captain Oliver and Lieutenant Pizer. Slept
quite well most of the night, but toward morning was so cold I had to
go out to the fire for a fresh supply of coals for my "heater". Rather a
depressing kind of Christmas Eve. There were no stockings hung up,
and there were few who had any fit to hang in this camp.

December 25th, 1863

Cold and disagreeable, but I was cozy and comfortable in my tent
with my charcoal fire. Was a bit homesick, to be out in this bleak country on Christmas day, but my health is fine and I am feeling first rate. My
coming out here, living in the open and roughing it, has been just the thing
for me. If I had left the service when home, don't believe I would have
lived long. Dan, the caterer of our mess, is a "brick" and gave us a fine
Christmas dinner of roast chicken and potatoes. Where in the world he
got them, or how, we can't imagine, and Dan isn't telling. The country
around here has been foraged to death, and we are certainly not draw-
ing chickens and potatoes as rations.

December 26th, 1863

Pleasant but cold. Was busy most of the day writing letters and making improvements in my tent. Lieutenant Colonel Barnes and Lieutenants
Whitman and Conant came back from leave and we were glad to see
them. Three of the very best officers we have, and we always feel better
when Barnes is with us, as we have no confidence whatever in Pierce's
judgement, ability, or courage in action—that is those of us who are not
Pierce's creatures. At night, rain and sleet, but my little tent held fast and
did not leak.

December 27th, 1863

Rainy, cold and very disagreeable. We had orders to break camp at
half past eleven and move over to some woods where we will be shel-
tered and more comfortable, but the weather was so bad the orders were

countermanded. At night we had a hard storm, wind and rain, but I was nice and cozy in my tent. Now that Longstreet has been driven off, and the communications open, things are brightening up, and we hope soon to have the regiment properly clothed and equipped and get more and better rations.

December 28th, 1863

Still storming hard so we did not move our camp. Passed the day reading and writing letters.

December 29th, 1863

A pleasant day after the storm. Broke camp and moved over about a mile to some woods on higher ground. A very good place for a camp. Made my tent as comfortable as possible, but did not sleep much, the ground was so wet and cold. Shelter tents are not the most comfortable habitations for winter in the mountains of east Tennessee, but I reckon things might be much worse.

December 30th, 1863

Pleasant and not so cold. Improved my tent by having logs put along the sides, and filling in with cedar twigs to keep the wind from getting in under. During the night the weather changed and was bitter cold, so did not get much sleep.

December 31st, 1863

This morning was very agreeably surprised to see Captain Brooks of my company, who has just come from leave. He was at once put in arrest by the Colonel, so I remain in command of Company D. I don't think Brooks has been treated right by Pierce, but he does not treat anyone right, except those who toady to him. Took Brooks in with me, although it is a little crowded, and will try to make him comfortable. He takes camp life a bit hard, but he is a good fellow and I like him. We were mustered for pay today. In the evening, played Poker with some of the officers and came out about even. Conditions here are quite different from those of a year ago when we were at Falmouth, Virginia, with good quarters and plenty to eat. I hope a year from today I will be home.

January 1st, 1864

Bitterly cold and blowy. The only way we can get anywhere nearly comfortable is by standing close to a big fire, and then can warm only one side, while the other is freezing, and making it necessary to "change front" pretty often. The new year opens very shivery, and the only bright spot on this New Year's Day was dinner, for which our Dan found a turkey. He roasted it at the company fire, and although not cooked quite as much as it might have been, and although there were no "fixings", it passed.

January 2nd, 1864

Quite cold in the morning, but by noon it was warmer and I did not suffer so much. Worked over my tent a while and wrote some letters. The payroll blanks came today and I will have to go to work on them tomorrow. There is a lot of talk and excitement in camp over a proposition from the War Department in regard to re-enlistments. If three-fourths of an old regiment, like the 29th, re-enlist for three years, the officers will remain with it, and the regiment consisting entirely of the re-enlisted men, will be designated Veteran Volunteers, and go home on a thirty day furlough. The men who do not re-enlist are to be transferred to the 36th Massachusetts to serve out the remainder of their term, which will be to next spring. A number of men have agreed to re-enlist, but I find my company does not take to it very strongly.

January 3rd, 1864

Worked on the company payrolls all day, as I am my own company clerk, and at night finished them. Feel quite satisfied with my day's work, and guess I am ahead of most of the officers. The excitement regarding the re-enlistment proposition still continues. It is reported among the men that the required three-fourths have signed and the regiment is to go on its veteran furlough as soon as arrangements can be completed. Wish it were true. I would like to get a square meal once more, and am awfully tired of short rations, but nothing official has come yet. Slept very comfortably in my cozy tent with the help of my charcoal fire. It is great.

January 4th, 1864

Did not feel very smart today, but had a lot of work on rolls and papers connected with the new enlistment business. Am getting mighty tired of this place and way of living. Have not had a chance to change my clothes for a long time, nor to have a decent bath, and I am exceedingly itchy, which is very common in camp. Some of the men say they do not object so much to the unwelcome visitors they have on them, as they are kept warm scratching. We turn in early, there being no candles.

January 6th, 1864

Felt poor today and have a severe headache, but was busy with numerous rolls and other papers made necessary by the veteran volunteer movement. All sorts of stories are flying around, among others, one that we are to go home sometime during the month for thirty days and are to remain in Massachusetts for a month or two longer to recruit up the regiment, which is now very small in number. At night my headache was worse and I felt miserable. Will get some medicine from the doctor in the morning.

January 7th, 1864

A thoroughly bad day—rain, sleet and snow. Am still busy with the volunteer rolls. No one seems to know just how they should be made, and it is rather blind work. Took some medicine the doctor gave me and at night felt better. We have to go to bed at dark or sit up in the dark, and generally prefer the former; it is warmer anyway. We learned today that sixteen men were lacking to make the required three-fourths for re-enlistment. Rather discouraging after all the talk, work and fuss.

January 8th, 1864

Four inches of snow on the ground, and the camp surely does look like a second Valley Forge. The men are suffering from want of blankets, clothing, shoes and proper food. I can't see any reason for this condition, but I suppose there is one somewhere.

January 9th, 1864

Very decidedly winterish. Did not feel like moving around much and kept pretty close to my blankets. Did a little work on papers, and played a little Casino. Captain Brooks appeared before a Court Martial today, but his trial is not yet finished. The charges against him, "Absence without leave", "neglect of duty", etc. are pretty tough and I fear it will go hard with him. Our mess was broken up today and I don't know just what to do; my boy, Frank, can cook a little, in his way, but I can't quite fancy his way, and we haven't many cooking utensils. Presume I can get along on hard tack and coffee, if I can get them.

January 10th, 1864

A disagreeable cold and hungry day. Had the blues of the worst kind all day, but after my evening smoke and the captain and I had our regular evening sing, I felt better. Lieutenants Braden and Carpenter joined today from leave and are looking tip-top. The talk today is that we go home in ten days. Maybe, but I will believe it when we head for Boston.

January 11th, 1864

A remarkably fine day for the season, and for this forsaken country. In the forenoon had a good wash, an incident worthy of note. Was in better spirits than yesterday. In the afternoon was before the Court Martial as a witness for Captain Brooks, and did the best I could for him. In the evening was in Braden's tent playing "Whiskey Poker" for a while, then had a sing and went to our blankets.

January 12th, 1864

Another pleasant day. Wrote some letters, and kept quietly in my tent all day. We have little duty, and there is nothing new in regard to the furlough. Our daily ration is four ounces of flour, made from a poor kind of grain, which they call here "sick wheat". We can mix with water and make flapjacks of it, but it does not go very well. If we are not a ravenous crowd, there never was one.

January 13th, 1864

A dull, dreary, depressing sort of day and that is just the way I have felt. Did some company writing and played a little Casino. At night two of my men, who had been out all day on a foraging expedition, came in with a lot of nice biscuits they had got a woman to bake for them and let me have four dozen, and a couple of tallow candles, all of which are great luxuries here. I also got a piece of mutton from another foraging party, and am all right for a few days, anyway. Went to bed with a full stomach, and consequently in better spirits.

January 14th, 1864

A fine day and felt quite cheerful, probably on account of having enough to eat. Passed the day writing letters and playing cards. The latest news is that our two divisions of the Ninth Corps are under marching orders. If true, it is too bad. We have got the necessary number of men to re-enlist, and have been expecting to go home on the veteran furlough, as was promised. Perhaps some emergency has come up and we are needed. The men are much disappointed. Some of them say they only re-enlisted to get home and escape starvation.

January 15th, 1864

Drew some clothing this morning, a pretty scant supply, and issued it to the men needing it most. At night we received orders to be ready to move at half past nine tomorrow morning, and it is said we go to Strawberry Plain or Mossy Creek; if the latter, it probably means a fight. The men are very much disgusted, and some say they will not go into a fight, but that kind of talk doesn't amount to anything. I am as disgusted as anyone, but orders are orders.

January 16th, 1864

We started on the march at ten, crossed the Holston River, and at four arrived at Strawberry Plain which is a little station on the East Tennessee and Virginia Railroad. We camped not far from the railroad bridge, which is an important point and has been burned and rebuilt several times. This march, although but eight miles, was one of the very hardest we have ever had. The route was partly over ploughed ground, which frozen at night, thawed during the day, and the mud was ankle deep and sticky. Many of the men were so weak from lack of proper food they could hardly stagger along. Brooks and I did not put up our tent, but rolled up in it on the ground. I was so beastly tired I slept first rate until reveille.

January 17th, 1864

In the morning started to lay out my company street and to put up my tent and make things as comfortable as possible, when Colonel Barnes, who is now in command, thank heaven, told us we would probably move our camp today or tomorrow, so we did not attempt to do much. The weather is very sharp and we are all cold, hungry and miserable. At night orders came to be ready to move at six tomorrow morning. This means going to the front. Good bye visions of furlough for the regiment.

January 18th, 1864

Reveille was sounded early, tents were struck, baggage packed, and we were ready to move at the hour named, when much to our satisfaction, the marching orders were countermanded and we put up our tents again. It was very cold and I remained most of the day rolled up in my blankets. Just after taps tonight, orders came to pack everything and be ready to move at a moment's notice. This was rough enough. The night was very cold and frosty, and to have to turn out of the blankets, where one was, at least warm, was not pleasant. Sent our baggage to the wagons, but I decided to take chances, and did not strike my little tent, but crawled into my blankets again and laid down, expecting every minute to hear the order to fall in. Nothing happened, however, and I slept until morning.

January 19th, 1864

Woke up this morning and found three inches of snow on the ground, and a cold biting wind blowing. Concluded I would be more comfortable in bed than out, so kept my blankets most of the day, cold even there. Ventured out once or twice, but not for long. Expected orders to move today, sure, but none came. I can't understand what is going on, but it looks very much like a "skedaddle", as the bridge over the river has been all fixed ready to burn. We hear we of the Ninth Corps are cooperating with General Sheridan's Fourth Corps in some kind of a movement, but it does not look like an advance.[3] This has been a most miserable, uncomfortable day, but I console myself by thinking it can't last always.

January 20th, 1864

A better day than yesterday and I felt first rate. Have detailed James Ball of my company to cook for the captain, who has not yet been released from arrest, and me. Ball is a character, a big goodnatured Irishman, with a big round head so large that no cap I can draw from the Quartermaster will fit him and he has to cut a slit in the back to get one on. He is not much as a soldier, but as a forager he is great, and if there are eatables to be had within a day's journey, he will find them. Food of all kinds is mighty scarce and I can't see why we are not given regular rations. Our allowance for the past five days has been eight ounces of flour. The men can't live in this way and be good for much, either marching or fighting. At sundown we were ordered to fall in under arms, and after standing a while, were ordered to fall out and strike tents, and then were ordered to pitch them again, but to be ready to fall in at the word. Fortunately our little shelter tents are easily put up and taken down. I did not pitch my tent, but rolled myself up in it before a fire and slept very well, until awakened by the Adjutant at eleven, with orders to be ready to move at six tomorrow morning.

January 21st, 1864

I had not been asleep more than an hour, after the Adjutant's call last night, when he came around again with orders to move at once. We formed in a hurry, crossed the river, and then stood awaiting an hour or so by reason of the stupidity of Colonel Pierce, who being temporarily in command of the brigade, had marched off with a part of it, leaving us waiting for orders. At last we got started, marched three miles and camped on the border of a cedar grove. I rolled up in my tent and blankets and slept a cold sleep until morning. Later we moved into the grove and it was a fine place for a camp, if we could only stay here. During the forenoon, we could hear our batteries back at the bridge, shelling the enemy, and there was considerable infantry firing along the river banks. Ball got some pork, salt and flour, so we will be all right for a day or two. Turned in early, but did not sleep very soundly as I expect we may have orders to move at any moment. We certainly seem to be about to retreat.

January 22nd, 1864

Soon after midnight last night we were routed out, as I expected, but instead of heading toward Knoxville, we turned to the rear and marched back about three miles toward the river, and halted. The morning air was quite sharp and we felt it keenly. We hear that the army is falling back upon Knoxville, and that our regiment and the 79th New York Highlanders, a fine regiment, are to form the rear guard. We remained halted near the river until the troops that had been out to the front had passed with their wagons and artillery, and followed on. We found two brass guns on the road, abandoned by the artillery of the 23rd Corps, and our men manned the drag ropes and hauled them over the rough frozen roads for several miles, until relieved by horses sent back from the front. While hauling the guns, we had to move slowly, and could not march fast enough to keep warm. At noon word came back from Corps Headquarters two or three miles away that the army was to halt for dinner, and we to govern ourselves accordingly. We didn't have much for dinner, but stretched ourselves on the ground for a rest, which we did not get, for suddenly sharp firing was heard at the rear, showing that the rebs had followed us up pretty closely and had struck our skirmish line, which today happened to be from the 79th. We at once deployed and soon had a strong line of skirmishers out, when we saw the Highlander's line coming down the hill, retiring steadily and in good order. They formed in line with us, and a few minutes later a large body of cavalry came charging over the hill with sabers drawn, shouting and giving the familiar "rebel yell", but one volley from our fellows sent them back to the cover of some woods. They soon reappeared in a large field. We moved some of our men into a road alongside the field, and as the enemy came up on the run, shouting to us to surrender, they got a fire in front and on the flank which broke them up and sent them back to the woods again. Word was at once sent to headquarters that we were attacked, and orders came back to retire slowly and hold the enemy in check. They tried to flank us once, but didn't succeed as their move was expected, and we had a line formed all ready for them. We fell back slowly, skirmishing all the way, through woods, over fences and across streams and fields, for nearly seven miles, until within about three miles of

Knoxville, when we made a stand and the enemy left us. The cavalry, after their first attempts to ride us down, dismounted and skirmished with us on foot. Our whole movement, of skirmishing in retreat, was carried out beautifully by our regiment and the 79th New York. The last part, just before the enemy retired, was in a large field on the slope of a hill, and every move of the enemy and of our men, could be seen distinctly. Our first line of skirmishers would hold the enemy while slowly falling back through a second line, already formed several hundred yards in the rear, each front line falling back alternately through a second line while keeping the enemy at a safe distance. Everything on our side went like clock work, and all hands agreed that it was one of the prettiest little fights we had ever seen. I happened to be in command of a division (2 companies) today, which deployed made quite a line, and I was kept pretty busy. I had on a fairly good overcoat in the morning, but in running back and forth along my line to see that the men kept the alignment and did not fall back too quickly or until ordered, I got tangled up a number of times in bushes of what is called down here "wait a bit thorns", and at the end of the skrimmidge was decidedly ragged. We went into camp without moving any further after the enemy left, and everybody was glad to rest. My cook, Ball, is missing, and as he was out foraging, I am afraid he has been captured by the cavalry. As I have nothing eatable, I went to bed without supper.

January 23rd, 1864

A fine day. We moved back a short distance into the woods, and camped. Ball came in some time during the night, but came very near being captured. He was successful in foraging, so we have something to eat. Laid around all day, reading and taking things easy. At night slept on the ground in front of the company fire. Did not pitch my tent. We have orders to move tomorrow at eight.

January 24th, 1864

Felt first rate this morning when we started out, which was quite early. We headed for Knoxville and after marching a few miles were halted and clothing and rations issued to the men. This looked rather ominous and might mean a fight, or a retreat. We marched through the city with bands playing and colors flying, and the old Ninth Corps made a fine appearance, our tattered flags attracting a good deal of attention. We took the London road and after going some four or five miles, turned into a big field for a camp. We were told we would probably stay here for some time. Had a good supper and rolled up before the fire in my blankets; had just fallen asleep when orders came to prepare to march at an early hour tomorrow morning, in light marching order, to go on a foraging expedition.

January 25th, 1864

Our 29th regiment was sent out alone this morning with seventy wagons foraging, to collect hay, corn, and anything in the way of supplies, for the whole corps. The day was fine and we all rode, going out, in the wagons, and enjoyed the trip immensely. After getting out into the country, some of the men did a little foraging on their own account, and got some "corn dodgers" and biscuits. My man Ball found among other things, a little butter, which did taste good. We went out about eighteen miles to the Clinch River and camped for the night at Mr. Black's plantation at Black's Ford. We got a lot of corn here. When we take forage from citizens, we give written receipts which enables them to get their pay from the Government, upon proving their loyalty, which some, I fancy, would have some difficulty in doing. We had a fine supper, but as the officers had been ordered to leave tents and blankets behind, I slept very cold during the night.

January 26th, 1864

Another fine day. After a good breakfast, we crossed the Clinch and moved on. During the forenoon, the regiment was divided into a number of small parties, each with wagons starting in a different direction to forage. Lieutenant Whitman and I with ten men and eleven wagons went together, and this just suited me. I like to cut loose from the crowd once in a while, and Whitman is a mighty nice fellow to travel with. We had pretty good luck during the day and at night stopped at a farmer's house for supper. Slept in the barn on shucks, and they make a good bed. Am enjoying this trip much, but have a slight internal disturbance, probably from gorging after being half starved.

January 27th, 1864

After a good breakfast, our little party started out and five miles of marching brought us to the place of a Mr. Jones, said to be a rebel. We filled two wagons here and by the time everything was loaded up, it was nearly noon, so we decided to stop here for dinner, and had a good one. At sunset, we tied up for the night at a house at Beaver Brook. Had a good supper and a bed to sleep in. This is the first real bed I have been in for a long time and it did feel good.

January 28th, 1864

A lovely day. We started early to return to camp with our loot, and overtook several of our detachments that had been out on different roads. About noon, while Ball and I were scouting a short distance ahead of our train, it turned off into another road and left us, so we kept on alone to camp, which we reached about four in the afternoon. The rest of our party, with the wagons, did not get in until some hours later. I was glad to get back to camp, but I did enjoy our foraging trip immensely, and am pleased with the result. We brought in for our private mess three pecks of meal, and a lot of corn dodgers and biscuits, also some pork and chickens. We will live high for a while, sure. In the evening, Lieutenant Davis of the 11th New Hampshire called to see me and we had a real nice chat about mutual friends. Received letters from home.

January 29th, 1864

Almost perfect weather. The nights are cold, but the days are mild and springlike. We have a good camp at a little place on the railroad called Erin Station, and it looks as if we may stay here a while. Have had my tent logged up and fixed to be very comfortable. At night had orders to have the men of my company, who have not re-enlisted, ready at eleven o'clock tomorrow, with the required rolls and other papers, to be transferred to the 36th Massachusetts to serve out the remainder of their term of original enlistment. This looks as if the promise of a veteran furlough to the rest of us is about to come true.

January 30th, 1864

Worked hard all the morning on rolls, invoices, receipts and other papers, but not one of us company commanders could get everything ready to transfer our men at eleven o'clock, as directed, so the order was changed to nine tomorrow. The nights have been beautiful with moonlight lately, and the brigade band plays every evening, so things are very pleasant. Colonel Barnes had a letter today from Mary asking if I were sick as neither she nor Mother had received any letter from me for a long time. Can't understand this. Have written quite often, but presume the mail service here is in keeping with everything else in this forsaken country down here.

January 31st, 1864

At nine o'clock this morning, we formally transferred our men, who have not re-enlisted, to the 36th Massachusetts Regiment. Colonel Barnes made a feeling speech to them, bidding them good by and God speed. We all felt bad to part from the men who have been our comrades so long and in all kinds of service, and they felt equally sorry to leave the old regiment. It has been a sad day all around. It took us to nearly night to get things straightened out with the Quartermaster of the 36th, who had to receipt to us for the ordnance and quartermaster's stores turned over with the men. We felt, at first, that we would now start for home on the promised furlough, but we hear that the 23rd Corps, which has been out to the front somewhere, had stirred up a fight and got more than they wanted, and that our 9th Corps is to go to help them.[4] We have no orders yet, however, except to draw three day's rations, which looks ominous.

Chapter 14

HARD TIMES AND A DEPLETED COMPANY

Since only four of the men in Ayling's company re-enlisted, he found himself in command of a Sergeant and three men. The furlough promised them for re-enlistment was indefinitely postponed, which naturally lowered morale. Winter weather, inadequate food, shelter, clothing, and equipment combined to make this duty in Tennessee the hardest to endure of all Ayling's war experience. There was little action other than shifting camp from place to place to counter enemy threats that never materialized. Finally, in late March of 1864, Ayling is detailed to leave by rail for Cincinnati in charge of convalescents and baggage of his brigade. The men were to march over the mountains on their way on furlough.[1]

February 1st, 1864

In the forenoon was busy with company papers. I have all my company writing to do myself, for although entitled to a company clerk and have detailed Ball as such, he can't even sign his name, but he can forage, and I am willing to do the writing for the grub he collects.[2] In the afternoon, was sitting in the sun, enjoying a smoke, when orders came to get ready to move at once in light marching order, all officer's baggage to be left in camp. We did not move until almost night, but when we did, it was a forced march and we hurried like the deuce. The night was thick and cloudy, and dark as pitch, the mud ankle deep, with lots of slippery stones, and we went slipping and staggering along, with someone falling flat every once in a while, when the air would

Bridge over Holston River, Knoxville, Tennessee.
From *Harper's Weekly,* Mar. 12, 1864.

be blue with remarks. We passed through Knoxville, crossed the Holston, and moved out several miles and then halted for the night. This night's hurried march made me think of the retreat from the front at Richmond in '62, and the forced march to Jackson, last summer. There were many muttered and some quite loud curses aimed at the 23rd Corps, the cause of all the trouble.

February 2nd, 1864

In the morning, instead of moving out to the front as we expected, we turned back and marched to our old camp where we arrived at about noon, and glad to get there. Was busy in the afternoon cleaning up, and repairing clothing, etc. At night we had a regular hurricane with a hard rain. Expected my tent would go, but I managed to hold it down. Later the storm cleared off very cold.

February 3rd, 1864

Did not feel very well today. Have a sore throat, so kept rather quiet. Wrote some letters and read. No orders for home, and there is a good deal of grumbling among the men as they were assured that, upon re-enlisting, they would at once be given a furlough. Felt poor at night, as if I was going to have a bad cold, or something.

February 4th, 1864

When I attempted to get up this morning, found myself quite sick, all my bones seemed to ache and I had a sore throat and headache, so felt pretty mean. All this is probably the result of our little excursion the other night. Kept in my blankets all day.

February 5th, 1864

Felt a little better today, but my throat is quite sore. Weather cold and disagreeable. No signs of going "over the mountains", and every-body is discouraged. We were ordered to get our men in as good a shape as possible, and camp cleaned up, ready for a review and inspection, so I had to turn out and look after things, but did not feel like it a little bit. We got all ready, but for some reason, General Foster who was to review us did not appear, so I went back to my blankets.[3] I promoted Private Joe Madigan to be Sergeant.[4] He is one of my four men who re-enlisted, and is a bright little fellow.

February 6th, 1864

Felt somewhat better, but the cold and sore throat hang on. I kept housed all day, the weather is so cold and rainy. Wrote some letters and played cards a little.

February 7th, 1864

Made out my ordnance returns for Washington and did some company writing. Everybody cross and growling because the regiment is not sent home as promised. Can't blame them much, but I presume there is some good military reason for keeping us here. Everybody is hard up, and we can't buy any eatables, even when we have a chance. The regiment has not been paid for six months. Why, I wonder?

February 8th, 1864

I received today a tremendous great blank to be filled out and completed. It is in connection with the re-enlisting business and is a nuisance. It took me all day to finish it. Hang this re-enlistment business; I am sick of the very sound of it.

February 9th, 1864

Got permission to leave camp for a few hours, and went in to Knoxville this morning, taking Frank with me. Borrowed an old horse, but did not dare to ride him for fear he would fall under me. Went around the city seeing what little there is to be seen, and had a shave, the only luxury I can afford just now. Did not stay long in the city, as Knoxville has mighty few attractions for me. Got back to camp about two, and found a fresh lot of blanks to be made, some to be ruled. This blank making is wearing out my patience. I have made out and ruled some twenty-five or thirty blanks, and don't see any signs of going home yet.

February 10th, 1864

Cold, but pleasant. Wrote letters, read and played cards. Made a bet with Whitman of a dinner for four at Young's in Boston, that we do not start on the furlough inside of one week from today. The four to be Whitman, Conant, Braden and myself. Hope I lose. I heard that the 2nd Michigan, which is a re-enlisted regiment like ours, is to go home tomorrow. In evening sat at the company fire until quite late listening to my men telling stories and experiences.

February 11th, 1864

Beautiful weather. Worked hard all day on blanks—confound them. Had a lot of ruling to do, which was not easy with the tools and coveniences at hand. The 2nd Michigan left today by rail for London on their way home. Well, I suppose our turn will come sometime.

February 12th, 1864

Another fine day. Worked most of the day on the blasted blanks, and hope I am through with them. This re-enlistment business being a new thing, the War Department does not know, evidently, just how to handle it, and has no proper blank forms, so we have to make them as best we can.

February 13th, 1864

We are certainly blessed with splendid weather here now, and appreciate it. No news today. Passed the time writing and reading. In the evening, Ball, my wonder of a forager, came in loaded down. He brought eight dozen eggs, four chickens, two pounds of butter, and meal, biscuits and molasses. He is surely the star forager of this regiment, and I am envied by the other officers. Colonel Barnes said, in a joking way, that he was going to detail Ball as forager for the headquarters mess. Anything very appetizing is mighty scarce about here, and Brooks and I fully appreciate our good things, and feel fine to see our larder so well stocked.

February 14th, 1864

The lovely weather still holds, and it is remarkable to have such mild pleasant days like spring at this season. Did not do much but lie around in the sun, taking things easy. In the afternoon, Hardy, our hospital steward, came to my tent with a song book and we had a little sing.[5] After supper, sat until quite late, with Whitman and Conant, around the fire, talking and telling stories. Sometime in the night, the Sergeant Major woke me up with orders to move at eight tomorrow. At first I thought it was for the long-looked-for homeward move, but on second thought, knew it could not be, so turned over and went to sleep again, after notifying the sergeant. Am disgusted to think we must go off on a tramp again.

February 15th, 1864

Our good weather has left us. It was too good to last. We did not move at eight, as first ordered and it was nearly noon when we got away. It rained very hard all day. We took the Knoxville road, and plodded along in the rain and mud until sometime after dark, and it was pitch dark when we halted for the night in a cedar grove two miles from the city. The officer's tents were behind with the wagons and we were wet and cold. Frank finally got a fire started and Brooks and I stood shivering before it, for a while, when as there were no signs of the wagons coming, we crawled into Sergeant Madigan's tent and had a cold, wet night of it.

February 16th, 1864

Did not rest very well last night, my feet were soaking wet and the blankets were wet and cold, so woke up this morning feeling anything but happy. The weather has cleared, but it is cold and windy. Brooks and I walked into Knoxville and called on Lieutenant Jones, who gave us a drink of good whiskey, which warmed us up some, and we returned to camp. Ball and the wagons came in soon after and we had grub and tents. After supper got into my blankets, and shivered until morning. The night was cold.

February 17th, 1864

Pleasant but cold and windy. No news or orders of any kind. Put a lot of cedar boughs in my tent and made it quite comfortable so had a good sleep at night and a rest I needed.

February 18th, 1864

Just after breakfast this morning, was washing and changing my underclothes, when before I was half through, orders came to move at once. This was exasperating, just as I have my tent all nicely fixed, so I can sleep with any comfort, but such is military life. We only moved about three miles nearer west of Knoxville, and went into camp in a very good place, well wooded, but the ground is rough and rocky. Got my tent up and slept, or rather laid, cold all night. The weather for the past few days has been uncomfortably cold and blustering. A big change from the fine days we had while at Erin Station a week ago.

February 19th, 1864

Pleasant, but beastly cold. Had Ball and Frank work on my tent to make it livable. In the forenoon we had division inspection which lasted a couple of hours. When I marched my company out everybody smiled, as I had only one sergeant and three men. I have some trouble in keeping peace between my two servants. There seems to be eternal war between Ball (Irish) and Frank (colored). Ball is the bigger and stronger and bullies Frank who when he can't stand it any longer, pulls a knife and I have to step in and smooth things. I think Ball is most to blame, usually, and I would send him back to the company, but he is so good at foraging, I can't spare him. The Commissary had whiskey today and we got some for the mess.

February 20th, 1864

Cloudy and cold. We had a dress parade in the evening, the first for a long time, and when I marched out onto the line with a sergeant and one man, the other two being on guard, giving my orders in a loud voice as if I had a full company, there was a snicker along the whole line.

February 21st, 1864

Snowed hard all the morning, but cleared off at noon. All day we have been expecting orders to march; most of the baggage has been sent to Knoxville. The Commissary has gone and the Quartermaster's wagons have been standing all day, hitched up, ready to take the rest. This looks like a retreat or a fight. We hear there is some apprehension of another attack on Knoxville, and I fancy our movements around and near the city, have something to do with its defense. Colonel Barnes sent a communication to headquarters today in relation to our promised veteran furlough, but what the results will be we can only guess.

February 22nd, 1864

The day passed quietly. Read and played cards, but expecting every minute to hear the "assembly" sounded. The teams were kept standing all last night and day today, ready to pull out at short notice. Things look mighty uncertain about here just now.

February 23rd, 1864

Fine weather once more, mild and springlike. Everything quiet today, and the alarm, whatever or wherever it was, seems to be over. I read in the *Atlantic Monthly* an article by Oliver Wendell Holmes "My Hunt for the Captain", which I enjoyed much.[6] In the evening, Conant was in my tent, and we were enjoying a pleasant talk, when we were suddenly disturbed by the appearance of the Adjutant with orders to move at daylight tomorrow, in light marching order, with four day's rations and sixty rounds of ammunition for each man. It looks as if there was a job of fighting for us, somewhere.

February 24th, 1864

We started at daylight and took the road to Strawberry Plain. Weather fine after the shower of last night. My company being so small, the men were temporarily transferred to Company G, so I tramped along with Conant. He is one of the best fellows in the regiment, clean, straight and intelligent. I enjoy being with him. He can talk of other things than rum and women, which some of the crowd usually choose as a topic of conversation. I really enjoyed the march today, although by noon my feet began to be rather sore and at night were quite painful. We marched until sundown and halted about three miles beyond the Plain. Was somewhat tired and had several large blisters on my feet, but after supper and a smoke, felt first rate. General Schofield, who is in command of the Department, I believe, and other general officers passed us today.[7] Everything looked as if we were going to have a fight, but nothing happened. We made twenty miles today, a pretty good march. I shared Ball's blanket and slept cold.

February 25th, 1864

Contrary to our expectations, we did not get orders to march this morning. Kept quiet all day resting and nursing my sore feet. The weather is good and we have a pleasant camp, from which we have a fine view of the Holston. Conant gave me some lessons in phonography, and I think I will study it in my leisure hours.[8] He came to my tent after dinner and we had a confidential chat, he telling me of a love episode in his life, in return for my story of the other evening. Toward evening, the regiment marched to the station at the Plain to get their knapsacks which had come from Knoxville by railroad. I did not have to go, having no company, but sent for my tent, and pitched it, when it came. Heard that some of the regiments were laying out camps as if for a stay here. I will have my tent fixed tomorrow.

February 26th, 1864

After breakfast had my tent logged up and carpeted with cedar boughs. Passed the day comfortably and counted on having a comfortable night, but alas for the uncertainty of military affairs. In the afternoon orders came for the men to carry their knapsacks back to the cars and officer's baggage to go also. We are to move at seven tomorrow morning, with fifteen day's rations, and I reckon there is a long tramp ahead for us. I sent back everything but one blanket and a piece of tent, so was rather cold all night. Have given up all hopes of getting home at present.

February 27th, 1864

We were to start at seven, but did not get away until nine. Marched to the Plain and crossed the Holston in boats, the bridge having been burned. We halted on the bank of the river until the 23rd Corps had crossed, and it was a lively sight. At noon we marched a few miles and camped for the night. We have only made about six miles today, and it does not look like a very hurried movement. Slept first rate before a big fire.

February 28th, 1864

Broke camp at nine this morning and although the sun, at noon, was quite warm, and my tent and blanket weighed down some, we had a very decent day's march. We reached and passed through New Market, rather an attractive little place, about noon, and all the inhabitants, including a lot of pretty girls were out to see us pass, with the usual accompaniment of the colored population of every size and shade. We arrived at the little settlement of Mossy Creek at sundown, passed through and went into camp two miles beyond. Marched thirteen miles today and are to move at seven tomorrow morning.

February 29th, 1864

Rained hard all day. We were hustled off in such a big hurry this morning there was no time to get any breakfast, nor did I have anything to eat all day. Had rather a hard day of it. The roads were muddy and slippery, and my boots were nearly "played out" and hurt my feet. About five in the afternoon we passed through Morristown and went into camp a mile out from the town. It rained hard all night, but after I had my tent up, Ball found some boards for me to lie on, out of the mud, and with a big fire in front, had a very comfortable night. An attack is expected here and orders have been issued to be prepared. Our march today was about the same as yesterday, only thirteen miles, but the rain, slippery mud, sore feet and nothing to eat, made it seem a good bit longer.

March 1st, 1864

For a wonder, we did not move today, and I was glad, as it rained hard. My tent leaks, but I am better off than some of the officers, who have no tents at all, and had to stand around in the rain all last night and today. It cleared off cold in the night and I did not get much sleep. Everything in this department seems to be in a muddled condition, and without a competent head to direct affairs. There is certainly no apparent reason for the privations and discomforts officers and men have to bear. They do things better over in the Army of the Potomac. We are to move at half past three tomorrow morning.

March 2nd, 1864

We started long before daylight, and took the road back, instead of forward, very much to my surprise, although there have been rumors that we were to retreat. I suppose it's all right, but if there is any enemy out front, why don't we "go for him"; if there is no enemy, what are we here for? The weather has been fine today, but the muddy roads made the marching hard. Early in the afternoon, we arrived at our old camp at Mossy Creek to remain for the night. In the evening was detailed for picket, to my disgust, as I was pretty tired. I went out about two miles from camp, with thirty men from the regiment, and a Lieutenant and ten men from the 46th New York, who reported to me. Instead of an aide from brigade headquarters going out with me, as is the custom, to show me where I was to picket, and with what other pickets I was to connect, I was left to find the proper position by myself, which after a lot of trouble in the darkness I succeeded in doing, establishing my line so that it was in touch with other lines on my right and left. Soon after an aide came out to me and said we would probably be attacked during the night, cautioning me to be on the lookout, and to hold my line, if attacked until reinforcements came to my assistance. I placed my reserve in the rear, where there was plenty of fence rails, then visited each post and cautioned the men to keep wide awake, and watchful, and then went back to my reserve, lighted my pipe, and sat down for a quiet night, for I don't believe there is any enemy within miles of us. Soon after midnight, I was much surprised to see the Lieutenant and the detail from the 46th New York, which was on my right flank, appear at the reserve. He told me a mounted officer had ridden up to him and ordered him to take his men back to camp, after transmitting the order to me. He also told me that the pickets on his right had been withdrawn. I did not like the looks of this a bit, and can't understand it. Sent my sergeant to the left flank and he came back and reported that there was no one on our left. This left my line with both flanks in the air. I sent a man back to headquarters to find out what it all meant, and he returned with the report that a big mistake had been made, and that I had done just right in remaining where I was. Soon after a Lieutenant and thirty men reported to me to strengthen and extend my line, so I had quite a good command. The night passed quietly and we did not have a chance to fire a shot at anybody.

March 3rd, 1864

A lovely day and everything quiet at the picket line. Was relieved at three this afternoon, and when I reported at camp, Colonel Barnes complimented me for sticking to my post and not obeying that fool order last night to withdraw my pickets. Had my tent pitched and made things comfortable for the night. Had Ball out foraging, and he came in at sundown with biscuits and eggs. Enjoyed a good supper, and then a good night's rest, which I needed. Orders came today for us to make requisition for clothing and supplies for a thirty days active campaign. A very singular order. Aside from the fact that there has been no fighting of any account, if marching back and forth all about the country, almost continually for the past thirty days, is not active service, I would like to know what is. We certainly have not been passive.

March 4th, 1864

All quiet today, but we were all the time expecting sudden orders to march. The air is full of rumors of all kinds, and there seems to be a feeling that we will not go with the rest of the corps on the thirty days campaign. One thing is certain, if the re-enlisted men are not sent home pretty soon, they cannot be held for another three years, for the term of their first enlistment will have expired before the government can fulfill its part of the contract, and give them the promised furlough. It rained hard all night, but although my tent leaked, I managed to keep fairly dry, and fairly comfortable.

March 5th, 1864

The active campaign doesn't seem to materialize to any great extent, and things were quiet all day, except in the afternoon our pickets were driven in and we had a little skirmish with some cavalry. There was a ripple of excitement for a time, but the affair did not amount to much, and soon everything was quiet again. Ball was out again today, and brought in some biscuits. How that fellow manages to escape capture, I can't see, for the enemy's cavalry are constantly raiding the country. Am afraid he will go out once too often.

March 6th, 1864

This noon we had orders to be ready to move at short notice. We at once packed up and were ready for the order to fall in, but no order came, and I laid down on my blanket and slept most of the afternoon. Wonder what it all means. We are not likely to start for home on such orders, although some think we are. This is the darndest place for orders I ever was in; we are getting them most of the time.

March 7th, 1864

Beautiful day. At noon we struck tents and moved camp about a mile to a place where wood and water are more plentiful. Did not get my quarters fixed up until nearly night when I curled up and slept very comfortably. Was disturbed once in the night by hearing an orderly, or some mounted man, ride up to the Colonel's quarters, and soon after hearing a call for the Sergeant Major. Thought marching orders had come, sure, and laid waiting for the summons, but everything was serene and I went to sleep again.

March 8th, 1864

Fine weather and nothing stirring. Wrote letters and played cards. Ball was out today, and brought some biscuits, and what is much better and a luxury, some butter.

March 9th, 1864

The usual routine today, and nothing new. Played a few games of cards and lounged around. There is a strong feeling of discontent in the regiment, and marching or fighting would be better for the men, who are getting restless.

March 10th, 1864

Cloudy and windy. The usual amount of loafing around and growling. At night Captain Taylor came to my tent and we had a chat about old times at Newport News in '62. We have orders to have two drills a day, hereafter, until further orders. We had a dress parade this evening with eighty-five men out.

March 11th, 1864

More orders today. The drills are to be suspended and we are to move tomorrow morning. Taylor came around again at night to resume our talk. Ball foraged today, and had his usual good luck in finding provisions.

March 12th, 1864

Broke camp at half past four this morning and moved on in the direction of Knoxville. The roads were good and although quite chilly when we started, the weather, after the sun came up, was just right for marching. Soon after dinner, we came to Morristown, moved a mile outside and went into camp on the slope of a hill, in a fine location. Was very agreeably surprised at halting here, as we had been told we would not stop until reaching Russellville, eight miles beyond. I was mighty glad to stop, my feet were sore and the new government shoes I had on had made a number of blisters. Pitched my little tent under a big tree, and after attending to my sore spots, as well as I could, had a little supper, a good smoke, and then a good sleep all night. For a wonder no orders came for us to march tomorrow, and there is a chance that we may stay here a day or so. Colonel Pierce has gone home sick, we hear. Hope he will never return to the regiment, upon which he is an incubus. Colonel Barnes has been assigned to the command of the brigade, which leaves Major Chipman in command of the regiment. Two fine officers and gentlemen, who should and would be promoted if that Pierce would get out.

March 13th, 1864

The payroll blanks were sent around this morning and I worked on those for my company most of the day, but did not quite finish them. The orders did not come to move, but just at sunset the assembly sounded and we formed in a hurry, when Major Chipman told us that there had been an alarm, and the brigade had gone out to the front, but that we were to stay back as reserve and guard the camps. We were then dismissed and broke ranks, after being cautioned to be ready to spring into line at short notice. The "29th luck" is still with us, and saved us a march of some miles for really nothing. The brigade was back in camp shortly after dark, and we learned the alarm was caused by some of the enemy's cavalry getting in between our cavalry vedettes and infantry pickets.[9] It doesn't take much to create an alarm down here.

March 14th, 1864

Was busy over my payrolls this morning, when we were ordered to fall in quickly, which we did, and leaving the tents standing, marched out some three or four miles to the front, to where several roads come together, and remained there until night, when we returned to camp. All hands looked for a fight, but we neither saw nor heard anything. It seems we were out as a support to the brigade, which had gone out on reconnaissance. I think we all would have been glad to have a little scrimmage for a change. On the way out this morning, we passed the biggest tree I have ever seen. It had been cut down and lay beside the stump, which was estimated to measure seven feet in diameter. What anyone wanted to cut down so magnificent a tree for, I can't understand. It was wicked.

March 15th, 1864

A quiet day, and uneventful, no alarms or orders, for a wonder. Finished the payrolls all ready for the Paymaster, who will be welcome. Received letters from home. Mother and Mary have been expecting, for some time, to see me, I having told them we were to go home on veteran furlough.

March 16th, 1864

We had snow today for a change. Nothing stirring about here. The principal talk in the regiment, as it has been for two months, is about the promised furlough, and we don't get it. Bet Whitman a box of cigars that we do not start for home inside of ten days. We had orders at night to move early in the morning.

March 17th, 1864

Commenced our march at five this morning. The weather fine and just cool enough for marching. Felt first rate, and for the first twelve or fifteen miles, really enjoyed the tramp. For some reason, we avoided the main roads, which would have been shorter and easier, and made our way through woods and fields. At noon we halted just long enough for the men to make coffee, and then continued the march until late in the afternoon, when we halted for the night near Newmarket. Did not go through Mossy Creek, but passed to the right of it. I was quite tired and foot sore when we halted. We marched twenty-three miles today. A pretty good march.

March 18th, 1864

Started at half past six, and moved toward Knoxville, crossing the Holston on pontoons. For the first few miles I got along pretty well, but after a while my feet became sore and kept getting worse and worse, and it was all I could do to keep up with the regiment, but I managed to limp along until we halted. Camped for the night in a very good location, about six miles from Knoxville and near Fort Sanders. Found my feet to be badly blistered, and very sore. My great trouble in marching has always been that my feet get blistered and sore. They seem to be remarkably tender, and in spite of the best care I can give them, blister very easily. Am decidedly sick of infantry service, and would much prefer the cavalry for mine.

March 19th, 1864

Continued our march this morning, and early in the afternoon arrived at the suburbs of Knoxville. We did not go through the city, but passed to the south and west. My feet were very sore and it was hard work to keep up, and it seemed as if we would never get to our camping ground, after we had halted. Finally after a number of mixed up and contradictory directions, we were assigned a position on the side of a bleak hill, some distance from wood and water, and where the cold wind had a good sweep. At night was tired, lame and rather used up. Captain Clarke gave me a good drink of whiskey, which helped some.

March 20th, 1864

Orders came today to send in to headquarters the names of all convalescents, sick and others who are unfit to march over the mountains. This looked encouraging in one way, that the regiment is at last to head for home, but it seems a little tough to make us take the long hard march over the rough roads when other re-enlistment regiments have been sent home the quickest and easiest way by railroad. I heard this evening that I am to be sent, with two other officers, in charge of the convalescents and baggage of the brigade, by rail to Cincinnati, via Chattanooga. Sincerely hope this may be true for my feet are in bad condition for marching. Perhaps the doctor, who has been treating them has reported their condition to Colonel Barnes. We are under orders to march at six tomorrow morning. Expect I will have a hard time of it.

March 21st, 1864

Early this morning received an order from Colonel Barnes to report for duty to Captain Richardson, which order I very willingly obeyed, as the captain is to be in charge of the brigade baggage and convalescents, and goes by railroad to Cincinnati. Lieutenant Conant is to go with us, and I am delighted with the whole arrangement, which will save me from marching on blistered feet, and gives me pleasant companions. The regiment started off about seven, for home at last, and in good spirits, and our little detachment left behind felt equally happy. We are not to take the cars until tomorrow, so we had nothing to do. The captain and I went into Knoxville and got dinner, and I bought a pair of boots. In the evening we received orders to be at the cars with our detachment ready to load the baggage at six tomorrow morning. Have been happy all day over my good luck in not having to march, or limp, over the mountains and my car ride will give the blisters a chance to heal.

Chapter 15

THE END OF THE WAR

Ayling went home on furlough in April of 1864 and returned
to duty briefly before being mustered out of the service on
May 26, 1864. He returned to work at the J. C. Ayer Company, his former employer, in Lowell, where he reports the
impact of the news of the fall of Richmond, the surrender
of Lee at Appomattox, and the assassination of President
Lincoln in 1865.

March 22nd, 1864

Snowing this morning. We got the cars loaded, and started about
ten for London, where we are to stay tonight. Felt first rate when we
started, but soon after was taken with a severe chill which was one of
the worst and longest I have ever had, and lasted until we arrived at
London late in the afternoon. It was still snowing and Captain
Richardson, seeing my condition told me to go out and find some house
to stay in, where I would be more comfortable than in the car. Started
out, taking Ball with me, and tramped around some time before I could
get shelter. Finally found a house where I could get a bed, and went in
at once, without trying to get any supper, and had a good sleep. It will
be too bad if I am to be troubled with the miserable chills all the way,
for I have been counting on having a very enjoyable trip this time.

March 23rd, 1864

A fine day after the storm, and I felt all right, but I fear tomorrow will be another "chill day", as they usually come every other day, confound them. The train left London at ten, Captain Richardson sending me on with the baggage and a guard, while he and Lieutenant Conant, with the rest of the detachment, are to follow later. Had a pleasant day. I have Quartermaster Sergeant Joslyn of the 29th with me, and he is a fine, reliable man.[1] We arrived at Chattanooga before dark, and I had much interest in seeing the place and the nearby battlefields of Missionary Ridge and Lookout Mountain, which certainly look like bad places to attack.[2] Had a good supper at an eating house, and while sitting before the fire smoking, became acquainted with a Major Quigg of the 14th Cavalry, and discovered that he was a friend of a Lowell friend of mine, Tom Allen, and we had a very pleasant time together. We left Chattanooga at midnight. Sergeant Joslyn made a nice bed for me on the baggage and I slept soundly until morning.

March 24th, 1864

As I expected and feared, I had a bad chill early this morning and with the accompanying fever it lasted nearly all day. We passed the battlefields of Stones River and Murfreesboro, but I was too sick to look at them.[3] Joslyn says I was out of my head part of the time. We arrived at Nashville at dark, and I felt so poor, thought I would go to a hotel and get a bed, but everyplace was crowded full and I could not get in anywhere. Went back to the depot, but our car had been moved, and I could not find it in the dark. Made a bed on some bags of corn on the platform and as it commenced to rain, my boy Frank covered me with an old tarpaulin he found somewhere. Did not get much sleep or rest. It was a pretty tough night for me, and I don't want any more like it.

March 25th, 1864

This being an off day for the chills, I feel pretty well, considering last night's experience. Found, when I got up, that my belt and revolver had been stolen during the night. Started out and found my Sergeant, Joslyn, and we went for breakfast. Learned that we were to stay here all day, so went to a circus. Our train got away late in the afternoon and I made up a bed on the baggage and had a good night's rest.

March 26th, 1864

Arrived at Bowling Green, Kentucky, early in the morning and by reason of a smash-up on the railroad somewhere ahead, we had to stay here most of the day. For some reason, and to my delight, did not have the chill, as I expected, but I felt poor and did not go out to look around. Our train got away towards night, and I hope we will not have to be side-tracked again till we reach Cincinnati.

March 27th, 1864

When I opened my eyes this morning, found we were in Louisville, Kentucky. Took Joslyn and went out to get breakfast and to look around the city, which seems to be a very nice place, streets laid out well, and clean, and with some fine buildings. My instructions were to transfer here, across the river to Jeffersonville, Indiana, and continue by rail to Cincinnati. I left directions in regard to the baggage, and with Sergeant Joslyn went over to find our car and to wait for the detachment with the baggage. After waiting a while and seeing no sign of either, concluded there was a hitch somewhere, so we went back to Louisville and found that without notifying me, the program had been changed and we are to go to Cincinnati by boat. Found my men and the baggage on the steamer, "General Buell", which was just about to start, and had Joslyn and I been a bit later we would have been left. Had a very pleasant trip up the Ohio. At night had a cot in the cabin and slept fine.

March 28th, 1864

Arrived at Cincinnati early in the morning. My instructions being simply to come to this city, I waited on the boat some time for further orders, but none came. Landed and went to the Gibson House for breakfast and met there several of our officers who have come on ahead of the regiment, and who had told me the brigade would probably be in Covington in a day or two. Went back to the levee and learned that the men and baggage had been sent to the barracks at Covington, and are all right. Went up town and met the officers, and went to the Buckeye Billiard Saloon for billiards. This is the finest place of the kind I have ever seen, sixteen tables, and everything in good taste. In the evening went to Wood's Theater and saw Proctor in "The Duke's Motto". Very good!

March 29th, 1864

Being relieved from the charge of the baggage, and being under

nobody's orders, I have nothing to do until the regiment arrives at
Covington, which will be in a day or two probably. Was around with
the officers all day. Played some billiards, and in the evening went to
the Opera House, and then to the beer gardens "Over the Rhine", as
the German part of the city is called.

March 30th, 1864

Heard that Captain Richardson had arrived at Covington with his
detachment, and went over early this morning to see him. Found him
nicely fixed at the U.S. Barracks, which in time of peace are used by
the regulars as an Army Post. Everybody is comfortably quartered and
the baggage nicely stored, and everything all right. Went to the city
for dinner, and in the afternoon played billiards. In the evening we all
went to the Palace Theater, which is a sort of "free and easy" place,
and very much "off color". I fancy I will have to go on duty at
Covington tomorrow, but am not anxious to leave Cincinnati just now.

March 31st, 1864

In accordance with orders received this morning, went over to the
barracks and reported to Captain Richardson, relieving Lieutenant
Conant. Our quarters here are very comfortable, with good bunks and
we can get good meals from a man who brings them to us. I fancy I can
have a pleasant time here. Kept pretty quiet all day and went to bed early,
as I am feeling the effects of my late hours recently in Cincinnati.

April 1st, 1864

Heard this morning that the brigade had arrived and was in camp
half a mile from the barracks. As I have not yet been relieved from duty
here, did not report to the regiment. Went over to the city, got dinner at
the Gibson House, played a game of billiards and returned to the barracks. Found that the regiment is to move over to Cincinnati with all the
baggage. As soon as the wagons came, had all our stuff loaded and rode
over on the load. The men are to be quartered at the 6th Street barracks
and the officers at the Clifton House, directly opposite. Took supper there,
engaged a room and went to the theater. When I got back, found my room
had been given to someone else, so had to sleep in a room with four others, which I did not like. Colonel Pierce, who has been home, ostensibly
recruiting, hearing the regiment was coming to Boston, has arrived here

to take command, which is just like him. If we were to go into active service, with the prospect of a fight, I do not believe he would have come.

April 2nd, 1864

I understand the regiment is to remain here until the paymaster, who has our rolls, comes to pay us. This is not so bad, although we are all anxious to get home. We have no duties to perform, and officers and men have nothing to do but "kill time". Played cards and billiards and in the evening went to the theater.

April 3rd, 1864

Same as yesterday. No paymaster yet. Nothing to do but hang around. All hands are getting impatient to be on the way to Boston.

April 4th, 1864

The paymaster did not arrive today as was expected, but we learned that the officers could get their pay from a paymaster here, so went to Major Crow's office and received our money. In the evening went to the Opera House and saw "Lady Audley's Secret". Very good! Felt poor when I went to bed.

April 5th, 1864

Waked up feeling very miserable. Went out to buy some things I need, and then went back to bed and remained all day. Hope I am not to be sick and unable to go with the regiment, which will probably start tomorrow night.

April 6th, 1864

Felt a little better this morning and was up and around. The regiment was paid today and we are to start for home tomorrow. It seems almost as if we would never get out of this department, and I hope we will never get into it again.

April 7th, 1864

Formed line early this morning and marched to the railroad and boarded the cars, but did not get away until half past nine. At last we are headed for home. As my Company D is very small, it is temporarily consolidated with Company F, and I am assigned to the same company with Captain Tripp. Arrived at Cleveland quite late in the evening and after some delay, we're off for Buffalo.

April 8th, 1864

Did not get much rest last night and felt poor all day. Arrived at Buffalo at noon where I got some dinner, and telegraphed Mother that I am on the way and will meet her at Albany. Have felt quite sick all day and fear the chills are after me again.

April 9th, 1864

Arrived at Albany at two o'clock in the morning, but Mary was there to meet me. Learned that our train would remain here several hours, so went with Mary to the house to see Mother. Had a good visit of two hours and then Mary and I went back to the depot, and found the train had been moved across the river to Greenbush. Hurried over and got there just in time. Have felt miserable all day. Wonder if I am ever to be free from that Mississippi malaria. Arrived at Boston at four in the afternoon, and found Uncle Charles, Henry and Phillips were there to meet me. The regiment marched to the Beech Street barracks, where the men are to be quartered, the officers going to the U.S. Hotel. Uncle Henry took me home with him, and after supper, I felt so poor I went to bed. The regiment is to be given a reception on Monday.

April 10th, 1864

A very bad day—snow and rain. Stayed at Uncle Henry's and in doors all day. Got the clothing accounts of my men fixed up and the rolls ready for them to sign tomorrow. Am not feeling well at all.

April 11th, 1864

Went in town quite early this morning and took breakfast at the U.S. Hotel. All our officers were there and we had a jolly time. At eleven we formed, and with the First Corps Cadets as escort, marched through some of the principal streets to the State House, where Governor Andrew joined us, and then to the American House, where Major Lincoln welcomed us in behalf of Boston and invited us to partake of a very good dinner.[4] Speeches were made by the Governor, the Mayor and several of our officers, after which we marched back to the barracks and after making out the furlough for the men, they were dismissed for thirty days, and the long-looked-for veteran furlough had come at last.

May 13th, 1864

My thirty days have passed quickly and pleasantly with Mother and Mary in Albany, relatives in Boston and friends in Lowell. Had lots of invitations to dinner, supper and for over night, and longer. Was quite surprised to be invited on April 14th to dinner by Dr. J. C. Ayer, my former employer, and had a very pleasant time. Felt quite complimented, as this is the first time, so far as I know, he ever invited any employee or ex-employee to dinner. On the 15th of April a lot of the 29th officers came up to Lowell on a sort of "bat", and I had my hands full showing them around, and entertaining them. They were a pretty lively crowd. All too quickly the time has passed and the thirty days have gone, and our furlough expired today. Took the morning train from Lowell and reported at the U.S. Hotel, as ordered, and found all hands there. No one knows just where we are to go or when we are to start. If Colonel Pierce knows he will not tell. I got leave for twenty-four hours and went to Grantville with Uncle Isaac and spent the night.

May 14th, 1864

Came in town early with Uncle Isaac and reported at the hotel. No orders to move yet. Was about the hotel all day and in the evening went to Morris Brother's Minstrel Show. It was fine, and is considered the best of its kind.

May 15th, 1864

Loafed around the hotel all day. Heard we are to start for the front tomorrow, and hope we may, as this hanging around the hotel is getting to be tiresome.

May 16th, 1864

Orders finally came today and at five in the afternoon we formed line and marched to the depot, taking the cars for Fall River. Everybody felt rather "blue" at leaving home and the ride was not very lively. At Fall River we went on board the steamer, "Metropolis", bound for New York. A fine boat. We had staterooms and a good supper. We don't know where we are going.

May 17th, 1864

Arrived at New York early this morning, landing near Castle Garden. We went on another steamer and were taken to Jersey City, where we took the cars for Philadelphia, arriving about four in the afternoon after a dusty, tiresome ride. We were taken to the Soldier's Home and treated splendidly. Philadelphia is far ahead of any city I have seen, as regards the care and comfort of soldiers passing through. After a good wash and a fine supper, we all felt pretty good. The 79th New York Highlanders, of our brigade, on their way home, came in just as we were leaving, and we formed and presented arms as they passed. We marched about a mile to the Baltimore depot, everybody waving flags and handkerchiefs to us as we passed. We did not leave until sometime after dark.

May 18th, 1864

Arrived at Baltimore sometime in the forenoon, and marched to the Washington depot, but did not leave until two o'clock. Captain Tripp and I went out and got dinner, and looked around a little. Arrived in Washington at six, the men going to the "Home", and the officers to the U.S. Hotel. In the evening played a few games of billiards and then, with a few of the officers, went to my room and had some mint juleps.

May 19th, 1864

We are not to leave until tomorrow, so some of the officers went to the Paymaster General's office to see if we can get our pay. Met here John Watkins, who succeeded me as "boy" in Ayer's office. We were sent to a paymaster here who paid us to May 1st. In the evening John and I went to Canterbury Hall, then around town. Got to bed about one.

May 20th, 1864

When I waked up this morning, found I had overslept and the regiment had gone. Hurried out and was delighted to find that my captain, Tripp, was in the same predicament. We took a carriage and drove to the landing, arriving just as the regiment was going on board a steamer. Had a pleasant trip down the Potomac and got to Belle Plain at two o'clock. Landed and pitched camp for the night on a bluff overlooking the river. After supper and a smoke, turned in on the ground and felt quite comfortable and contented. It seems like old times. We expect to move tomorrow, somewhere, but no one seems to know just where.

May 21st, 1864

An order has been issued by the Secretary of War that all officers who have served three years must be mustered out, and seven of our oldest and best officers who come under the order have prepared a petition asking that they be mustered out. They are good, clean men and among those whom I like best, and I decided to sign the petition with them. I can not stand, any longer, Colonel Pierce, and his injustice, inefficiency and low instincts. He has made sergeants and corporals captains over me, and I feel there is little hope of my promotion, unless I join Pierce's gang and toady to him, which I cannot do. I have, as First Lieutenant, commanded several different companies, and I think, successfully, and feel that I have earned a captaincy. The officers who have signed the petition are all disgusted with Pierce and his methods, and if he were out, and Barnes Colonel, I doubt if they would leave the regiment. I certainly would not, and as it is, I hate to go and would like to stay until the end of the war. At night our petition came back approved, giving us permission and transportation to go to Washington to be mustered out. We go tomorrow noon.

May 22nd, 1864

At noon we took the boat for Washington. A lot of the officers and men came to see us off, and seemed to feel bad to have us go, and we felt bad to leave the old regiment. Our party consists of Captains Leach and Oliver, and Lieutenants Whitman, Braden, Conant, Darby, Goodwin and myself. Arrived at Washington after dark and went to the American House, and found it very bad, but we concluded to stay over night. Went out and had supper, and then to bed.

May 23rd, 1864

We went to the War Department early with our papers. We were the first to apply for muster out under the order, and the authorities were somewhat in doubt as to whether it meant three years as an officer or three years, including service as an enlisted man. Quite an important matter, for five of us had been promoted from the ranks. Finally, after considerable delay, we were given transportation to Boston to be mustered out there. We had to take the night train, but I got a berth and had a good sleep.

May 24th, 1864

Arrived in New York early and found the baggage of some of our party had not come, so we waited for another train for Boston, where we arrived about nine. Went to the Hancock House, got supper and went to bed.

May 25th, 1864

Went to the office of Captain Maloney, the Mustering Officer, who gave us a lot of rolls to make out, which took all the forenoon, and when we went back with them were put off until tomorrow.[5] The Captain is evidently as uncertain regarding the meaning of the order as they were in Washington. He gave us a new lot of rolls to make out.

May 26th, 1864

When we went to Captain Maloney's office this morning, he told us he could not muster us out, and he interpreted the order to mean that we must have served three years from the date of our last commission. This was the worst yet. We talked and argued quite a while, and finally the Captain, to get rid of us, I guess, mustered us out of the service. Feel glad to be free from the restraint of military life, but sorry to have left the old regiment.

May 27th, 1864

Am invited to a reception given tonight by the people of Sandwich, to my old Company D, most of the members being home, few having re-enlisted. Took the afternoon train for the Cape, and was much interested in seeing the country, which seems to be mostly marsh and sand. Company D was composed largely of men employed in the Glass Works, and was considered a pretty tough lot, but I never had any trouble with them, and when I arrived, they gave me a most sincere and cordial welcome, and I was certainly glad to see my "boys". There was a dance at night and it was kept up until four o'clock in the morning, and was a pretty lively affair. Did not go to bed at all, but walked around and sat in the hotel until breakfast, and then took the train for Boston. Bought a suit of citizens' clothes, and made some calls on my Uncles and others. It is hard to realize, after three long years, that I am no longer in the service. Am both glad and sorry, and more sorry than glad. Feel sort of lost and out of place, but I presume this feeling will pass after a while, and I get settled down. After a day or two in Boston, went to Lowell, and had a few weeks of picnics, excursions, fishing, driving, and a general good time, then went to J. C. Ayer's office and Doctor Ayer offered me my old place on the books, or a position as Assistant Cashier, advising me to take the latter, which I did.

The rest of the year 1864 was uneventful and passed quietly. The work at the office runs smoothly and it is good to be back there with the old crowd. I have a good boarding place, and everything is very pleasant, but there is a feeling of regret , all the time, that I left the regiment, and I often find myself wishing I was back with my old comrades.

November 8th, 1864

Today was Election Day, and I cast my first vote, and for Abraham Lincoln for President. I feel that I may be proud, sometime, that I voted for "Uncle Abe."

January 14th, 1865

Received notice today from the Adjutant of the Twenty-ninth that I am reported absent without leave. Very pleasant. Immediately wrote the Mustering Officer in Boston, asking that he send the proper papers to

Washington and to the regiment to relieve me from the charge, and to show that I was honorably mustered out.

February 17th, 1865

Received the third degree in Masonry in Ancient York Lodge tonight, and am now a Master Mason. Liked the ceremony very much. It is beautiful and impressive.

February 26th, 1865

In the evening was out calling on some young ladies, and did not start to go home until nearly twelve. As I was passing the Merrimack House, I heard a crackling sound and saw a very bright light in the basement. Upon investigating, there was a lively fire in the laundry, which was all ablaze. Gave the alarm and waited to see the engine come and go to work. The fire was extinguished after a while, but I think it was mighty lucky I happened along just at that time, for the streets were deserted and not a soul in sight. Had the fire gotten a little more headway, it might have made things bad for the sleeping guests of the hotel.

April 3rd, 1865

We heard today that Richmond had fallen and there was a great rejoicing. After nearly three years of trying, our troops are at last in the rebel capital, and Jeff Davis and his cabinet are fleeing south. It is great news, and looks like the beginning of the end.

April 9th, 1865

More good news. Lee has surrendered to General Grant. Everyone was jubilant. The streets were crowded with people cheering and congratulating each other that the war is over, for with Lee and his Army of Northern Virginia out of it, there will not be much fight left in the other armies of the Confederacy.

April 14th, 1865

There is to be a big parade on the nineteenth at the dedication of a monument to Ladd and Whitney, two Lowell men who were killed when the Sixth Regiment went through Baltimore in '61, and I received today an invitation from Colonel Sawtell,[6] the Chief Marshall, to serve on his staff, which I accepted, and have engaged a horse.[7]

April 15th, 1865

Today the city is wild with grief and anger over the report that President Lincoln was assassinated last night by a southerner, Wilkes Booth. Coming after the good news of a few days ago, when everyone was elated, it is a terrible shock. All flags are at half mast, public and private buildings draped in black, and business is suspended. Lowell is a city of mourners. It is all a man's life is worth to show any feeling but sorrow or anger.

Chapter 16

POSTWAR DUTY IN RICHMOND, VIRGINIA

In April of 1865, Ayling was offered a commission as First Lieutenant and Aide de Camp on the staff of General R. S. Foster, commanding the First Division of the Twenty-fourth Corps in Richmond, the fallen Capital of the Confederacy. Ayling eagerly accepted the commission and went to Richmond, where he soon found himself appointed Judge Advocate and undertook the responsibility of trying court martial cases.

After General Foster left Richmond, Ayling became Adjutant of the Twenty-fourth Massachusetts Regiment under Lieutenant Colonel Thomas Edmands.

April 22nd, 1865

Received a nice letter from Colonel Davis, my old Captain, with whom I enlisted in '61, and who is now Adjutant General on the staff of General R. S. Foster, commanding First Division, Twenty-fourth Corps, stationed near Richmond.[1] Colonel Davis wrote he would arrange to have me commissioned in the Twenty-fourth Massachusetts Volunteers and assigned to duty on the staff with him as Aide de Camp, if I would like the arrangement.[2] Wrote at once that I certainly would like it, and thanked him.

May 6th, 1865

In the morning paper saw my name in the list of commissions issued

Lieutenant Colonel Phineas A. Davis, 1865.
Centerville Historical Society Archives.

and will go to Boston and get mine at once and as soon as I can get things at the office straightened out, will start for Richmond.

May 15th, 1865

Went to Boston this morning, where I met several officers of the Twenty-ninth. There seems to be considerable doubt about my being mustered in, when I get to Richmond, as the war is practically over, but now I have started will keep on and take the risk. Dined with Uncle Phillips who gave me a pass to New York and return, in case I could not get mustered. Took the boat train at half past five for New York.

May 16th, 1865

Left New York at eight this morning and arrived at Washington at half past five. After supper called at the hotels to find General Foster, upon whose staff I am to be, and who is here as a member of the Court Martial to try the conspirators in the murder of President Lincoln, but did not find him.

May 17th, 1865

Tried this morning to find General Foster, but did not succeed. Have not been able to get the balance of pay due me when I left the Twenty-ninth, and find I am held up for a bayonet which it is claimed I have not accounted for properly and which I know I have. Put the matter in the hands of a claim lawyer here and left some affidavits signed in blank, and don't care much how he fills them out.

May 18th, 1865

Took the train for Baltimore, but there were delays so we did not arrive in time for the Fort Monroe boat, so had to stay here all night.

May 19th, 1865

Had a whole day in Baltimore as the boat does not leave until six in the evening. Called on some of the old friends of '61, when I was Provost Marshal on the boat between here and the Fort, and had a very pleasant day. When I went to take the boat, found it was the old "Louisiana", one of the boats upon which I was Provost Marshal and I felt quite at home.

May 20th, 1865

Arrived at Fort Monroe at seven this morning and everything looked very familiar and took me back to the time I landed on the sandy beach four years ago. Transferred to the "Georgianna", and had a very delightful

Lieutenant Colonel Thomas Edmands, 1865.
Centerville Historical Society Archives.

trip up the James River, only I would have enjoyed it more, if I felt sure of being mustered when I get to Richmond. Early in the afternoon came in sight of the first rebel works from there. Things were particularly interesting. Became acquainted with a young man in the Quartermaster's Department, who had been up and down the river many times, and could point out the interesting places. Saw General Butler's Dutch Gap Canal, Drewry's Bluff, and other places of historical interest.[3] Arrived at Richmond quite late in the afternoon, and was most agreeably surprised to find Colonel Davis at the landing to meet me, and he relieved my mind by saying he had everything arranged for my muster and detail. We took the headquarters ambulance for camp, stopping at the Twenty-fourth Regiment, in which I am commissioned, where I was introduced to my colonel, Ordway, and some of the officers.[4] Colonel Ordway is vastly different from Pierce, my former colonel, being a gentleman in every particular. He is on duty in Washington, and Lieutenant Colonel Edmands is in command of the regiment.[5] He, like the colonel, is a thoroughbred, and an officer and gentleman with whom it would be a delight to serve. At dinner met the staff and later there was quite a celebration in honor of my arrival at Colonel Davis' quarters, where I slept.

May 21st, 1865

Upon turning out this morning, found the headquarters to be in a delightful place, in a grove about two miles from Richmond on the Brook Road, not far from the Mechanicsville Pike and battlefield.[6] The wall tents are pitched on three sides of a square, and each tent has an awning of evergreen in front of the entrance. Everything is neat and clean, and it is the handsomest headquarters I have ever seen. General Foster being temporarily on duty in Washington, General Osborn, one of the brigade commanders, is in command, and he is a pleasant gentleman.[7] The ten members of the staff are: Lieutenant Colonel Davis, Adjutant General; Major Barlow, Surgeon; Brevet Major Sellmer, Inspector; Brevet Major Carruthers, Provost Marshal; Brevet Major Waddell, Judge Advocate; Brevet Major Sampson, Quartermaster; Brevet Major Thompson, Commissary; Brevet Major Byrnes, Ordnance Officer; Brevet Captain Frye, Aide de Camp; and Brevet Major Sawyer, Mustering Officer.[8] The staff is a pretty gay crowd, and with some exceptions, rather fast, I fancy. All hands are very nice to me and I will like them, I am sure. My fellow Aide, Frye, is a nice quiet fellow and does not drink at all. In the afternoon, took a horse from the corral and rode in town with Colonel Davis. Richmond is a hard looking place now, the rebel rear-guard having fired a part of the city, which is now only a lot of blackened ruins. Before the war, this must have been a beautiful city. Saw Belle Isle where many Union prisoners were confined, and the notorious Libby prison.[9]

May 22nd, 1865

Rode over to the Twenty-fourth with Colonel Davis to get a certificate of the vacancy which I am to fill, but when we got back, found it was not quite right, so cannot be mustered until tomorrow.

May 23rd, 1865

This forenoon we were all invited to the headquarters of General Fairchild, commanding the First Brigade of our Division.[10] The Colonel had a keg of lager tapped and gave us a little collation. The brigade has a fine band and we had some good music, which I always enjoy.

May 24th, 1865

The whole division turned out at seven this morning, formed, and marched into Richmond, taking position to receive the Sixty Corps, which marched through on the way to Washington to take part in a grand review of all the armies, except our corps, which is to be kept here to preserve order in the city and surrounding country, and a pretty tough job it is. Was in the saddle four or five hours, and not being used to it, was rather sore.

Libby Prison, Richmond, Virginia (misspelled above). From *Harper's Weekly,* Oct. 17, 1863.

May 25th, 1865

In the afternoon rode in town with General Osborn and some of the staff, the General having been invited to be present at a reception to the newly appointed Governor, Pierpont. General Devens and the Staff of the Third Division were with us and there was to be a grand turnout, military and civic.[11] We rode to the landing and waited until dark, but no Governor appeared. At the invitation of Mr. Morrison, correspondent of the *New York Herald,* we went to his quarters and had a drink or two, after which the General dismissed us and we started for camp at full gallop through Main Street. There were thirty in the party, and we made some clatter.

May 26th, 1865

I find there is a possibility that I may see some active service yet, in Mexico. Taking advantage of the fact that the U.S. was busy at war, the Archduke Maximilian of Austria, with the connivance of the Emperor of France, Louis Napoleon, and the support of a small party of the natives, declared himself Emperor of Mexico in 1864, and French troops have been sent to help him. The United States does not approve of this arrangement to set up a foreign monarchy next door, and it is generally believed that troops will be sent to drive the foreigners out.[12] Colonel Davis told me that if any troops are sent, our division is sure to go, and I hope we may.

May 28th, 1865

Went to church with Byrnes and Carruthers, the Episcopal Church that Jeff Davis attended, and in the pew in front of us was General Lee. I recognized him from pictures I have seen of him, and was so much interested in looking at the man who had held us off for four years, I did not give much attention to the sermon. He had a sad, careworn face.[13]

May 29th, 1865

The Corps badge of our Twenty-fourth Corps is a heart, red for the First Division, white for the Second, and blue for the Third. Our

Division was reviewed this evening by General Gibbon, the Corps Commander, and there was a big crowd of officers and ladies and gentlemen from the city to see the "Red Heart Division", as it is called, which made a fine appearance, as it has always done.[14]

June 3rd, 1865

After dinner this evening, rode with the General and some of his staff over to see a review of the Second Division, and were entertained with the usual hospitality.

June 6th, 1865

Colonel Davis and I went to look at some horses that had just arrived at the corral. I liked the looks of a gray very much, but they tell me he is balky and tricky, but I think I will try him tomorrow.

June 7th, 1865

Rode in town in the morning and called on some Lowell friends. Like my gray horse very well, but he is green. Was back in time for lunch, and read all the afternoon until dinner, after which rode with the General and staff over the river to Manchester to see a review of the Third Division. Met an old Lowell friend, Colonel Donohoe, who commands one of the brigades.[15] My gray acted badly at the review and backed me into and through a group of officers, in spite of my efforts, and liberal use of spurs. Felt pretty cheap, but think I can break him of his bad habits. I fancy the numerous reviews we are having are to keep up discipline, which under the present conditions is getting a little lax.

June 10th, 1865

Rode over to Corps Headquarters this morning on business for the General. A review of the Corps is ordered for this evening, and Major Byrnes and I were directed to start ahead and form the Division line. Rode up and down Broad Street from one end of the line to the other several times, and as it was raining hard, was getting well soaked, when an aide from Corps Headquarters rode up and told us the review was postponed. Rode back to General Osborn and gave him the information, then a lot of us went to the Spottswood, and remained until the rain ceased.

June 11th, 1865

After dinner Captain Frye and I rode around the suburbs of the city, and enjoyed the ride very much. The view from the bluff, opposite Belle Isle, is magnificent. We rode through Hollywood Cemetery, which is the most beautiful I have ever seen.

June 13th, 1865

The Grand Review of the Twenty-fourth Corps by General Gibbon came off today, and it certainly was a grand review, between ten and twelve thousand men, with the batteries—all seasoned veterans. It was a magnificent spectacle. After the review there were presentations of medals, and then we were invited to Corps Headquarters, where refreshments were served in the shape of crackers, cheese, salt fish and a most insidious punch. Being very tired and thirsty, I took more of the punch than I realized, and have no idea how I got back to camp. It was the first and only time I was ever in such a condition.

June 14th, 1865

Felt decidedly used up this morning. The staff have the laugh on me, for according to all accounts I must have been pretty well "set up". Some of the staff were, however, in equally bad shape, or worse, and did not get to camp at all last night. We have found out that the punch was made of mixed liquors, well sweetened, and "doctored" for the special purpose of knocking out the division staff, and it succeeded. Shall fight shy of mixed drinks in the future.

June 15th, 1865

Accompanied the General to the First and Third Brigade. Was out till lunch. We are going to lose Major Waddell, Judge Advocate, who has resigned, and I am sorry. I like him very much. Colonel Davis told me tonight he was going to appoint me to Waddell's place, and I am scared blue, for I know very little about court martials, and told the

Colonel so, but he said he had guaranteed that I will fill the position, and now I must not go back on him, so I suppose I will have to take it, but have many misgivings. Major Waddell turned over to me a copy of "Benet on Courts Martial", a pretty good sized volume, with the contents of which I am supposed to become familiar.[16] Some studying for me, I reckon.

June 21st, 1865

Have been quite busy lately helping Major Sawyer examine the rolls of the regiments of the division, and he was glad to accept my offer of assistance. He is a fine fellow, and I quite enjoy going with him and visiting the different commands. We have regiments from Maine, Massachusetts, Connecticut, New York, Pennsylvania, Ohio and Illinois, and it is interesting to see the different ways of doing things. Received today the order appointing me Judge Advocate of the Division, quite an honor, but I have fears as to my ability in that line. Will have to put in all my time studying Benet, as a court is to be convened in a few days, and my first case will be that of a commissioned officer, Captain Botsford of the 39th Illinois, who is charged with misbehaving one night in a theater, or as Benet requires the charge to read, "conduct unbecoming an officer and gentleman".[17] He is to be defended by counsel, and I don't fancy the prospect of having to contend with a lawyer. I find that a Judge Advocate is a prosecuting officer and counsel for the defense, all in one. All questions to witnesses are put through him, and he must keep a record of them and the answers. The whole object of a court martial is simply to get the exact facts without any quibbling or bulldozing of witnesses, as occurs in ordinary courts, and to give an impartial verdict.

June 24th, 1865

The court met today, but the place of meeting not being satisfactory, we adjourned until the day after tomorrow. Was busy enough all day conferring with Captain Botsford, summoning his witnesses, and making up the case. Went to church last evening.

June 26th, 1865

The court met this morning, and I was considerably nervous, but went to work, bound to make a success or a glorious failure. Things went better than I expected, and the President of the Court, Colonel McArthur, told me I did first rate.[18] We adjourned at three o'clock, and I was greatly relieved.

June 29th, 1865

After three tiresome days, the case of Captain Botsford was finished this afternoon, and court adjourned to July 1st.

June 30th, 1865

Was busy all day writing up the record of the Botsford case, as my clerk is no good as such, and will have to find another somewhere. Have a tent all to my self now, and like it. Colonel Davis came to my tent today and laid fifty dollars on my desk, telling me to use it until I got my pay. This was mighty kind, as I am broke.

July 3rd, 1865

Since the Botsford case, have tried several enlisted men, mostly on minor charges, and feel quite encouraged after my experience of a week. Think I have done fairly well and guess I can run things all right now. Tonight there was a "Grand Ball" given by the leader of the *Demi Monde* of Richmond, and a lot of us went out of curiosity, and to see the fun. There were a lot of officers present, and a crowd of "cits" from town. The "ladies" were all of a kind, and the whole affair "laid over" anything in my experience. In one particular it certainly was unique, for the Provost Marshal fearing there might be trouble between some of the Union officers and ex-Confederates present, had stationed guards in uniform with rifles at intervals around the hall to preserve order. It was something new to me in the way of balls, and I soon got enough and left for camp. On the way back, my horse stumbled and fell and I came near to getting an ugly fall, as I was going quite fast, but escaped with a shaking up and a few bruises.

July 4th, 1865

Went in town in the morning with the General and staff to the Spottswood Hotel. We went up on the roof where a large flag was raised. We had a band and lots of champagne. General Osborn made a very good speech. Went back to lunch and then laid down, but it was too hot to sleep. In the evening went in town to see some fireworks, but they were nothing much.

July 5th, 1865

At court as usual, but tried only one case. Colonel Davis' wife and friend, Mrs. Milward, arrived at headquarters today. After dinner was sent to the First and Third Brigades with orders for bands for tomorrow, when we are all going down river to meet General Foster, who is coming back to resume command.

July 6th, 1865

The General and staff went to Richmond early this morning, stopped at the Spottswood to pick up Morrison of the *New York Herald*, then went on board a steamer that had been engaged and started for a landing some distance down the river to wait for General Foster's boat. There were some fifty officers of our division in the party, two bands, and a number of baskets of wine. Mrs. Davis and Mrs. Milward were with us. While waiting at the landing, I noticed Colonel Davis, out one side, in earnest conversation with a crippled and dilapidated looking man in Confederate uniform. After a while the Colonel beckoned to me and others of the party whom he knew to be Masons, and told us he had found the man to be a distressed and destitute brother Mason on his way to find his family near Petersburg. We took up a subscription and the old fellow was made happy, with more good money than he had ever seen before, I reckon, and an order for transportation to Petersburg. When General Foster arrived, we took him on our boat and started back for Richmond. Mrs. Foster is with the General and is a very charming woman, and I like much the appearance of the General. There were many healths drunk on the way back, but everybody kept within bounds. I had a delightful trip, and arrived at headquarters about dark.

July 20th, 1865

The last few weeks have been busy ones for me, at court a good part of each weekday, and the rest of the time, including Sundays, studying cases, looking up witnesses, interviewing prisoners in Libby

General Robert Sanford Foster, 1865,
Centerville Historical Society Archives.

to see that they were furnished with copies of the charges against them, and what witnesses they wanted summoned. The court finished the last case today and adjourned for good. I was hoping to have a little leisure, but at night received an order detailing me as Recorder of a Board of Inquiry, to investigate the death of a man of the 89th New York, who was killed a few nights since by a sentinel.

July 25th, 1865

Early in the morning started with Majors Sellmer and Carruthers and Captain Frye to visit the battle field at Fair Oaks.[19] Was able to locate the position occupied by my old regiment, the Twenty-ninth, in '62. There is little change and the elaborate entrenchments are almost intact. We rode to where General Foster's division was camped last winter and other places of interest and covered considerable ground. Stopped at several houses for food, melons, fruit, etc. Got back to camp about six, after a rather hard, but very pleasant day. Was quite tired and a little stiff and sore, and my neck is badly sunburned. We rode some thirty odd miles.

July 30th, 1865

Received an order today detailing me for Recorder of a Military Commission for tomorrow.

August 3rd, 1865

Captain Frye and I have been running headquarters mess, alternately, each taking it a week, but as Frye has gone home on leave, I will now have it all the time. At first did not fancy getting up at five o'clock every morning and going to market, but now I really enjoy the gallop in the cool morning air, and it is fun to watch the crowd and the colored people. All kinds and classes are there. One morning I rubbed against Ex-Governor Wise, and the next minute was jostled by a big, fat colored "mammy".[20] I have the ambulance take the servants, with baskets and pans, and like going around buying meat, fish, vegetables and fruit. In the evening played poker with General Foster and some of the staff, using beans for chips. I dropped about a hundred dollars, in beans, and had lots of fun.

August 4th, 1865

An order from the War Department, providing for the mustering out of certain General officers was received today and we were all very blue as this means that General Foster will soon be discharged and the staff and division broken up. I do not want to go on duty with the regiment, if I can help it.

August 9th, 1865

General Foster told me today he had recommended me to General Turner, whose division is to remain here, as Aide-de-Camp, for which I am very grateful.[21] Went in town in the forenoon and while there met

Colonel Edmands, who said he wanted me for Adjutant of the Twenty-fourth as soon as General Foster left. In the evening went in and played a few games of billiards.

August 10th, 1865

General Foster told me this morning that Colonel Edmands was over to see me last night and wants me for Adjutant. Am very much in doubt as to what I had better do, accept Colonel Edmands' offer, or go on General Turner's staff. In evening, was in town and saw the Colonel, who invited me to a dinner tomorrow evening.

August 11th, 1865

Went to market as usual this morning, and after breakfast had to go in town again on business. The rest of the day took things easy, it was so hot. In the evening went with Dr. Barlow and Major Sawyer to the Twenty-fourth headquarters and dined with Colonel Edmands, and the dinner was fine, one of the best I have ever eaten. After dinner, we went out and saw Dress Parade, which was excellent. Had a good talk with the Colonel, and told him I felt it to be a rather delicate situation for me to go to the regiment as Adjutant, being an outsider and having seen no service with it, and that I felt the position belonged to one of the regimental officers, but he said none of them cared to take it, and told me to talk with them, which I did and they all urged me to take the position. I could not quite make up my mind, but promised to decide tomorrow. Had a delightful evening.

August 12th, 1865

Decided to accept Colonel Edmands' offer to appoint me Adjutant, and notified him of my decision. Will try it a while and if I don't like it, can go on General Turner's staff. In the morning accompanied General Foster to the city, returning for lunch. In the evening went in to the Spottswood and played billiards.

August 13th, 1865

A very blue day for us all, for General Foster leaves tomorrow and the staff will be broken up. Life on the staff has been exceedingly pleasant and I have enjoyed it very much. Everybody from the General down has been nice to me. The quarters are comfortable and pleasantly located. The mess congenial and jolly, and we have had a band to play evenings while we were at dinner. Staff duty, particularly with a Corps or Division, is the poetry of military life, and although in active service it would be harder and things would not be so pleasant, yet if there is another war, I will try for a staff position.

August 14th, 1865

Early in the morning, all the staff went in town and to the boat to see General and Mrs. Foster off. Had breakfast in town and then went to the Spottswood and stayed a while. In the evening a lot of officers came over and there was a very lively time. We buried the big headquarters demijohn, with imposing ceremonies. Morrison of the *New York Herald* delivered the eulogy, and I was undertaker. The band played a dirge and all joined hands and circled around the "grave". It was a decidedly convivial occasion, and some were pretty well soaked, but I managed to keep out of the worst of it, as did our staff.

August 15th, 1865

Was in town a short time in the morning, then came back and packed up. I will report to Colonel Edmands tomorrow. Tonight received an order to report to General Turner for duty as Judge Advocate of a General Court Martial.

August 16th, 1865

Reported to Colonel Edmands this morning, and he issued an order appointing me Adjutant, although I can not go on duty as such, until I am relieved from the Court Martial. The regiment is nicely quartered in wooden barracks, and the Colonel has a building with quarters and office for himself, and room for the two Surgeons and the Adjutant. Am much better pleased with all the arrangements here than I expected, and am sure I will like it. Could not find the Judge Advocate I am to relieve, so could not get copies of the charges I am to try. In evening, played *Vingt et un* with the Colonel and Surgeons.

August 17th, 1865

Received the copies of the charges to be tried by the Court, but

First Lieutenant Augustus D. Ayling as adjutant of the 24th Massachusetts
Volunteers, 1865. Centerville Historical Society Archives.

could not do anything today as I must have time to prepare them. Rode
in town with Captain Stoddard, my predecessor as Adjutant.[22] He is
a fine fellow and I like him much. Called on Colonel Davis, who is now,
since the division was broken up, Adjutant General of the District of
Henrico, which includes Richmond. He is to have a horse sent to me
from the corral, and will give me a mounted orderly.

August 18th, 1865

The Court met and I tried one case. Got along all right, and rather enjoy the duty. Was busy after adjournment interviewing prisoners in Libby, Castle Thunder and the city jail.[23] I have a lot of cases to be tried, and don't know when I will finish them. Colonel Edmands has had some gymnastic apparatus fixed up, and evenings we exercise on the flying rings, and horizontal and parallel bars.

August 19th, 1865

No court today, but I was busy enough. The horse sent me from the corral is no good, and if I can find one that suits me, will buy.

August 21st, 1865

No quorum at court today, and I was glad as it gives me more time to get cases ready. Captain Reynolds of the court is going to bring over a mare tomorrow for me to try, and if I like her, may buy.[24] Don't like the corral stock.

August 22nd, 1865

Managed to get the court to try two cases today. Captain Reynolds brought over a beautiful mare for me to try. She belongs to an ex-officer of Fitzhugh Lee's rebel cavalry.[25] After court, rode her to the city and like her very much. The price is $125.00, and everybody says buy, and I think I will after trying her a little more.

August 24th, 1865

Gave the mare a good trial yesterday, and am much pleased with her. After lunch Colonel Edmands and I rode to town and over to Manchester to see her owner. He warrants her to be sound and free from tricks, and perfectly broken to the saddle, but never had a harness on her. He felt bad to part with her, when I decided to take her, saying she was a pet, and tears came to his eyes when he said, "Good bye, Mollie."

August 25th, 1865

Tried some cases in the forenoon and we then adjourned. It is so hot the court gets enough of it by noon, and usually adjourns. In the afternoon rode in town with Captain Stoddard, who has been, and is still acting as Adjutant, while I am on Court Martial duty. He is a good chum, and

I like him much. Tomorrow we go to town to escort the 10th Connecticut to the boat, as they are going home. I am to go as Adjutant as Stoddard wants to go in command of his company. Colonel Edmands and I are invited to the 8th Maine for next tuesday evening.

August 26th, 1865

At eight o'clock this morning, I formed the regiment and we marched in to Richmond where we met the 10th Connecticut and escorted them to the boat they are to take on their way home. It was a perfect day, the 24th looked and marched splendidly, and I was proud to be Adjutant of such a regiment. My Mollie behaved finely, and the occasion was very enjoyable. In the evening, rode with the Colonel over to the 4th Massachusetts Cavalry on business, and on returning to camp had our usual game of cards.

August 29th, 1865

At court in the morning, after which had to go to town. This court business keeps me on the jump, but I like to be busy. In the evening, Colonel Edmands took the regimental band and glee club to Manchester to visit Colonel True of the 8th Maine as per invitation.[26] There were lots of young ladies present, and I had a very good time. Got home about twelve.

August 30th, 1865

Went in town to see the 11th Maine escort the 100th New York to the boat, and we rode to the landing with them. They made a good appearance, but no regiment here can compare with the 24th. Court adjourned at noon as usual, and in the afternoon took a rest and read and slept until dinner. In the evening was busy with court matters.

September 1st, 1865

After lunch rode in town and met Colonel Davis who told me there were some Lowell people, George Pray, who was enlisted in the same company with me in '61, and the Misses Howe, sisters of another comrade, were at the Ballard Hotel. In the evening, called on them with Colonel Davis and had a very pleasant time. They were intending to go home tomorrow, but we prevailed upon them to stop one more day and promised them a serenade for tomorrow evening by our band.

September 2nd, 1865

Tried but one case today. After lunch went in town and arranged for Colonel Davis and the Lowell party to go to camp immediately after dinner. Called at the Ballard and was invited to dine with Pray and the ladies. After dinner Colonel Davis took the party in a carriage and started for camp. I rode Mollie and all thought she was a beauty, and she certainly is a very fine animal. Every time I ride her I like her better. We went directly to the parade ground to see the dress parade, which was fine, as usual. Then we went to the quarters and met Colonel Edmands. The party returned to town about eight o'clock, the Colonel and I following and taking the regimental band, which we stationed on the bridge over the street connecting the two sections of the Ballard where it gave some very beautiful music, which was much enjoyed by our party, the guests of the hotel and others. Our band is a remarkably fine one, and was organized and drilled by P. S. Gilmore, the celebrated band leader, and is largely supported by the regimental officers, although the members are all enlisted men, carried on the rolls as company musicians.[27] We got back to camp about half past eleven, after a very delightful evening.

September 8th, 1865

The past week has been an unusually busy one, with court each day, riding all over the district hunting up witnesses, and getting cases ready for trial. Have had lots of writing to do evenings, but have managed to have some good games of whist, euchre, etc. with the Colonel and Drs. Wheeler and Parsons, our Surgeons.[28] I go in to market at five o'clock mornings with Colonel Edmands. When we get back we exercise on the horizontal bar, then after a bath, am ready for breakfast with a good appetite. I find I have not forgotten some of the stunts I used to do in the gymnasium in Lowell. Orders came today dissolving the Court Martial and appointing a new one, with Colonel True as President and me as Judge Advocate. The people at headquarters must be satisfied with my work, I think, by the way I am kept at it. There is one good thing about it. I get a dollar and a quarter a day extra pay. I am much pleased to have Colonel True as President in place of Colonel Hardenburg, the President of the last court, whom I did not like.[29] He was a Pennsylvania Dutchman or German, who thinks he knows it all. I had to object to his ruling several times and when I quoted Benet to show he was wrong, he did not like it a bit. Colonel True is a different kind of man. One of the pioneers of the regiment, a first class carpenter, has made for me a desk of black walnut, and it was a surprise, and a very pleasant one.

September 9th, 1865

Rode in town this morning with Stoddard, and called on Colonel Davis who told me Will Farrar, who was 1st Lieutenant of the company in which I enlisted in '61, was to be here in a few days.[30] Will be glad to see him. He is a good friend of mine. In the evening, rode to Rockets with Dr. Wheeler to look at a horse he thinks of buying. Made up and sent to headquarters the last of the cases tried by me before the old court.

September 10th, 1865

Stoddard and I went to the city on court business this morning. Have had thirty new cases turned over to me and guess I have all I can do this month. Was busy all the afternoon, and in the evening the Colonel, Surgeons, and I had a comb concert.

September 16th, 1865

Have been awfully busy the past week with the new cases, some of which are pretty serious, such as murder, rape, highway robbery, etc. I like Colonel True as President of the court. He helps me instead of bothering, as Hardenburg did. While in town this morning, met Billy Farrar and Mr. Hosford of Lowell. Was right glad to see them, especially Billy, who is an old friend. Dined with them at the Spottswood.

September 17th, 1865

Sunday and no court. Rode in town to see some witnesses, and met Colonel Davis, who invited me to go with him and the Lowell party to see Fort Darling and Drewry's Bluff, two former rebel strongholds.[31] We took a tug at Rocket's Landing and went down to the Bluff and then to

Richmond, Virginia, 1865. Mathew Brady photo, from *Mr. Lincoln's Camera Man,* 1946. Reprinted by permission of Russell & Volkening.

the Fort and examined the strong works the rebels had constructed to command the river and approach to Richmond by water. It was a very pleasant and interesting trip. Got back to camp about three, and read until dinner. In the evening Colonel Edmands called with me to see Farrar, but could not find him at the Spottswood or Ballard.

September 18th, 1865

We had Colonel Davis, Farrar and Hosford out to dinner this evening, and to see the parade. A very pleasant time.

September 19th, 1865

Got the court to adjourn at eleven and went to town. Had an ambulance for Farrar and Hosford, and I rode my pet, Mollie. Took them over to Manchester, to Libby, Castle Thunder and other places of interest. Dined with them at the Spottswood.

September 22nd, 1865

One of the tailors in Richmond has a lot of gray homespun cloth made for the rebel government, and all the officers are having suits made from it. I was measured today for a suit and it will be just the thing to wear when I go home. It is very cheap too at $19.50 for a whole suit.

September 23rd, 1865

After lunch rode to Manchester with Colonel Edmands to see the 4th Massachusetts Cavalry reviewed by General Terry.[32]

September 24th, 1865

Sunday, so had no court to attend. After breakfast, took the ambulance, which, with its fine pair of horses, is our headquarters carriage, and took Dr. and Mrs. Wheeler and Dr. Parsons to Fair Oaks and showed where my regiment was camped in '62, and found the tree, close by our camp, into which railroad spikes were driven, where we used to watch the captain of a battery climb to direct the fire of his guns. We drove out to Savage's Station, but I could not locate the position of the 29th. We returned to Fair Oaks and drove over to Gaines's Mill, which was familiar ground, and then to Mechanicsville, where the first of the Seven Days Battles was fought. Got back just in time for dinner. A delightful, but rather tiresome day.

Chapter 17

LAST DAYS IN RICHMOND

Ayling continued duty in Richmond with the double responsibility of adjutant of his regiment and judge advocate, trying
court martial cases. He was mustered out of the service on
January 20, 1866, and returned to Lowell, Massachusetts.

September 26th, 1865

In the evening Colonel Edmands, Dr. Parsons and I went in to the
theater, but neither the play, "The Streets of New York", nor the ac-
tors amounted to much. Lieutenant North, our Quartermaster, returned from leave today.[1] Can't say I am particularly delighted, for
he is the only one of the Field and Staff I very much dislike.

September 29th, 1865

Felt as if I had a chill coming on this morning. Dr. Wheeler gave me five
grains of quinine and after lying down a while, felt better. In the evening,
Captain Wiley and I talked Masonry.[2] We are going to visit one of the Richmond Lodges next week if we can get in after being examined.

October 1st, 1865

Dr. Parsons and I went to church this morning, the one in which Patrick
Henry delivered his celebrated speech.[3] It was very interesting, and as I sat
in the old fashioned pew I thought of the exciting time when the old walls
had echoed with the eloquent words which aroused his hearers to action.

October 2nd, 1865

Colonel True was taken ill in court and we had to adjourn. Put him in bed in my quarters until he felt better. Commenced to run the mess this morning, and will continue through the month.

October 3rd, 1865

In the evening, Captain Wiley and I walked to town and visited Richmond Lodge No. 10, to which we were admitted after a proper examination. Enjoyed the meeting very much. The bretheren were all in the Confederate gray, and we in the Union Blue. It was a very peculiar situation. We were treated first rate, and nothing was said or done to show anything but the kindliest brotherly feeling toward us. Such is Masonry, for only a few months ago, they would have been glad to shoot us, as we would to shoot them. It was a fine night and Wiley and I enjoyed our walk home.

October 4th, 1865

A cold, disagreeable day. After court, had a fire in the fireplace in my quarters and sat by it the rest of the day. Have been bothered and delayed in trying cases recently by the absence of members of the court, on account of sickness, or for some other reason. I am beginning to feel that I want to get through with court and take up my duties as Adjutant.

October 11th, 1865

The usual routine the past week. Trying cases where there are enough members present and evenings in town playing billiards, or at camp playing cards. Felt this morning as if I was going to have a chill and Dr. Wheeler gave me five grains of quinine. After lying down a while felt better. The Colonel was to have battalion drill this afternoon and I was going out as Adjutant, but it was postponed. Bought a pair of trousers at $18.50, pretty steep.

October 12th, 1865

I have been told that Mollie is of running stock, and I thought I would try her, so after dinner, rode her to the racetrack near camp, and let her go around once. She surely can run.

October 13th, 1865

This afternoon went out on battalion drill as Adjutant, and felt very nervous and awkward. It is a long time since I have seen a drill, and I never had any experience in equalizing companies, which is quite a job, and must be done quickly and on the field. Managed to get along fairly well and the Colonel spoke encouragingly. Am glad the ice is broken; will not dread it so much next time.

October 16th, 1865

No court. Members absent. Rode over to the camp of the 12th Infantry U.S. Army, some four or five miles on court business, and had a pleasant time with the army officers. In afternoon, went on battalion drill. Rather like it. In the evening, went with a lot of the line officers to town in the ambulance. Captains White, Wiley and I visited Richmond Lodge again, receiving the same courteous treatment as before.[4] After the Lodge we joined the rest of the officers at the "Magnolia", where we were all invited to a supper at eleven. We left at one o'clock, and as we were about to start for camp, the military police seized our ambulance in accordance with orders to take any U.S. ambulance standing in front of a public house after eleven o'clock. Wiley and I walked to camp. The others went to police headquarters and after some trouble, got the ambulance released.

October 17th, 1865

In the evening, Captain Wiley and I visited Richmond Randolph Lodge No. 19 and had a good time. When the Lodge was closed, we were invited to a collation and to come again.

October 23rd, 1865

While at court this forenoon, was called out, and found my friend Eli Hoyt and wife from Lowell. Sent my orderly with them to my quarters where I joined them as soon as court adjourned. Went with them out on Mechanicsville Pike to see the strong works made by the rebels to defend Richmond. They returned to the city and I joined them later and dined with them at the Spottswood, and remaining until they left for Washington. Tried to get them to stay a day longer and dine at camp, but they had to go.

October 25th, 1865

After court, rode in to Richmond to interview a Miss Virginia Crenshaw, one of the "F.F.V's" who alleges she was knocked from her horse by a drunken cavalryman.[5] Was treated with cold politeness, which was all I expected. Am to try the case tomorrow.

October 26th, 1865

Finished the Crenshaw case and when we adjourned, I had but two cases to try and was congratulating myself when I received a batch of thirteen new cases. Was not much pleased, but suppose it is all right. Was on battalion drill today, and like it more and more.

October 30th, 1865

No court. Too many members absent. In the evening with Captains White and Wiley, went to a Masonic Lodge we had not visited, Henrico Union Lodge No. 130. Nearly all the members in the Confederate gray as in the other Lodges, and we three in the Union blue. We had a delightful time. When the Master closed the Lodge, he requested all to remain seated, informally. This gave us an opportunity to have a good talk with some of the members regarding their service, the fights they were in, etc. After a while the Marshall was directed to form the line for the banquet hall, and we were escorted to a nice collation of oysters, hot coffee, etc. The particularly kind and fraternal feeling shown us by all the Masonic bodies was made more impressive from the fact that all the Lodges were heavily draped in black in memory of the District Deputy Grand Master, a very old man, who was killed one night a short time since by one of our sentinels, who challenged, and the old man being deaf probably did not hear the challenge, and the sentry fired. It was a most unfortunate affair and must have caused much feeling in Richmond as well as among the Masonic fraternity, but no unkind allusion to it was made or any feelings of resentment shown us in any way. Surely the Masons of Richmond have the true Masonic spirit.

October 31st, 1865

Finished my tour of duty as caterer, and will not have to get up so early mornings. I commence tomorrow to mount guard, and form for dress parade. Am not obliged to while on court duty, but it will please Colonel Edmands. Must confess I dread it some.

November 1st, 1865

Mounted guard this morning and was a little nervous, but got along all right. Was at court in the forenoon, and commenced to try thirteen mutineers of the 67th Ohio. In evening went on dress parade, and was so nervous I could hardly speak, but thank goodness the worst of it is over, and I will not dread it so much the next time.

November 3rd, 1865

Cold, with rain, but not enough to prevent Guard Mount. Captain Stoddard turned over to me the property of the Adjutant's office, and has been relieved as acting Adjutant. I will be pretty full of business now as the court is still running. In evening played "Loo" with the doctors.

November 7th, 1865

Received orders today to finish up and send in all the cases I have tried, and all cases untried, when the court will be dissolved. Am glad, as I will not be so confined.

November 8th, 1865

Rode over to the 11th Maine on business and was invited to dinner by Major Adams.[6] In the evening, went with Dr. Parsons and Quartermaster Dadd to the Casino and from there to a "Rag Masquerade" in Locust Alley.[7] Pretty tough!

November 10th, 1865

Captain Stoddard has been appointed Judge Advocate of a court and I went with him to the various prisons to see prisoners and post him up on some of the business.

November 12th, 1865

After dinner rode in town with Dr. Wheeler to see Captain Foster, whom we hear has been hurt by a fall from his horse. He is painfully, but not seriously injured.[8]

November 13th, 1865

J. C. Ayer & Company have sent me an account against Purcell, Ladd & Company, wholesale druggists of Richmond, for goods bought before the war, asking me to see if I can collect anything. Called on them today, but could get no satisfaction. Guess they are pretty hard up.

November 17th, 1865

Major Carruthers and Lieutenant North are boarding at a house nearby and invited Colonel Edmands and a lot of officers to a party there tonight. There were some young ladies present, but the affair was like all others of the kind here, still and formal. Our Glee Club gave several songs, and was the best part of the "show". Met there the former Adjutant of the 12th Mississippi Confederate Regiment. He seemed to be a very good fellow and we had a nice chat about our service.

November 19th, 1865

Sunday. The Reverend Mr. Clark of the Christian Commission held service at the quarters today. He preached a short sermon on The Lord's Supper, which was very fine indeed, and did me good.

November 22nd, 1865

Beautiful weather. Rode in town and around the suburbs, just for the pleasure of riding. In the evening, the Colonel and I went to Pizzini's, where we have been all summer for ices, and now go for oysters. It is a fine restaurant. While there a fire broke out a few blocks away and we rode over and watched it.

November 24th, 1865

Dr. Parsons and I borrowed a light wagon and harness to see how my mare would behave, she never having been harnessed. It was funny to see her trot along a few steps and then stop and look back, as if to say, "What is this arrangement? I don't understand." I would say, "It's all right, Mollie," and at the sound of my voice, she would trot a few steps more. We got to Richmond finally, and coming back she did better. On our way to camp, we were run into by a country team and I went over the dasher, striking on my shoulder, but was not hurt much. Mollie did not run away, and was not frightened.

November 26th, 1865

Wonderfully fine weather. Rode over to say good bye to my friends in the 11th Maine. They leave for Fredericksburg today. In the evening, there were services in the quarters, but not quite so interesting as a week ago.

November 29th, 1865

On getting up this morning was surprised to see the ground covered with snow. We have had such delightful weather lately, the sudden change is very disagreeable. Spent the day overhauling and fixing up the office books and papers.

November 30th, 1865

Rode in town with Colonel Edmands. A beautiful day but sloshy travelling. The Colonel went to a jewelry store for something and I saw a pretty scarf pin, carbuncle, which I bought for $7.00.

December 1st, 1865

Rode in and called on Colonel Davis, who told me he would have to put me on court martial duty again, at District Headquarters, and gave me the order and some cases. The 20th New York left today for Norfolk and we are glad to see them go, for they have been trying hard to have us sent so they might remain here.

December 2nd, 1865

Rode in to court at District Headquarters. Tried four cases, a pretty good day's work.

December 4th, 1865

Wonderfully fine weather for December, like spring. We have doors and windows wide open and go around our quarters without coats or caps. The court finished all the cases and we adjourned *sine die.*[9]

December 5th, 1865

Cold and very disagreeable. Very much a change from yesterday. Wrote Eli Hoyt, ordering for Dr. Wheeler an electric machine to use on Captain Foster's arm, which is quite lame from his accident.

December 7th, 1865

Today is Thanksgiving Day as ordered by Governor Andrew. Rode in town in the morning and played billiards with some officers of the 11th U.S. Infantry. Came back to lunch, and then played cricket with some of the line officers until dinner. We had a big dinner with cocktails, sherry, etc. After dinner, Colonel Edmands read the Governor's proclamation in his inimitable style, and gave a witty talk. We had a jolly good time.

December 11th, 1865

In the afternoon, a lot of us rode to Fairfield Race Course to see a running race, the first of the kind I have seen. Five horses with little colored jockeys, all yelling and shouting. It was quite exciting. Time two minutes and six seconds for the mile.

December 13th, 1865

Rode in town with the Colonel, and arranged with a French gentleman to come to camp and give us, and Drs. Wheeler and Parsons, lessons in French.

December 14th, 1865

In the evening, our French teacher, Captain Blum, came and gave us our first lesson, after which we all sat by the fire smoking and talking. Found that Captain Blum commanded a battery under Longstreet, and in several battles was opposed to us, on the same part of the field as that on which my regiment was placed.

December 19th, 1865

This afternoon our band and one from the city united and gave us a fine concert, which I enjoyed much. We had Colonel Ordway and Major Macomber to dinner and a jolly time.[10] We are still at our French.

December 20th, 1865

My clerk, Washburn, is absent and we fear he has deserted.[11] I am in a peck of trouble, as it will be hard to fill his place, and will put lots of extra work on me.

December 23rd, 1865

Rode in town to get boots and trousers, ordered some time since, and when I got back, found I had lost my pocketbook with all my money. I may have left it at the tailor's. Hope so.

December 25th, 1865

Christmas! Pleasant but muddy travelling. Made a number of calls in town, played a few games of billiards, and had lots of egg-nog. Found my pocketbook at the tailor's and was mighty glad. They have a funny way of celebrating Christmas down here by firing crackers, fireworks, etc. as we do on the Fourth of July. It is a great day for the darkeys.

December 28th, 1865

My clerk came back today and I am very glad. His coming relieves me of much work, and as he was absent but a few days, I will not have him punished.

December 29th, 1865

This evening attended a grand concert at the theater, and it was fine. The music was operatic and classical and I enjoyed it very much. The audience was of the upper class and very swell. Have not seen so much beauty and style since I have been in Richmond. Pratt, of our band, played the accompaniment for Madame Ruhl's songs.[12]

December 31st, 1865

A dull, cheerless day. We had inspection and muster. In the evening, Colonel Edmands and Dr. Parsons were in my quarters, and with the help of some Medical Department brandy, managed to see the old year out in proper form.

January 1st, 1866

The new year did not come in very smilingly. It was cold, dark and stormy, raining all day. There was a report that the negroes were going to rise and smash things tonight, and the whites in Richmond were quite nervous. We put on extra guards, and kept patrols out all night. There was a little excitement on the streets but nothing serious, and the night was fairly quiet. We were all ready to move into the city at once, if necessary.

January 2nd, 1866

We are ordered to go to Norfolk and everybody is blue. We are comfortably fixed here, and if possible would like to remain until mustered out, but orders must be obeyed.

January 7th, 1866

Have been awfully busy the last few days. The order for Norfolk has been countermanded and we are ordered to prepare muster-out rolls, and get ready to start for Massachusetts. Went in town with the Colonel to buy trunks, and in the evening, packed up and am ready to leave at short notice. We were inspected today.

January 8th, 1866

It has been growing cold lately, and today was the coldest yet. Had to go to town on business for the Colonel, and thought my ears would freeze. I assembled the men in one of the barracks, and the Colonel made a nice speech to them about going home. The roof of our quarters caught fire from the chimney tonight, and we came near to being turned out in the cold. All hands rallied to our assistance. I climbed to the roof and with water passed up soon had the fire out.

January 9th, 1866

Rode to District Headquarters with Colonel Edmands and learned that the order for our muster out had been suspended. Was glad. In evening, Dr. Parsons and I went to the Casino but soon left disgusted. Too little fun and too much indecency.

January 10th, 1866

In town with the Colonel, as usual, and found new orders. The order suspending our muster out has been countermanded, and we are to go on and make out the rolls. Colonel Edmands and I have invitations to a ball to be given by the officers of the 11th Infantry U.S.A. on the night of the twelfth. We think we will go.

January 11th, 1866

Attended a concert for the benefit of Stonewall Jackson's widow.[13] All the female rebels were there, of course.

January 12th, 1866

Went to headquarters for instructions this morning and we are not to be mustered out until we arrive in Boston, but are to have the rolls all ready. We are to start a week from today. At night Colonel Edmands and I attended the 11th Infantry ball, arriving about nine o'clock. The dancing was in one of the barracks, which was tastefully decorated with swords, rifles, bayonets and flags. We had a fine supper and an elegant time. Danced eight or ten times and got back to camp about four in the morning.

January 14th, 1866

Rode in to headquarters with the Colonel on business. They are trying to get us off in three days, but I don't see how it can be done with so many rolls and other papers to be made out, property turned over, and many other things incidental to the final discharge to be done.

January 15th, 1866

An awfully mean day, cold with snow and sleet. Had to go in town on business, but did not enjoy it much.

January 16th, 1866

Pleasant but very bad travelling. Did not have to go to town, for a wonder, and was glad. Colonel Terry, Inspector General, was here all day inspecting our books and papers.[14]

January 18th, 1866

My mare is not feeling quite right, but we have given her medicine, and think she will be well before we start for home. Have sent word to have her sharp shod. Had to go to town twice. In the evening, rode one of the team horses, and in the afternoon the Quartermaster Sergeant's horse. Not much like Mollie, either of them.

January 19th, 1866

The "powers that be" have changed their minds once more, and we are to be mustered out tomorrow. Was in Major Martin's office three hours this morning, then came back and packed everything but blankets. Have had a lively time the past two weeks with rolls, clothing accounts, invoices and receipts for our headquarters and band, and in addition showing the line officers how to make their rolls and papers. Have had to go in town once or twice every day and have discovered that there are occasions when an Adjutant is a very useful as well as busy member of the regimental staff, and has many details to attend to and look out for.

January 20th, 1866

Major Martin came to camp this morning and mustered us out. At three in the afternoon, we marched to Rocket's Landing and went on board the "City of Albany". Mollie absolutely refused to be led down on to the boat, but when I mounted her, she went down the steep planks all right without trouble. We did not get away until nearly dark and the captain did not dare attempt to run by the obstructions in the river in the dark, so anchored off City Point for the night.

January 21st, 1866

On the boat all day. Will not get to Baltimore until tomorrow morning. Passed the time very pleasantly, as I always do on the water.

January 22nd, 1866

Arrived at Baltimore in the morning and went with Colonel Edmands across the basin to see the Quartermaster about transportation, then got the regiment off the boat and marched to the Philadelphia depot and took the cars. Arrived in Philadelphia after dark. Marched across the city to the ferry, which we crossed and took cars on the Camden and Amboy Railroad for New York. Travelled all night and managed to get a little uneasy sleep.

January 23rd, 1866

Did not reach New York until afternoon. Had to be sidetracked pretty often for the regular trains, but passed a very pleasant day. The regiment went to Battery Barracks, and Colonel Edmands and I went up town and had a lunch. At four o'clock we went on board the "Empire State". The Colonel took me with him into his stateroom, and the captain of the boat invited us to take supper with him. I find travelling as Adjutant is quite different from travelling as a line officer. In the evening, we had our band and Glee Club in the saloon, and the passengers were much pleased with the music.

January 24th, 1866

We arrived in Boston about eight and marched to Boylston Hall where we had a collation, after which we marched to Commercial Wharf and took a boat for Gallop's Island where the regiment was put into barracks. This island may be all right in the summer, but it is a mighty cold, bleak, desolate place in January. We may have to stay here several days for the officers to make out the discharges and other papers. After we got things all straightened out and the men as comfortably fixed as possible, the Colonel gave me leave to go to Boston. On the way up town, met Harry Braden, formerly of the 29th, who invited me to spend the night at his home in Washington Village. He had some young people there and we had a pleasant time.

January 25th, 1866

A hard snow storm. Went to the wharf and found that the boat for the island had started out on account of the storm, and there would be no other boat today. Went to the Custom House and called on Colonel Barnes and had a good chat. Met George Long also of the 29th, who invited me to his house in Charlestown for the night.

January 26th, 1866

Got the boat for Gallop's all right this morning, and found everything all right. The regiment was paid today, all but the officers who are to get their pay in Boston, a queer arrangement. Was quite busy all day on various duties.

January 27th, 1866

At half past ten the regiment left the island for the city, and with the Cadets as escort, marched to the State House and turned over our colors to Governor Bullock, then marched to Faneuil Hall, where a very fine collation was served and lots of speeches made. We certainly had a good reception. The 24th is the last Massachusetts regiment to be mustered out, and we were told we have had one of the biggest receptions given any regiment. I was quite proud to ride through the streets of Boston as Adjutant with Colonel Edmands. Saw Uncle Henry with Bert and Arthur on the sidewalk as we passed. After the regiment was dismissed, went to the Adams House with some of the officers for a while, and to Uncle Henry's for the night, and had a pleasant time.

January 27th, 1866

This ends my three years and eight months of military service. There have been times that were pretty hard, and many that were very pleasant, particularly the past eight months. I enjoyed much my duties as Aide de Camp and Judge Advocate on General Foster's Staff, and my service in the 24th Regiment, as Adjutant, has been delightful as it naturally would be with a commander like Colonel Edmands. The relations of an Adjutant with his chief should be intimate, confidential and in every way pleasant. Mine with him have certainly been exceedingly pleasant. He is not only a thoroughbred gentleman and splendid officer, but one of the most lovable men I have ever met. I will always have a warm affection for Colonel Tom Edmands.

January 28th, 1866

Was at the Adams House, where most of the officers are staying, a good part of the day. We are all invited to Colonel Edmands' tomorrow evening, and it is proposed to make the Colonel a present of a fine watch and the officers asked me to receive the subscriptions and buy the watch. Was at Uncle Henry's for the night.

January 29th, 1866

Was around town during the day and in the evening all the officers met at the Adams House and took carriages for Colonel Edmands' house, where we received a cordial welcome from the Colonel and his sisters. Major Macomber presented the watch, taking the Colonel absolutely by surprise. We had a fine supper and the affair was very pleasant, but we all felt pretty blue at having to sever the relations that have been so pleasant. Stayed at the Adams House for the night, and will go to Lowell tomorrow to see about getting to work again. Will leave Mollie here for a few days, and come down and ride her back. Have arranged with my friend, Eli Hoyt, to keep her in his stable for a while. Will miss Mollie and my daily rides when I sell her, as of course, I must. There have been few days in the past eight months when I have not ridden from five to fifteen or twenty miles, and it has been a great pleasure. I want to put off as long as possible the day when I must say, "Vale Mollie".

Epilogue

After being mustered out of the service in January 1866, Augustus Ayling was once more employed by the J. C. Ayer Company of Lowell, but he took residence in Nashua, New Hampshire, and operated from there as a traveling wholesale distributor for the company. In that capacity he came to Centerville on Cape Cod, and while there met his future wife, Elizabeth Cornish, daughter of John F. Cornish, a captain of a coastal vessel.

Elizabeth Cornish was the niece of Sarah Cornish Crosby and lived close by Crosby House, a residence and small hotel owned by Gorham Crosby, who was my wife's great-grandfather. While in Centerville, Ayling stayed at Crosby House and there met Elizabeth, whom he eventually married in Centerville on December 22, 1869. It thus happens that my wife, Melvina Crosby Herberger, is distantly related to Elizabeth Cornish, Augustus Ayling's wife, and preserved family letters and memories have provided me with some personal accounts of Ayling's courtship and of his retirement years in Centerville.[1]

While in Nashua, Ayling joined the New Hampshire National Guard and was commissioned as a first lieutenant, Company F, 2nd Regiment, on October 23, 1877. On July 1, 1879, he was promoted to the rank of Captain with the same regiment.[2] His exceptional abilities as an officer and organizer were recognized, and accordingly Governor Nathaniel Head of New Hampshire appointed him adjutant general and chief of staff on July 15, 1879, and thereafter he served full time in Concord, New Hampshire, in command of the state's guard.[3] This position gave him the rank and authority of a major general. He had found the role most congenial to his aspirations and abilities as a career army officer. He moved from Nashua to Concord, the

General Augustus D. Ayling in 1904.
Centerville Historical Society Archives.

capital, where he took office with a staff of assistants. In addition to military administration, this office put him in the position of a close associate of the Governor and consequently he had a conspicuous part in many statewide civic affairs and public celebrations.

His appointment was at the discretion of the governor and was renewed over a period of more than twenty-seven years by fourteen successive governors. When he retired on January 3, 1907, he was the senior ranking adjutant general in the United States.[4]

It is fortunate that General Ayling maintained a record of major events in his career by keeping a scrapbook of four bound volumes containing newspaper clippings and other mementos of his military activities. He also preserved all of his official letters and general orders during his command. These are now in the Archives of the Centerville Historical Society.

I shall call attention to a few events recorded in this rich collection that reveal the energy and devotion with which he pursued his duties as commander of the State National Guard. No doubt his most remarkable achievement was the compilation of the *Register of the Soldiers and Sailors of New Hampshire in the War of the Rebellion,* a work of 1,347 pages based on ten years of research and published in 1895.[5] In his own opinion, this work was the contribution he was most proud of, as may be seen from the following remarks recorded by a reporter for the *Boston Journal* who interviewed him on November 11, 1893. Ayling said, "I have given my best services to this work with perfect love, loyalty and enthusiasm. Year in and year out it has been the thought uppermost in my mind by day, and I may add, of my dreams at night. I have constantly striven to make it the great effort of my life, in the hope that it will be found worthy of full appreciation by New Hampshire's surviving soldiers, as well as by patriotic generations yet to come."

It was published at state expense and distributed free to every public library in the state and Grand Army Post and was available at cost to individuals from the state librarian.[6]

In the many years of his tenure as adjutant general in Concord, New Hampshire, he was called upon to take a prominent part in military and ceremonial affairs of all kinds—the annual encampments for training of the guard, military inspections, dedication of war memorials, military balls, national holiday celebrations, visits of celebrities, and gubernatorial inaugurations. All of these are chronicled in his scrapbooks in great detail and documented by dated newspaper clippings.

A few of these events are of special interest from a historical point of view. For instance, on November 26, 1883, he rode in a carriage with Governor Samuel Hale of New Hampshire in a grand parade down Fifth Avenue in New York headed by a carriage carrying President Chester A. Arthur and ex-President Grant and consisting of the governors of ten eastern states and their state guards honoring Civil War veterans.[7] On another occasion, on August 15, 1889, General Ayling personally met and greeted President Benjamin Harrison on his arrival by train at Concord, New Hampshire, in behalf of Governor

Major General Philip H. Sheridan. From *Harper's Weekly*, May 14, 1864.

Goodell.[8] At the outbreak of the Spanish American War, he trained New Hampshire Guardsmen, who were sent for further training to Lexington, Kentucky, but never saw action.[9] He also played a part in the official reception of President Theodore Roosevelt at Concord on August 27, 1902.[10] And he was present as a military escort of the Russian and Japanese delegations negotiating the Peace Treaty of Portsmouth, New Hampshire, on August 8, 1905, at the end of the Russo-Japanese War.[11]

Most of the material in Ayling's scrapbooks is made up of newspaper clippings, but tucked in among them I was delighted to find a brief scribbled pencil note on scrap paper of a very personal sort. It concerns a reunion of Civil War veterans at Weirs, New Hampshire, on August 28, 1884, at which General Phil Sheridan was the honored guest. Ayling writes, "I went with Governor Hale and staff to the Veteran's Reunion and took my son, Charles, with me as I wanted him to see the veterans and particularly General Sheridan, who was the honored guest. I joined the party at Concord and after being presented to the General, said I would like to present my son, and he took Charles on his knee and talked with him. It will be something for Charles to remember that he had sat on the knee of Phil Sheridan, the outstanding cavalry leader and hero of Winchester and Five Forks—General Phil Sheridan."[12] It appears that this little personal incident meant more to Ayling than the many public parades and ceremonies he participated in during those years at Concord.

Upon his retirement General Ayling was honored at a reception and banquet attended by all the living ex-governors of New Hampshire and the staff members of fourteen administrations under which he served. He was presented an engraved gold watch with diamond and pearl-studded chain in remembrance of his many years of service.[13]

At Concord, every summer he spent his three-week vacations at Centerville on Cape Cod. He and his family set up camp in a tent not far from the sea, as a personal letter in my possession from him to my wife's grandfather, Aaron Crosby, reveals.[14] But upon his retirement in 1907, he moved into a modest frame house near the shore in Centerville, which he called "The Barracks."[15]

In his retirement years he was an active participant in many local Cape and village affairs. He was president of the Centerville Village Improvement Society, president of the Barnstable County Council of the Boy Scouts, a member of the G.A.R., the Military Order of the Loyal Legion, and a Mason and Knight Templar.[16] His daughter, Edith, lived in Hartford, Connecticut. His son, Charles, who became a very prosperous businessman in Boston, had a large estate and home in Centerville and in his retirement years, he became a very generous philanthropist to whom Centerville and Cape Cod are much indebted.

General Ayling died at the age of seventy-seven on March 9, 1918, at his home in Centerville. He was known to young and old in the village as "the General" and much loved. He and his wife, who was born in Centerville, had many friends and were welcome guests at village social affairs, which they attended with pleasure. Everyone in the village knew that at his death they had lost a good citizen and a dear friend.

The diary of Augustus Ayling is remarkable for a number of reasons. Few Civil War veterans experienced fighting in three different theaters of the war; Ayling served in Virginia with the Army of the Potomac, in Kentucky and Tennessee under Burnside, and with Grant at Vicksburg. His reporting on the situation and conditions in Richmond after the fall of the Confederacy are of interest to students of the Reconstruction period. The readiness of the Union forces to maintain order under the threat of an expected rising of the black population is interesting. The beginnings of reconciliation between northern and southern whites revealed in the bonds of Freemasonry is enlightening.

But above all the Ayling diary is significant for its many vivid pictures of what it was like to be a soldier in that tragic war of brother against brother that almost tore this great nation apart. It portrays a tapestry of close-ups of clamorous battle, and of quiet campfires, of the pomp of parades, and of crumpled bodies on the field of strife, of poignant partings, and of joyful reunions, of moments of elation, and days of boredom—and above all that paradox of heroic sacrifice and loathsome horror that is war. Ayling, of course, was not without human weaknesses. He was often impatient, sometimes impulsive, and he candidly admits that on a few occasions of celebration he had too much to drink. But on the whole he was a man of character and integrity, of loyalty and industry, a good soldier and a good comrade, one who loved to sing in his tent with fellow officers, and who felt united in friendship and kindness with his erstwhile enemies in the spirit of Masonic brotherhood. Such a man was that Yankee at arms, Augustus Ayling.

Notes

Introduction

1. Obituary in the *Boston Globe,* Mar. 12, 1918. Ayling's scrapbook, 4:
   1.
2. *Boston Herald,* Mar. 12, 1918. Ayling's scrapbook, 4: 67. This unsigned
   piece is probably by a drama critic.
3. Obituary in the *Boston Evening Transcript,* Mar. 12, 1918. Ayling's
   scrapbook, 4: 73.
4. *Boston Journal,* July 20, 1895. Ayling's scrapbook, 2: 171–72.
5. *Manchester Union,* July 11, 1895.

1. Enlistment and Fort Monroe

1. On April 15, 1861, President Lincoln declared that "insurrection" ex-
   isted, and called for seventy-five thousand three-month volunteers. *Encyclopedia of American History,* ed. Richard B. Morris (New York:
   Harper and Brothers, 1953), 230.
2. George F. Richardson (1829–1912) was a prominent lawyer in Lowell,
   Massachusetts. He was a brother of William A. Richardson, secretary of
   the treasury under President Grant. He was also president of the Prescott
   National Bank of Lowell and director of several companies, including the
   Vermont and Massachusetts Railroad. He was noted for his philanthropy,
   and at the outbreak of the Civil War he organized the "Richardson Light
   Infantry." Frederick W. Coburn, *History of Lowell and Its People* (New
   York: Lewis Historical Publishing Co., 1920), 1: 40–43.
3. On April 19, 1861, the 6th Massachusetts Regiment arrived in Baltimore

by railroad. It was necessary to pull the railroad cars by horses through the city to the depot for departure for Washington. The cars were attacked by a mob throwing stones and other missiles. Nine cars reached the depot in safety, but two cars were held up. The troops left these cars and attempted to proceed on foot, and while exposed to attack by the mob, two soldiers were killed and eight wounded. No order was given to fire on the mob, but some men did, and seven of the rioters were killed. J. T. Headley, *The Great Rebellion: A History of the Civil War in the United States* (Hartford, Conn.: Hurlbut, Williams and Co., 1863), 1: 73–74.

4. Morris, *Encyclopedia of American History,* 231.
5. Captain Henry A. Snow, 1st Massachusetts Regiment, *Official Army Register of the Volunteer Force of the United States Army,* pt. 1, 149. Published by Order of the Secretary of War, March 2, 1865.
6. Captain Thomas W. Clarke, 29th Massachusetts Regiment, *Official Army Register,* pt. 1, 195.
7. Major General Benjamin Franklin Butler, USA (1818–1893), was in command of the District of Annapolis and Fort Monroe in early 1861. Mark M. Boatner III, *The Civil War Dictionary* (New York: Random House, 1991), 109. Unless otherwise stated, hereafter all identifications and historical information are from this source.
8. Since Ayling's diary was lost, he is apparently relying on some other sources for the daily entries he makes for 1861.
9. General James Ewell Brown Stuart, CSA (1833–1864), known as "Jeb" Stuart, was a colorful cavalry officer who made several daring raids in the course of the war. Here the reference is to his exploit of June 12–15, 1862. General Lee ordered him to reconnoiter McClellan's right flank, but Stuart exceeded his orders and completely rode around McClellan's entire army astride the Chickahominy. In so doing, he alerted McClellan to the need of changing his base.
10. The Battle of Big Bethel, Virginia, June 10, 1861, was the first land battle of the war. The federal forces of 4,400 men under Colonel E. W. Pierce engaged 1,408 Confederates principally under Colonel D. H. Hill of the 1st N.C. The Union forces lost 76 men, including Major Theodore Winthrop and Lieutenant J. T. Greble, while the Confederates lost only 11.
11. Simon Cameron (1799–1889), secretary of war under Lincoln.

2. The *Monitor* and the *Merrimack* and Newport News

1. William Henry Seward (1801–1872) was secretary of state under Lincoln

and Simon Cameron, secretary of war. Senator Henry Wilson was from Massachusetts; William H. Osborne, *The History of the Twenty-Ninth Regiment of Massachusetts Volunteer Infantry in the Late War of the Rebellion* (Boston: Albert J. Wright, 1877), 109.

2. Second Lieutenant John E. Smith, 29th Massachusetts Regiment, *Official Army Register,* pt. 1, 195.

3. "Contraband" was a slang term for a runaway slave. Three slaves of a Virginia owner sought refuge at Fort Monroe, Virginia, on May 23, 1861, and the owner demanded their return under the Fugitive Slave Acts. General Butler refused, saying that since Virginia had seceded, she had no right to the Federal laws. In a report to the secretary of war, Butler referred to the slaves as "contraband of war," and the name came into usage to refer to an escaped slave.

4. Lieutenant Colonel Joseph H. Barnes, 29th Massachusetts Regiment, *Official Army Register,* pt. 1, 195.

5. General J. K. F. Mansfield, USA (1803–1862).

6. George Von Schack, a colonel in the Union Army (d. 1887), was in command of "Steuben Rifles." He came to the United States on a leave of absence from the Prussian army. Later he became a U.S. citizen.

7. Elmer Ellsworth (1837–1861) was the Union officer famous for organizing a regiment of Zouaves, troops wearing uniforms modeled after the French Algerian light infantry with baggy trousers, gaiters, short and open jacket, and a turban or fez. He was killed by the proprietor of a tavern in Alexandria, Virginia, for taking down the Confederate flag from the roof of the building.

8. General John Bankhead Magruder, CSA (1810–1871).

9. Captain James H. Osgood, 29th Massachusetts Regiment, *Official Army Register,* pt. 1, 195.

10. John Albion Andrew (1818–1867) was governor of Massachusetts from 1860 to 1866.

11. Major General John Ellis Wool, USA (1789–1869).

12. Colonel Ebenezer W. Pierce had been a brigadier-general of the Massachusetts State Militia before the war. When commissioned colonel in command of the 29th Massachusetts Regiment, he chose two inexperienced young officers, First Lieutenant Freeman A. Tabor and First Lieutenant John A. Sayles over older and experienced officers to command existing companies. For this reason and for other acts of favoritism in promotion, he was generally disliked by many in his command. The historian of the 29th Regiment, William H. Osborne, explains this and writes, "It would be useless to attempt to conceal the fact that the appointment of the colo-

nel [Pierce] of the regiment was exceedingly distasteful to the officers and men of the Battalion." Osborne, *History of the Twenty-Ninth Regiment,* 307. Osborne does not report the charges of the court-martial.

13. Colonel George Nauman, USA. See Brigadier General Fred C. Ainsworth and Joseph W. Kirkley, *The War of the Rebellion: Compilation of the Official Records of the Union and Confederate Armies,* General Index (Washington, D.C.: Government Printing Office, 1901), 691.

14. Hannibal Hamlin (1809–1891), vice president under Lincoln.

15. The troop movement referred to here was the beginning of McClellan's Peninsula Campaign.

16. General Silas Casey, USA (1807–1882). *Official Army Register,* pt. 1, 195.

17. First Lieutenant Henry A. Kern, 29th Massachusetts Regiment, *Official Army Register,* pt. 1, 195.

18. Captain Charles Brady, 29th Massachusetts Regiment, *Official Army Register,* pt. 1, 195.

19. First Lieutenant Thomas H. Adams, 29th Massachusetts Regiment, *Official Army Register,* pt. 1, 195.

3. An Infantry Officer in the Army of the Potomac

1. Major General Benjamin Huger, CSA (1805–1877).

2. Stephen W. Sears, *To the Gates of Richmond: The Peninsula Campaign* (New York: Ticknor and Fields, 1992), 51–209; and General George B. McClellan, *McClellan's Own Story* (New York: Charles L. Webster & Co., 1887), 253–409.

3. Corporal Alonzo B. Fisk, Company K, and Corporal John A. Tighe, Company K, 29th Massachusetts Regiment, Osborne, *History of the Twenty-Ninth Regiment,* 366–67.

4. Second Lieutenant John P. Burbeck, 29th Massachusetts Regiment, ibid., 366.

5. Captain Lebbeus Leach, Company C, 29th Massachusetts Regiment, ibid., 352.

6. Captain Samuel H. Doten, Company E, 29th Massachusetts Regiment, ibid., 356.

7. Captain William A. Pray, 29th Massachusetts Regiment, *Official Army Register,* pt. 1, 195.

8. First Lieutenant Alfred O. Brooks, 29th Massachusetts Regiment, *Official Army Register,* pt. 1, 196.

9. General Edwin Vose Sumner, USA (1797–1863).

10. General Israel Bush Richardson, USA (1815–1862).

11. Brigadier General Thomas Francis Meagher, USA (1823–1867); An Irish American leader who raised an "Irish Brigade" in New York City.

12. Major General Joseph Hooker, USA (1814–1879).

13. General Fitz-John Porter, USA (1822–1901); In command of V Corps.

14. General William Henry French, USA (1815–1881).

15. Second Lieutenant Thomas A. Mayo, Company E, 29th Massachusetts Regiment, Osborne, *History of the Twenty-Ninth Regiment,* 356.

4. McClellan's Retreat and the Hospitalization of Lieutenant Ayling

1. Sears, *To the Gates of Richmond,* 210–336, and McClellan, *McClellan's Own Story,* 253–458.

2. After the Battle of Gaines's Mill, McClellan ordered a retreat of the army to the James River. Three corps, including Sumner's in which Ayling's regiment was, were to pull out at night and constitute a rear guard. General Lee gave orders to pursue the retreating Federals. General Magruder's troops attacked the rear guard on June 29 at Peach Orchard. Sumner delayed the Confederates until 11 A.M. and then withdrew to Savage's Station. The Federal troops suffered heavy losses but delayed the advance long enough to ensure the safe retreat of the main army.

3. General Sumner's corps destroyed the bridge at White Oak Swamp, preventing General Jackson's troops from crossing. Other positions at White Oak Swamp were attacked by the Confederates but with limited success and McClellan was able to withdraw his entire force during the night of June 30th to Malvern Hill. Sears, *To the Gates of Richmond,* 273–307.

4. Sergeant Ansel B. Kellam, Company G, 29th Massachusetts Regiment, Osborne, *History of the Twenty-Ninth Regiment,* 381.

5. Corporal Thomas F. Darby, Company D, 29th Massachusetts Regiment, ibid., 354.

6. Sergeant Benjamin H. Hamlin, Company D, 29th Massachusetts Regiment, ibid., 354.

7. This was the site of the Battle of Malvern Hill on July 1, 1862. McClellan held a strong defensive position and his artillery destroyed the Confederate batteries before they could effectively support infantry attack. The result was devastating to Confederate troops attempting to advance. The Federals lost 3,214 men while Lee lost 5,355 men. That night McClellan withdrew to his new base at Harrison's Landing on the James River where he had Union gunboats to support him. Sears, *To the Gates of Richmond,* 328–36.

8. Captain Charles T. Richardson, Company G, 29th Massachusetts Regiment, Osborne, *History of the Twenty-Ninth Regiment,* 360.
9. First Lieutenant Ezra Ripley, Company B, 29th Massachusetts Regiment, ibid., 350.
10. Chaplain Henry E. Hempstead, 29th Massachusetts Regiment, ibid., 347.
11. First Lieutenant Nathan D. Whitman, Company C, 29th Massachusetts Regiment, ibid., 352.
12. Major Charles Chipman, 29th Massachusetts Regiment, ibid., 347.
13. First Lieutenant John B. Collingwood, 29th Massachusetts Regiment, ibid., 347.
14. Bedloe's Island in New York harbor is now the site of the Statue of Liberty, which was presented in 1884 and dedicated in 1886. *The Columbia Encyclopedia,* 2d ed. (New York: Columbia University Press, 1950), 1130.

5. Lieutenant Ayling on Sick Leave

1. First Lieutenant Henry S. Braden, Company K, 29th Massachusetts Regiment, Osborne, *History of the Twenty-Ninth Regiment,* 365; 2nd Lieutenant William R. Corlew, Company H, 29th Massachusetts Regiment, ibid., 362.
2. The J. C. Ayer & Co. of Lowell was a pharmaceutical firm.
3. The passage from St. Paul's Epistle to the Ephesians, 2:12, refers to pagans of Ephesus before conversion to Christianity as being without hope of salvation. Ayling's allusion to it implies that he thought he had no hope of winning this young lady. Apparently Ayling knew his Bible rather well.
4. *Jubilee.* Unidentified in chapter 26 (Song Books) of the *Cambridge History of American Literature.*
5. General Harvey Brown, USA (1796–1874), was at this time in command of the defenses of New York harbor and the city.
6. Colonel Martin Burke, USA, was in command of Fort Hamilton at this time.
7. Surgeon George B. Cogswell, 29th Massachusetts Regiment, Osborne, *History of the Twenty-Ninth Regiment,* 347.
8. Private Charles Walker, Company K, 29th Massachusetts Regiment, ibid., 367.
9. Although the State of Tennessee joined the Confederacy, there was a Union Department, and the Army of the Tennessee was created on October 16, 1862. The department included Cairo, Forts Henry and Donelson, northern Mississippi, and portions of Kentucky and Tennessee west of the Tennessee River. The army was commanded by Major

General U. S. Grant. However, Ayling appears to be in error about the regiment here, for there was no Federal 61st Tennessee.

10. In the early part of the war, prisoners on parole were exchanged by both sides. However, Secretary Stanton suspended the exchange of officers on December 28, 1862, and General Halleck stopped all exchanges on May 25, 1863.

11. General Ambrose Everett Burnside, USA (1824–1881), relieved General George Brinton McClellan, USA (1826–1885), as commander of the Army of the Potomac on November 9, 1862. It was a coincidence that Lieutenant Ayling happened to be on the same train with General Burnside at this time and also to see the train carrying General McClellan away from the front.

12. First Lieutenant Charles D. Browne, Company G, 29th Massachusetts Regiment, Osborne, *History of the Twenty-Ninth Regiment,* 360.

6. The Fredericksburg Campaign

1. William Marvel, *Burnside* (Chapel Hill: University of North Carolina Press, 1991), 175–200.

2. First Lieutenant Charles A. Carpenter, Company G, 29th Massachusetts Regiment, Osborne, *History of the Twenty-Ninth Regiment,* 360.

3. Captain Israel N. Wilson, 29th Massachusetts Regiment, *Official Army Register,* pt. 1, 195.

4. Captain Willard D. Tripp, 1st Lieutenant Thomas H. Husband, 29th Massachusetts Regiment, Osborne, *History of the Twenty-Ninth Regiment,* 358.

5. First Lieutenant Abram A. Oliver, 29th Massachusetts Regiment, ibid., 364.

6. Colonel Benjamin C. Christ, USA, of the 50th Pennsylvania Regiment.

7. The Battle of Fredericksburg on December 13, 1862, was costly for Burnside's army. In the morning Franklin's Corps crossed the Rappahannock only to be repulsed by Stonewall Jackson's force defending Prospect Heights. In the afternoon Sumner's and Hooker's Corps crossed to face devastating fire from Longstreet's Confederates firing down upon them from Marye's Heights. The Federals lost 12,700 men killed or wounded while the Confederates lost only 5,300.

8. General William Buel Franklin, USA (1823–1903).

9. Captain George H. Taylor, 29th Massachusetts Regiment, *Official Army Register,* pt. 1, 195.

10. General William Wallace Burns, USA (1825–1892), was in command of the First Division of the IX Corps at Fredericksburg.

11. Second Lieutenant Peter Windsor, 29th Massachusetts Regiment, *Official Army Register,* pt. 1, 195.

7. Winter Camp and Transfer to Newport News

1. First Lieutenant Baldwin T. Peabody, First Lieutenant Dudley M. Prescott, First Lieutenant Caleb Philbrick, First Lieutenant Joseph P. Thompson, 33rd Massachusetts Regiment, *Official Army Register,* Part 1, 202. Hospital Steward Freeman B. Shedd, Sergeant Charles A. Bailey, 33rd Massachusetts Regiment, *Record of the Massachusetts Volunteers, 1861–1865* (Boston: Wright & Potter, 1870), 2: 698 and 706.
2. Second Lieutenant George H. Long, Company H, 29th Massachusetts Regiment, Osborne, *History of the Twenty-Ninth Regiment,* 362.
3. On January 26, 1863, General Hooker replaced General Burnside as commander of the Army of the Potomac.
4. Private Malvin Gear, Company H, 29th Massachusetts Regiment, Osborne, *History of the Twenty-Ninth Regiment,* 362. This man later deserted on January 12, 1865. *Record of the Massachusetts Volunteers,* 601.
5. First Lieutenant John M. Deane, 29th Massachusetts Regiment, *Official Army Register,* pt. 1, 195.
6. Captain Edward G. Park, 35th Massachusetts Regiment, *Official Army Register,* pt. 1, 205.
7. The "Scotchman" was apparently the name of a local tavern.
8. General John Adams Dix, USA (1798–1879), was in command of the Department of Virginia and the VII Corps.
9. Captain Albert Pinder, 6th Massachusetts Regiment, *Official Army Register,* pt. 1, 155.
10. Colonel Albert S. Follansbe, 6th Massachusetts Regiment, ibid., 155.
11. Private Bernard Molino, Company B, 29th Massachusetts Regiment, Osborne, *History of the Twenty-Ninth Regiment,* 351.
12. *Charles O'Malley* (1841) is a novel by Charles James Lever (1806–1872). The novel deals with military life.

8. A Wartime Love Affair

1. William F. Fox, *Regimental Losses in the Civil War* (Albany, N.Y: Albany Publishing Co., 1898), 81.
2. Marvel, *Burnside,* 218–63.
3. Robert Penn Warren, *John Brown: The Making of a Martyr* (Nashville: J. S. Sanders & Co., 1993). John Brown (1800–1859) was a fanatic abolitionist, who in 1859 seized the U.S. Armory at Harper's Ferry with

a band of twenty-one men. A company of U.S. Marines commanded by Robert E. Lee captured Brown, and he was convicted of treason and hanged. In the eyes of Northern abolitionists he was regarded as a martyr of the antislavery cause.

4. Western Virginia was loyal to the Union and in consequence separated from Virginia on August 20, 1862, and was admitted as a separate state on June 20, 1863.

5. On March 19, 1863, the IX Corps under General Burnside was ordered to the Department of the Ohio, where the corps had two months of pleasant occupation duty in Kentucky.

6. Second Lieutenant Thomas Conant, Jr., Company C, 29th Massachusetts Regiment, Osborne, *History of the Twenty-Ninth Regiment*, 352.

7. "Lord Dundreary" is obviously a satirical literary character, but I have been unable to locate the source.

8. Corporal Isaac H. Taylor, Company H, 29th Massachusetts Regiment, Osborne, *History of the Twenty-Ninth Regiment*, 363.

9. Sergeant Willliam F. Pippey, Company H, 29th Massachusetts Regiment, ibid., 362.

10. Captain Daniel W. Lee, 29th Massachusetts Regiment, *Official Army Register*, pt. 1, 195.

9. Occupation Duty in Kentucky

1. Marvel, *Burnside*, 231–40.

2. Camp Dick Robinson near Danville, Kentucky, was an assembly point for Federal volunteers.

3. Private William P. Farnsworth, Company H, 29th Massachusetts Regiment, Osborne, *History of the Twenty-Ninth Regiment*, 362.

4. First Lieutenant Warren Goodwin, Company B, 29th Massachusetts Regiment, ibid., 350.

5. See chapter 5, note 3.

6. General John Hunt Morgan, CSA (1825–1864), was famous for his many daring cavalry raids.

7. Colonel Frank Wolford, USA, of the 1st Kentucky cavalry. *Battles and Leaders of the Civil War*, ed. Robert Underwood Johnson and Clarence Clough Buel (New York: The Century Co., 1887), 4: 415.

8. Assistant Surgeon Albert Wood, 29th Massachusetts Regiment, *Official Army Register*, pt. 1, 196.

9. *Waverley* (1814) is a novel by Sir Walter Scott.

10. "Patience is bitter, but its fruit is sweet."

10. Down the Mississippi and the Siege of Vicksburg

1. The Copperheads were Northern Democrats who opposed the war and favored a negotiated peace with the Confederacy.

2. Captain Jacob Roemer, USA, commanded the 34th New York Battery. Johnson and Buel, *Battles and Leaders*, 4: 815.

3. General John Pope, USA, captured Island No. 10 in April of 1862, opening the Mississippi River to Union forces as far as Fort Pillow.

4. Southern and Northern accounts of this action differ. Southern accounts maintain that Federal losses were incurred before the surrender. Northern accounts, including the House of Representatives Report No. 65, 38th Congress, 1864, state that a "massacre" did occur.

5. *The Drunkard or, The Fallen Saved* by William H. Smith (1844). This play, which was based on temperance tracts, was first performed in Boston on February 12, 1844. It became an important factor in the temperance movement and was performed in various cities during the Civil War. John Allen Kraut, *The Origins of Prohibition* (New York: Alfred A. Knopf, 1925), 254–55.

6. *Les Miserables* (1862) is a novel by Victor Hugo. It was very popular with both Union and Confederate soldiers at the time. Some Confederate soldiers called themselves "Lee's Miserables."

7. Second Lieutenant George W. Pope, 29th Massachusetts Regiment, Osborne, *History of the Twenty-Ninth Regiment*, 360.

8. *No Name* (1862) is a novel by Wilkie Collins.

9. General Joseph Eggleston Johnston, CSA (1807–1891), threatened to relieve General John Pemberton, CSA (1814–1881), who was besieged by Grant at Vicksburg.

10. General Nathaniel Prentiss Banks, USA (1816–1894), did not capture Port Hudson until after the fall of Vicksburg. However, its capture removed the last obstruction to Union navigation of the Mississippi River. Admiral David Glasgow Farragut, USN (1801–1870), led a fleet up the Mississippi River, which was instrumental in the fall of both Port Hudson and Vicksburg.

11. General Ulysses Simpson Grant, USA (1822–1885), captured Vicksburg on July 4, 1863. The day before at Gettysburg, Lee's invading army was repulsed with heavy losses. These two crucial Union victories were the turning points of the war.

12. General William Tecumseh Sherman, USA (1820–1891), becoming Grant's closest collaborator, would ultimately command the principal Union force in the West.

13. Sergeant Henry A. Kern, Company D, 29th Massachusetts Regiment, Osborne, *History of the Twenty-Ninth Regiment,* 354.
14. Jefferson Davis (1808–1889) was president of the Confederacy from February 1861 until its fall.
15. General Sherman laid siege to Jackson, Mississippi, and J. E. Johnston's forces evacuated on July 16, 1863. Ayling's regiment participated in this victory.

11. Occupation in Mississippi and Return to Kentucky

1. General John Grubb Parke, USA (1827–1900), was in command of the IX Corps from June 5 to August 25 of 1863 at Vicksburg.
2. Second Lieutenant Horace A. Jenks, Company E, 29th Massachusetts Regiment, Osborne, *History of the Twenty-Ninth Regiment,* 356.
3. Quinine and capsicum (from the pepper plant) are standard medications for malaria.
4. *Rob Roy* (1818) is a novel by Sir Walter Scott.
5. A guidon is a small flag carried by a regiment in battle as a guide for identification.
6. Second Lieutenant William F. Pippey, Company H, 29th Massachusetts Regiment, Osborne, *History of the Twenty-Ninth Regiment,* 362. Promoted from sergeant. See chapter 8, note 9.
7. First Lieutenant John B. Pizer, 29th Massachusetts Regiment, *Official Army Register,* pt. 1, 195.
8. Captain Harvey Heisinger, 50th Pennsylvania Regiment, Ainsworth and Kirkley, *War of the Rebellion,* General Index, 418.
9. Surgeon John Heister, Ainsworth and Kirkley, *War of the Rebellion,* General Index, 418.
10. Second Lieutenant Henry A. Hunting, Company K, 29th Massachusetts Regiment, Osborne, *History of the Twenty-Ninth Regiment,* 366.

12. Travel to Knoxville on Return from Sick Leave

1. Marvell, *Burnside,* 276–334.
2. General James Longstreet, CSA (1821–1904), was besieging Burnside's army occupying Knoxville, Tennessee.
3. Lieutenant Colonel William S. King, 35th Massachusetts Regiment, *Official Army Register,* pt. 1, 205.
4. General Speed Smith Fry, USA (1817–1892). Lieutenant Colonel Daniel F. Griffin, USA.

5. The Sibley tent was a large conical tent erected on a tripod holding a single pole. It would accommodate twelve soldiers and their gear. It was invented before the Civil War by Henry Hopkins Sibley, who was later an officer in the Confederate army.

6. "Bushwhacker" is a term applied to any backwoodsman, but during the Civil War applied to Confederate guerillas in particular.

7. First Lieutenant Charles Davis Jr., 11th New Hampshire Regiment, *Official Army Register,* pt. 1, 84.

8. Colonel James P. Brownlow, USA, of the 1st Tennessee Cavalry. His father was William Gannaway Brownlow, a Methodist minister, who violently opposed secession in 1861 and became a leader of Unionist elements in east Tennessee. Known as "Parson Brownlow," he published a pro-Union newspaper that was suppressed by the Confederate authorities. He was elected governor of Tennessee on the Republican ticket in 1865 and again in 1867. In 1869 he became a U.S. senator.

9. Cumberland Gap had been a Confederate stronghold, but it was captured by Union forces under Burnside on September 8–10, 1863.

10. Fort Sanders was the Union stronghold protecting Knoxville held by Burnside and attacked by Longstreet. The attack on November 29, 1863, was repulsed with heavy losses for the Confederates. The failure caused Longstreet to cease further efforts to take Knoxville.

13. Winter Camp in Eastern Tennessee

1. Marvel, *Burnside,* passim.

2. First Lieutenant James H. Atherton, Company D, 29th Massachusetts Regiment, Osborne, *History of the Twenty-Ninth Regiment,* 354.

3. General Philip Henry Sheridan, USA (1831–1888), was in command of the 2nd Division of the IV Corps at this time.

4. The XXIII Corps under General George Lucas Hartsuff combined with the IX Corps made up Burnside's Army of the Ohio in the operations against Longstreet in eastern Tennessee.

14. Hard Times and a Depleted Company

1. In the Union army a company comprised a maximum of 101 officers and men and a minimum strength of 83. An infantry regiment was ordinarily made up of 10 companies.

2. Private James Ball, Company D, 29th Massachusetts Regiment, Osborne, *History of the Twenty-Ninth Regiment,* 354.

3. General John Gray Foster, USA (1823–1874), was in command of the Department of Ohio from December 11, 1863, to February 9, 1864. Boatner reports that he asked to be relieved from this command to recover from injuries received in a fall from his horse and went on sick leave. It appears probable that he canceled his review of the IX Corps scheduled for February for this reason.

4. Sergeant Joseph J. C. Madigan, Company D, 29th Massachusetts Regiment, Osborne, *History of the Twenty-Ninth Regiment,* 355.

5. Hospital Steward John Hardy, 29th Massachusetts Regiment, ibid., 347.

6. Oliver Wendell Holmes, "My Hunt for the Captain," *Atlantic Monthly* 10 (62) (December 1862).

7. General John McAllister Schofield, USA (1831–1906), was in command of the Army of the Ohio from February 9 to November 17 of 1864.

8. Phonography is a system of shorthand writing based on sound.

9. Vedettes are mounted sentinels stationed in advance of pickets.

15. The End of the War

1. Sergeant Henry C. Joslyn, Company A, 29th Massachusetts Regiment, *Record of the Massachusetts Volunteers, 1861–1865* (Boston, 1870), 2: 585.

2. Ayling is referring to the Confederate defeat at Chattanooga in November of 1863. Union forces under Grant successfully attacked the Confederates under General Bragg at Lookout Mountain (November 24) and Missionary Ridge (November 25). The loss of Chattanooga was a severe blow to the Confederate cause since a vital line of lateral communications was lost and the stage was set for Sherman's move to split the Confederacy further by his march from Atlanta to the sea.

3. Ayling refers to the Stones River campaign of December 30, 1862, to January 3, 1863, in which Bragg's Confederate army of Tennessee attacked Union General Rosecrans's Army of the Cumberland. The result was indecisive for either side. At Murfreesboro, Tennessee, Forrest's Confederate Cavalry raided Union troops under Rousseau on December 7, 1864.

4. Major Rufus P. Lincoln, 20th Massachusetts Regiment, *Record of the Massachusetts Volunteers,* 2: 332.

5. Captain William B. Maloney, *Official Army Register,* pt. 1, 159.

6. Lieutenant Colonel Josiah A. Sawtell, ibid., 189.

7. See chapter 1, note 3.

Chapter 16. Postwar Duty in Richmond, Virginia

1. General Robert Sanford Foster, USA (1834–1903). A newspaper clipping of February 22, 1903, preserved by Ayling, reports his death and reads, "He commanded the 1st division of the 24th Corps in the Civil War and headed off General Lee at Appomattox, causing his surrender." He also served on the military commission that tried Lincoln's assassins.

2. Colonel Phineas A. Davis, *Official Army Register,* pt. 1, 143.

3. General Butler's Army of the James attacked Confederate forces under General Beauregard at Drewry's Bluff, Virginia, on May 12–16, 1864. The operation was a failure, for Butler's army suffered heavy losses and was forced to retreat. After this retreat, Butler's army was bottled up at Bermuda Hundred and Federal gunboats were blocked from passage up the James River. Butler constructed a canal at Dutch Gap to allow gunboats to pass. However, the project was not completed in time to be of military value.

4. Colonel Albert Ordway, 24th Massachusetts Regiment, Alfred S. Roe, *The Twenty-Fourth Regiment, Massachusetts Volunteers, 1861–1866* (Worcester, Mass., 1907), 450.

5. Lieutenant Colonel Thomas F. Edmands, 24th Massachusetts Regiment, ibid., 452.

6. The Battle of Mechanicsville, Virginia, on June 26, 1862, was one of the Seven Days battles of McClellan's Peninsula Campaign.

7. General Francis A. Osborn, 24th Massachusetts Regiment, Roe, *The Twenty-Fourth Regiment, Massachusetts Volunteers,* 450.

8. Major Charles Sellmer, 11th Maine Regiment, *Official Army Register,* pt. 1, 31; Major Robert Carruthers, 24th Massachusetts Regiment, Roe, *The Twenty-Fourth Regiment, Massachusetts Volunteers,* 455; Major Elijah J. Waddell, 16th Indiana Regiment, *Official Army Register,* pt. 6, 54; Captain William H. H. Frye, 11th Maine Regiment, *Official Army Register,* pt. 1, 31; Major James Thompson, 24th Massachusetts Regiment, Roe, *The Twenty-Fourth Regiment, Massachusetts Volunteers,* 453. Brevet rank was an honorary title awarded for meritorious action in time of war, usually having none of the authority or pay of full rank.

9. Belle Isle was a Confederate prison on the James River at Richmond used only for enlisted men. Libby Prison on the James River at Richmond was used for captured officers.

10. General Harrison Stiles Fairchild, USA.

11. General Charles Devens, USA (1820–1891), had a distinguished career in the army and later in political positions. He served on the Massa-

chusetts Supreme Court and then as attorney general under President Hayes. Camp Devens in Massachusetts is named for him.

12. In May of 1865, General Sheridan was sent with 50,000 troops to the Rio Grande. Secretary Seward then sent General Sherman on a mission to Juarez, the Mexican revolutionary leader, as a gesture of recognition. Then Napoleon III withdrew his troops in May 1866, leaving Maximilian to be overthrown and executed.

13. General Robert Edward Lee, CSA (1807–1870). After a brilliant career as the master strategist and field commander of the Confederate forces, Lee became president of Washington College, later named Washington and Lee University in his honor.

14. General John Gibbon, USA. *Battles and Leaders of the Civil War,* 4: 788.

15. Colonel Michael T. Donohoe, 10th New Hampshire Regiment, *Official Army Register,* pt. 1, 83.

16. Captain S. V. Benet, *A Treatise on Military Law and the Practice of Courts-Martial,* 4th ed. (New York: D. Van Nostrand, 1864).

17. Captain Reuben S. Botsford, 39th Illinois Regiment, *Official Army Register,* pt. 4, 278. The actual pertinent charges as the records of the Court Martial show, were "Disobedience of Orders" and "Breach of Arrest". The Court found the accused guilty of both charges. However, in reviewing the case, Major General A. H. Terry disapproved both findings of the Court, the first because the defendant had been improperly ordered to violate an Article of War and the second because the term of arrest had legally expired. Captain Botsford was exonerated and returned to duty. Copy of General Court Martial Orders, No. 86, Head Quarters Dept. of Virginia, Richmond, Va., Aug. 17, 1865. National Archives, Record Group 153 JAG (Army) Court Martial Number MM-2640.

18. Colonel William M. McArthur, 8th Maine Regiment, *Official Army Register,* pt. 1, 25.

19. The Battle of Fair Oaks, Virginia, on May 31 to June 1, 1862, was an encounter of McClellan's Peninsula Campaign.

20. Henry Alexander Wise (1806–1876) was governor of Virginia from 1856 to 1860.

21. General John Wesley Turner, USA (1833–1899).

22. Captain Benjamin F. Stoddard, 24th Massachusetts Regiment, Roe, *The Twenty-Fourth Regiment, Massachusetts Volunteers,* 453.

23. Castle Thunder was a Confederate prison in Richmond named thus by the inmates because of the sound of artillery fire. After the war, the Federals used it to hold Confederates charged with war crimes.

24. Captain William Reynolds, 24th Massachusetts Regiment, Roe, *The Twenty-Fourth Regiment, Massachusetts Volunteers,* 521.
25. General Fitzhugh Lee, CSA (1835–1899), was a nephew of Robert E. Lee. He had a distinguished career as a Confederate cavalry officer.
26. Colonel Edward A. True, 8th Maine Regiment, *Official Army Register,* pt. 1, 25.
27. Patrick S. Gilmore, Leader of the 24th Massachusetts Regimental Band, Roe, *The Twenty-Fourth Regiment, Massachusetts Volunteers,* 456.
28. Major Edward R. Wheeler, Surgeon; Assistant Surgeon John W. Parsons, 24th Massachusetts Regiment, ibid., 454.
29. Colonel Charles Hardenburg, Ainsworth and Kirkley, *War of the Rebellion,* General Index, 397.
30. First Lieutenant William E. Farrar, Massachusetts Light Artillery, *Official Army Register,* pt. 1, 143.
31. Fort Darling was the Confederate artillery battery at Drewry's Bluff.
32. General Alfred Howe Terry, USA (1827–1890).

17. Last Days in Richmond

1. First Lieutenant James N. North, 24th Massachusetts Regiment, Roe, *The Twenty-Fourth Regiment, Massachusetts Volunteers,* 453.
2. Captain William F. Wiley, 24th Massachusetts Regiment, ibid., 540.
3. Patrick Henry (1736–1799), the Virginia patriot, whose words, "Give me liberty or give me death," are so well known.
4. Captain Jarvis White, 24th Massachusetts Regiment, Roe, *The Twenty-Fourth Regiment, Massachusetts Volunteers,* 540.
5. "F.F.V." stands for First Family Virginian, meaning an aristocratic family.
6. Major Henry C. Adams, 11th Maine Regiment, *Official Army Register,* pt. 1, 31.
7. First Lieutenant Eben H. Dadd, 24th Massachusetts Regiment, Roe, *The Twenty-Fourth Regiment, Massachusetts Volunteers,* 517.
8. Captain Davis Foster, 24th Massachusetts Regiment, *Official Army Register,* pt. 1, 185.
9. *Sine die,* Latin for "without day," a legal term meaning "indefinitely."
10. Major George B. Macomber, 24th Massachusetts Regiment, Roe, *The Twenty-Fourth Regiment, Massachusetts Volunteers,* 457.
11. Private Justus W. F. Washburn, Company D, 24th Massachusetts Regiment, ibid., 495.
12. Private Charles E. Pratt, Company I, band member, 24th Massachusetts Regiment, ibid., 442.

13. General Thomas Jonathan Jackson, CSA (1824–1863), known as "Stonewall" because of his firm stand at the First Battle of Bull Run. He died in May of 1863 after being accidentally wounded by his own men. His widow was Mary Jackson. *Columbia Encyclopedia,* 989.
14. Colonel Ira C. Terry, *Official Army Register,* pt. 8, 193.

Epilogue

1. Charles F. Herberger, *Three Centuries of Centerville Scenes: Vignettes of a Cape Cod Village* (Centerville Historical Society, 1989): 94–105.
2. *Nashua (N.H.) Gazette,* June 4, 1879. Ayling's scrapbook, 1: 2.
3. *Boston Journal,* July 12, 1879, Ayling's scrapbook, 1: 4.
4. *Boston Herald,* Jan. 11, 1907, Ayling's scrapbook, 4: 26.
5. *Boston Journal,* July 20, 1895, Ayling's scrapbook, 2: 171.
6. *Manchester (N.H.) Union,* July 11, 1895, Ayling's scrapbook, 2: 170.
7. *New York Sun,* Nov. 26, 1883, Ayling's scrapbook, 1: 108–11.
8. *Concord (N.H.) Monitor,* Aug. 15, 1889, Ayling's scrapbook, 2: 47–52.
9. *Concord (N.H.) Patriot,* May 12, 1898, Ayling's scrapbook, 2: 214.
10. *Concord (N.H.) Patriot,* Aug. 28, 1902, Ayling's scrapbook, 3: 102–7.
11. *Concord (N.H.) Patriot,* Aug. 8, 1905, Ayling's scrapbook, 3: 198–200.
12. General Sheridan won important victories over General Jubal Early on September 19, 1864, at Winchester, Virginia, and over General Pickett at Five Forks, Virginia, on April 1, 1865.
13. *Concord (N.H.) Patriot,* Jan. 11, 1907, Ayling's scrapbook, 4: 28–29.
14. Herberger, *Centerville Scenes,* 102.
15. General Order, No. 2, State of New Hampshire, The Adjutant General's Office, Concord, N.H., Mar. 12, 1918.
16. *Boston Globe,* Mar. 12, 1918, Obituary of General Ayling, Ayling's scrapbook, 4: 1.

Bibliography

Ainsworth, Fred C. and Kirkley, Joseph W. *The War of the Rebellion: Compilation of the Official Records of the Union and Confederate Armies.* General Index. Washington, D.C.: Government Printing Office, 1901.

Ayling, Augustus D. Scrapbooks. 4 vols. Centerville Historical Society Archives.
———.Official Letters. Office of the Adjutant General, Concord, New Hampshire, 1879–1907.

Beard, Charles A., and Mary R. *A Basic History of the United States.* New York: Doubleday, Doran and Co., 1944.

Benet, Captain S. V. *A Treatise on Military Law and the Practice of Courts-Martial.* 4th ed. New York: D. Van Nostrand, 1864.

Boatner, Mark Mayo, III. *The Civil War Dictionary.* New York: Random House, 1988.

Coburn, Frederick W. *History of Lowell and Its People.* Vol. 1. New York: Lewis Historical Publishing Co., 1920.

Columbia Encyclopedia. 2nd ed. New York: Columbia University Press, 1950.

The Concise Cambridge History of English Literature. George Sampson. New York: Macmillan Co., 1941.

Duyckinck, Everet A. *National History of the War for the Union: Civil, Military and Naval.* 3 Vols. New York: Johnson, Fry and Co., 1868.

Harper's Weekly: A Journal of Civilization. Bound copies from 7 (314) (Jan. 3, 1863) to 8 (414) (Dec. 3, 1864).

Headley, J. T. *The Great Rebellion: A History of the Civil War in the United States.* 2 Vols. Hartford, Conn.: Hurlbut, Williams and Co., 1863.

Herberger, Charles F. *Three Centuries of Centerville Scenes: Vignettes of a Cape Cod Village.* Centerville Historical Society. Centerville, Mass., 1989.

Holmes, Oliver Wendell." My Hunt for the Captain." *Atlantic Monthly* 10 (62) (Dec. 1862).

Johnson, Robert Underwood, and Clarence Clough Buel, ed. *Battles and Leaders of the Civil War.* 4 Vols. New York: The Century Co., 1887.

Marvel, William. *Burnside.* Chapel Hill: Univ. of North Carolina Press, 1991.

McClellan, General George B. *McClellan's Own Story.* New York: Charles L. Webster and Co., 1887

Morris, Richard B. ed. *Encyclopedia of American History.* New York: Harper and Brothers, 1953.

National Archives, Record Group 153, Judge Advocate General (Army) Court Martial Number MM-2640, Captain R. S. Botsford, 6W4 7/4/A BX 1203, Copy of 51 pp.

Official Army Register of the Volunteer Force of the United States Army for the years 1861, 1862, 1863, 1864, 1865, Part I, Part VI, Part VIII. By the order of the Secretary of War, March 2, 1865.

Osborne, William H. *The History of the Twenty-Ninth Regiment of Massachusetts Volunteer Infantry in the Late War of the Rebellion.* Boston: Albert J. Wright, 1877.

Record of the Massachusetts Volunteers, 1861–1865. 2 Vols. Boston: Wright and Potter, 1870.

Roe, Alfred S. *The Twenty-Fourth Regiment, Massachusetts Volunteers, 1861–1866.* Worcester, Mass: 1907.

Sears, Stephen W. *To the Gates of Richmond: The Peninsula Campaign.* New York: Ticknor and Fields, 1992.

Trent, W. P., John Erskine, Stuart P. Sherman, and Carl Van Doren, eds. *Cambridge History of American Literature.* 3 vols. New York: Macmillan Co., 1943.

Warren, Robert Penn. *John Brown: The Making of a Martyr.* Nashville: J. S. Sanders and Co., 1993.

INDEX

A Yankee at Arms was designed and typeset on a Macintosh computer system using PageMaker software. The text is set in Sabon and the chapter openings are set in Fourier Ornaments. This book was designed by Kay Jursik, composed by Kimberly Scarbrough, and manufactured by Thomson-Shore, Inc. The recycled paper used in this book is designed for an effective life of at least three hundred years.